Working-class self-help in nineteenth-century England

Responses to industrialization

Eric Hopkins

University of Birmingham

UCL
PRESS

First published in 1995 by UCL Press

UCL Press Limited
University College London
Gower Street
London WC1E 6BT

and

1900 Frost Road, Suite 101
Bristol
Pennsylvania 19007-1598

The name of University College London (UCL) is a registered trade
mark used by UCL Press with the consent of the owner.

British Library Cataloguing in Publication Data
A catalogue record for this book is available from the British Library.

ISBNs:
1-85728-242-6 HB
1-85728-243-4 PB

Typeset in Sabon.
Printed and bound by
Biddles Ltd, Guildford & King's Lynn, England.

In memory of my late wife Barbara,
and for those three hostages to fortune, Ruth, Hedley and Valerie

Contents

Preface

When Samuel Smiles published his famous work *Self help* in 1859, the belief in getting on by one's own endeavours and without external assistance of any kind was already very familiar to many Victorians. It was a belief highly characteristic of an entrepreneurial age, and generally accepted by generations of middle-class public school boys. But what of the working classes? In fact, as they constituted the toiling work-people in the factories, workshops and mines of what was to be the world's first industrial nation, they had as much need, if not more, of self-help as the middle classes. This book therefore examines three aspects of working-class self-help in the long nineteenth century, that is, up to 1914. Greater space is given to the history of trade unionism than to the other two topics simply because the story is rather more complex and at times requires lengthier comment. The standard secondary sources have been used, together with a certain amount of research in government publications such as the reports of Royal Commissions and of Select Committees.

The choice of the three aspects named might surprise some readers, at least the inclusion of trade unionism. However, it seems to me that although friendly societies and the co-operative movement are obvious candidates for inclusion, trade unions are just as important as forms of self-help and self-defence in the developing industrial economy of the nineteenth century; and the reasons for choosing all three forms of self-help are explained and discussed at greater length in the Introduction. No especial difficulties arose in the course of writing this book, although a critical note is sounded from time to time. Nor has it proved at all difficult to maintain the customary historical impartiality in dealing with labour problems, although as a *soi-*

disant labour historian, I suppose I am to be classed as being "on the side of the workers" (as some of us used to say in Party circles in the 1930s).

I would like to record my thanks to Steven Gerrard, of UCL Press, and to two colleagues in the Department of Economic and Social History at the University of Birmingham – Peter Cain and Leonard Schwarz – who have had less to put up with than usual in replying to my often inane questions arising out of the writing of this book. Of course, I am solely responsible for all errors of commission and omission, and for all misconceptions and misapprehensions in what follows. Thanks are also due to our two excellent and always helpful departmental secretaries, Suzy Kennedy and Diane Martin.

Introduction

Extraordinary and far-reaching social changes took place in England during the course of the nineteenth century, changes unparalleled in the history of the country either before or since. The first of these changes was an increase in population. During the second half of the eighteenth century the population roughly doubled, while in the following century it increased nearly fourfold, from about 9 million to 36 million in 1911. No increase of this dimension had ever been seen before. At the same time, a striking change in the occupations of the working classes occurred, from employment for very many in agriculture at the beginning of the nineteenth century to employment by the end of the century in industry, commerce and the service industries. This was the consequence of the Industrial Revolution, the first of its kind to take place in any country of the world. Well before 1900, the majority of the nation were no longer country folk, but had become dwellers in cities and towns. Thus, society was transformed by sweeping demographic and economic change in little more than the lifetime of a centenarian born in the opening decade of the nineteenth century.

These historical facts are widely known, but they need to be emphasized if their impact on the ordinary working-class family is to be properly understood. A largely (but not exclusively) rural population in the mid-eighteenth century was overtaken by great urban conurbations in the next century. Millions had to adjust to town life, often in congested and insanitary conditions, particularly in the first half of the century. At the same time, millions grew up to spend their working lives in factories, workshops, mines and other industrial workplaces, whereas their forebears had worked in the fields. Furthermore, all those at work in the new industrialized economy had to contend with

1

the booms and slumps characteristic of industrial capitalism. Overseas trade, of course, had always been subject to variations due to the expansion, re-direction, or closure of markets, while internal trade suffered similarly from changes in market conditions, the delays inherent in a transport system previously reliant on roads and canals, and new patterns in consumer demand. Both external and internal trade were affected, sometimes very badly, by the great wars of the eighteenth century, and especially by the Revolutionary and Napoleonic Wars, 1793–1815. But to all these disturbing elements were added the strains and stresses of the new industrial economy. Put simply, in the mid-eighteenth century the average worker was an agricultural labourer, and his well-being depended very largely on the state of the harvest. After 1800, the average worker became more and more an industrial worker, and his future depended on the ups and downs of an industrialized economy.

How then was the worker in industry to protect himself against the loss of employment, due to the failure of his employer, or to sickness, or to a slump in trade? In the eighteenth century, the agricultural labourer was relatively secure in his employment. In times of need, especially in the winter months, he could go to the overseers of his parish, and commonly be given outdoor relief. There was also the possibility of additional charitable relief in kind given by local employers. In the nineteenth century, in the towns, it was different. Access to relief depended on having a settlement in the parish, and newcomers would be excluded. In addition, after the Poor Law Amendment Act, 1834, the aim was to stop outdoor relief and help only those willing to enter the purposefully forbidding workhouse. In these circumstances, it is clear that working men and women were increasingly thrown back on their own resources. They had to help one another, or die.

This is to put it somewhat starkly, of course, but it is to state a simple truth. Working people in almost any age have always helped each other, but the need was particularly urgent in the rapidly changing world of industrial England. Employment could be insecure, even for the highly skilled, and the hazards to health in the new industrial towns were immense – death rates in the towns were far higher than in the countryside. So in the absence of social services of the modern kind, working people had to help themselves, and this they did in a variety of ways. The nature of this self-help was necessarily somewhat different from what is taken to be the conventional form of Victorian self-help. Too often this is thought of in terms of individual endeavour, raising oneself by one's own boot straps, getting on by solid application and entrepreneurial zeal. The working-class self-help that is the subject of this book was rather different. Its strongest characteristic was not individualism, but *co-operation* – especially working together to safeguard employment, and to make provision for sickness and ill-health.

As a consequence, three major forms of working-class self-help emerged in the nineteenth century. First is the great expansion of the friendly society movement, a means of combining conviviality with simple insurance against ill-health, which for most of the nineteenth century had a far larger membership than the trade unions. Secondly is the trade union movement, initially designed to maintain and safeguard conditions at work, but later leading to working-class representation in the House of Commons. Thirdly, there is the co-operative movement, generally on a small scale in the first half of the nineteenth century, but expanding greatly from the 1840s onwards.

This introductory sketch is intended merely to set the scene for the newcomer to nineteenth-century social history. In fact, working-class self-help took many different forms. It could hardly fail to do so, given the absence of social services other than that provided by the Poor Law, a system of relief which, as we have noted, was drastically amended in 1834 so as positively to discourage application by persons in need. For the remainder of the century the Poor Law authorities were disliked and feared by working people. As a result, the working classes were thrown back on their own resources. Sometimes this amounted to no more than mutual assistance in times of need or distress – children would help their parents or siblings, friends would help each other, members of the same church or chapel would give what aid they could. More material assistance or long-term help might be gained by the individual through simple solidarity at the work place, or through saving. Both trade unionism and the friendly society movement started to expand on a considerable scale from the 1830s onwards as the new industrial society began to settle down, while the co-operative movement, after uncertain beginnings earlier in the century, took a firm hold with its concentration on retailing in 1844 and in the years that followed.

The role of the government in all these developments is interesting.

As one might expect, its attitude to trade combinations or trade unions in the early nineteenth century was one of suspicion and hostility. During the French wars, trade associations, which were already regarded with disfavour as being in restraint of trade, came under suspicion as possible cloaks for revolutionary conspiracy; they were actually illegal between 1799 and 1824, and it was not until the 1870s that they acquired a really firm legal status. Even then, further legal obstacles were placed in their path at the turn of the century. Friendly societies were viewed in a different light. Although they too might shelter conspiracies (and be trade unions in disguise), on the whole they were regarded as relatively harmless, and indeed, from the 1830s onwards they were to be encouraged as limiting the costs to the rates of Poor Law relief. Yet even here, it was not until 1870 that the government established a Royal Commission on friendly societies, and thereafter sought a more thoroughgoing regulation of their financial affairs. As for the co-operative movement, it was so small before the 1840s that it hardly merited detailed attention by the government. As it happened, some of the early societies were much more politically biased and shot through with socialist thinking than the average craft union, which often forbade the discussion of politics at meetings. Nevertheless, when the co-operative movement took off in the 1850s with the increasing success of consumer co-operation, the government was prepared to give legal recognition to co-operative societies as a form of friendly society, and to permit them to acquire limited liability. All in all, nineteenth-century governments with their great belief in free trade and *laissez-faire* were understandably on the side of employers and hostile (at least initially) to trade unions, although more favourably inclined to other forms of self-help.

To sum up, then: faced more and more as the nineteenth century progressed with a new mode of industrialized and urbanized life, the working classes were forced to buckle to and seek their own salvation. They had little alternative. The old-style paternalism of the village squire and parson (and even, it could be, of the overseers of the poor) was less and less available to them. They had to help themselves, and this book records some of their achievements.

In conclusion, it might be useful to the reader to set out the main stages of the development of working-class self-help in simple diagrammatic form (see diagram, p. 6). What follows is not intended to show comprehensively all forms of self-help, but merely to indicate the principal periods of development. Naturally enough, they are not mutually exclusive, and the small local organizations at the beginning of the century are still to be found at its end. In all three stages of the model, the extent of self-help is conditioned by prevailing economic conditions. For example, friendly society activity and growth were greater at the end of the century, obviously enough, when real wages were higher, than in the early decades of the century when the standard of living was still relatively low.

All in all, working-class self-help in the nineteenth century took a variety of forms, the vast majority being rooted in the simple human need to help one another in times of adversity. This was perhaps one of the outstanding characteristics of working-class life in the last century as men, women and children struggled to come to terms with the lifestyle imposed on them by the new industrial economy. Not all of them responded unselfishly, of course; some simply looked the other way and pursued their own narrow interests. But on the whole they did help each other, both in simple door-to-door transactions and in the organizations described in this book. Anyone who served in the ranks during the Second World War will know what comradeship means; it was always good to have an "oppo" – a mate or pal. So it was with the working classes in the Industrial Revolution as they adjusted to their new role as the protagonists in the burgeoning of the first industrial nation in the world.

Development of working-class self-help in the nineteenth century

1st stage: 1800–1830s

Informal development of small local organs of self-help

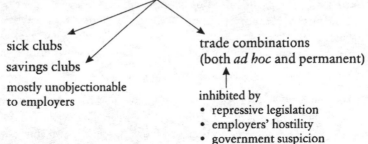

sick clubs

savings clubs

mostly unobjectionable
to employers

trade combinations
(both *ad hoc* and permanent)

inhibited by
- repressive legislation
- employers' hostility
- government suspicion

2nd stage: 1830s–70s

Multiplication and diversification of self-help agencies

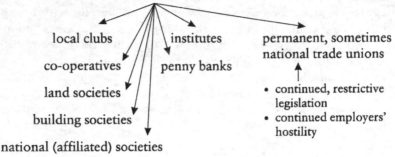

local clubs   institutes

co-operatives   penny banks

land societies

building societies

national (affiliated) societies

permanent, sometimes
national trade unions

- continued, restrictive
  legislation
- continued employers'
  hostility

3rd stage: 1880s–1914

Continued activity and extension of sphere of trade union activities

local clubs

growth of
consumer
co-operatives

further growth of
affiliated societies

trade unions – further growth
of national bodies

parliamentary representation
of labour

Labour party

new unionsim

- challenge of government
  welfare legislation

- employers' associations
- use of "free labour"
- adverse legal decisions

Part One

The friendly societies

Chapter One

Friendly societies in the late eighteenth and early nineteenth centuries

In their heyday in the nineteenth century, the leading friendly societies often claimed to have been founded many centuries previously, even as far back as Roman times, but literary evidence seems to show that they were first in existence far more recently than this. Certainly there were friendly societies in Scotland in the early seventeenth century, and also Huguenot friendly societies in London at the end of that century. In 1797, Defoe remarked that "another branch of insurance is by contribution, or (to borrow the term from that before mentioned) Friendly Societies; which is, in short, a number of people entering into a mutual compact to help one another, in case any disaster or distress fall upon them". Thus, Defoe described the Sailors' Chest at Chatham as being a friendly society, and some of the societies of the eighteenth century appear to have been formed to protect work people in more hazardous occupations. For example, there were two acts of parliament, one in 1757 and the other in 1792, the first setting up a compulsory scheme for assisting coalheavers on the Thames, and the second providing another compulsory fund for skippers and keelmen on the Wear. In both cases the basic idea seems to have been to reduce the cost to the local poor rates of supporting the sick and aged and their widows. Many friendly societies, however, were not confined in membership to any one occupation, but were simply a means of insurance against sickness or accident, with appropriate funeral benefits.

Such societies appear to have grown much more numerous during the last 40 years of the eighteenth century, and Professor Gosden has suggested that by the end of the century there were probably some thousands of these societies in existence. Sir Frederick Eden, the contemporary writer on the poor, put their number at about 7,200 societies in 1801, with a membership of 648,000 – a very substantial

Table 1 Friendly societies in England and Wales, 1803–15.

Year	No. of societies	Total membership
1803	9,672	704,350
1813	–	821,319
1814	–	838,728
1815	–	925,429

number out of a population in Great Britain of about 10.5 million. Subsequently, the returns of the overseers of the poor, although not to be relied on in detail, show increasingly large numbers (see Table 1). These figures were said at the time to represent nearly 8.5 per cent of the resident population of the country.

Why were friendly societies increasingly popular in the second half of the eighteenth century? Partly their increase in numbers may be attributed to the growth in population of the time, an increase, as we have already noted, of about 50 per cent between 1750 and 1801; but more significant, perhaps, was the development of the Industrial Revolution. It was very noticeable in the early nineteenth century that membership of the societies was most concentrated in industrial areas. Thus, according to the Poor Law returns of 1815, Lancashire, the seat of the fast-developing cotton industry, had 17 per cent of its population in friendly societies. The West Riding, home of the woollen cloth industry, had a similarly high membership figure, while industrial counties such as Leicestershire, Nottinghamshire, Staffordshire and Warwickshire, all had over 10 per cent in membership. By way of contrast, rural counties such as Dorset, Kent, Lincolnshire and Sussex, had less than 5 per cent of their population as members. It seems clear that industrial occupations with their greater risks of ill health and injury (not to mention the hazards to health in the insanitary conditions of the new industrial towns, where it was well-known that mortality rates were far higher than in the countryside) supplied compelling reasons for joining a friendly society.

The point is well-illustrated by the growth of friendly society activity in the Black Country, the industrial region to the west of Birmingham. In the southwest corner of this area, Stourbridge was a rapidly expanding, small industrial town manufacturing iron, glass and firebrick, and mining coal and clay. Its population more than doubled in

Table 2 Sick club membership in Stourbridge, 1810.

No.	Appellations	Date	Years	Membership
1	Cross, Swinford	1752	58	78
2	Mitre	1769	41	81
3	Pipe	1773	37	81
4	Vine	1777	33	126
5	Talbot	1778	32	136
6	Duke of Wellington	1778	32	40
7	Rose and Crown, Swinford	1779	31	60
8	Queen's Head, Amblecote	1779	31	71
9	Seven Stars	1780	30	57
10	Fish, Amblecote	1783	27	45 Fem.
11	New Inn	1784	26	40 Fem.
12	Swan, Swinford	1784	26	90
13	Presby. Cong. Prov. Soc.	1784	26	22
14	Mitre	1785	25	34 Fem.
15	Mitre	1785	25	121
16	Duke Wellington, Swinford	1786	24	60
17	Holly Bush, Swinford	1789	21	67
18	New Inn	1793	17	90
19	Bell	1799	11	130
20	Chawnell Inn	1800	10	61
21	Horse Shoe	1804	6	64
22	Indep. Cong. Christian Soc.	1809	1	13
				1,567

the first half of the nineteenth century. According to a reliable contemporary observer, sick club membership in the town in 1810 was as shown in Table 2.

William Scott, the compiler of these figures (a prominent local Unitarian), then divided up the societies into three areas – the town itself, and two outlying areas (see Table 3).

Table 3 Distribution of sick clubs in Stourbridge, 1810.

Area	No. of societies	Membership	Population	Proportion of population
Stourbridge township, Lye, Wollaston, Wollescote Upper Swinford	14	1,035	3,431	1 : 3
Upper Swinford	6	416	3,766	1 : 9
Amblecote	2	116	1,002	1 : 8
	22	1,567	8,199	1 : 5

Scott remarked on the very high proportion of societies in Stour-bridge itself, and commented that his figures for the township might include "many members probably resident in the country hamlets elsewhere, which may account for the great apparent disproportion between this and the other districts". There is the further point that Scott's figures are based on the 1801 Census and not the figures for 1811, which would be more appropriate. The 1811 figures would re-duce his Stourbridge fraction to a quarter, and overall from one-fifth to one-sixth. Nevertheless, the figures are striking enough.

Indeed, the figures are even more remarkable if a further simple analysis is attempted. In 1811 there were 3,940 males of all ages in the district. If membership of the female societies is excluded, there were 1,447 members of either male or mixed societies. It is a reasonable assumption that the majority of these 1,447 members were men – probably 1,000 or more. Thus, if Scott's figures are approximately right, one in four males in 1810 were members of friendly societies (and an even higher proportion if male children are deducted from the population figures). All things considered, it seems likely that Scott's own qualification regarding outside membership must be taken into account (and presumably there would be a small degree of multiple membership as well); but when all such considerations are weighed, it still seems clear that a wide membership of benefit socie-ties prevailed in this part of the Black Country. This membership was substantially above the national average of the resident population quoted earlier in this chapter of about 8.5 per cent in 1818.

Such societies traditionally had their meeting place in local inns, as the Stourbridge list makes clear. (About half of those listed are still in existence at the time of writing.) They were purely local affairs, run very informally under a variety of names, "sick and draw clubs" being a term often used in the Black Country. As such, they are to be distin-guished from the national, affiliated orders which will be discussed in the next chapter. A further distinction should be drawn between these sick clubs and other savings societies that often met in public houses, such as clothing clubs, boot and shoe clubs, and even watch clubs. The basic aims of the average club were simple: insurance against ill health, and a burial grant for a respectable funeral – something of great importance to working-class men and women.

There is no doubt that industrialization encouraged the growth of this kind of friendly society. A further example is provided by Birmingham, where benefit clubs were as common as in the Black Country. William Hutton, historian of Birmingham, writing in the 1780s, remarked disapprovingly of their habit of meeting in public houses:

> As liquor and labour are inseparable, the imprudent member is apt to forget to quit the clubroom when he has spent his necessary two pence, but continues there to the injury of his family.

Thomas Attwood, the Birmingham banker and reformer, told the House of Commons in 1812 that the help of the clubs was very great, and that there was hardly any industrial worker in Birmingham who did not belong to a club. This was obviously an exaggeration, for unskilled workers whose earnings were limited and irregular, could not afford to keep up the regular payments made necessary by membership. Nevertheless, clubs certainly were very numerous in Birmingham, and Rawlinson's Report to the General Board of Health on the town in 1849 lists 213 registered societies, of which about 159 met in inns, public houses, or beershops. These societies had at least 30,000 members (there were probably as many again in unregistered societies). Rawlinson gives the names of some of the societies, for example, the Sick Man's Friendly Society, Abstainers' Gift, Society of Total Abstinence and the Rational Sick and Burial Society. Some had even more striking names – the True Blue Society, the Honourable Knights of the Wood, the Modern Druids, the Royal Dragoons and the Society of Royal Veterans.

What was the attitude of the government and of the middle classes generally to friendly societies? In fact, opinions were divided. Some were decidedly hostile, because friendly societies were thought to be a disguised form of trade union activity and, as will be seen in subsequent chapters, trade combinations were actually made illegal under the Combinations Acts of 1799 and 1800. This belief was not entirely without foundation – a minority of benefit clubs were, in fact, a cloak for combination in particular trades. Again, middle-class hostility was still displayed in the mid-nineteenth century against the convivial practices of many societies. Rawlinson was as critical of this aspect as Hutton had been in the previous century, singling out the annual processions as a sheer waste of money:

> Vast sums of money are expended by these clubs on unmeaning,

gaudy and childish show. Once a year, usually in Whitsun week, they hold processions. More money is spent in processions, in loss of labour and in attendant expenses, than would pay the rent-charge of a full supply of water, and perfect sewerage.

On the other hand, the government was well aware that the genuine friendly society provided a form of self-help that was invaluable in keeping down the poor rates. There was increasing concern at the increase in poor rates as industrialization and the population grew in the early nineteenth century. It is not surprising, therefore, that the government was prepared to countenance the growth of friendly societies, provided that the local magistrates were able to keep an eye on them. Rose's Act of 1793 actually welcomed the growth of the movement:

> ... that the protection and encouragement of friendly societies in this kingdom for securing by voluntary subscription of the members thereof, separate funds for the mutual relief and maintenance of the said members, in sickness, old age, and infirmity, is likely to be attended by very beneficial effects ...

The act then went on to provide for the registration of societies with magistrates at Quarter Sessions, though this was not compulsory, so that smaller bodies such as Christmas clubs and slate clubs were not obliged to register. Furthermore, under Section 17 of the act, no member of a registered society could be removed to his place of settlement until he actually became chargeable to the poor rates. Removal of this kind was later abolished, but the close connection between friendly society membership and keeping the poor rates down can clearly be seen. As a result of this act, friendly societies could both sue and be sued in their corporate capacity.

Subsequently, during the Revolutionary and Napoleonic Wars (1793–1815) the friendly society movement continued to grow, although government suspicions of working-class conspiracies and secret societies remained strong (strictly speaking, the affiliated societies with their branches were illegal under the Corresponding Societies Act, 1799, while the Seditious Meetings Act, 1817, forbade all meetings of more than 50 persons without notice). Although the government approved of the principle of friendly society self-help, the problem seemed to be how to ensure that they were properly administered. Numerous proposals were made at the time for parochial sick clubs, including a bill brought in by Pitt in 1796 for a compulsory parish levy (it never became law). One proposal for the proper regulation of societies took the form of setting up county societies run by the clergy and gentry of each county. The first of these societies was the Essex Provident Society, established in 1818, to be followed in 1821 by the Hampshire County Society. Such societies were largely confined to southern England, and were not popular in industrial areas. By 1871, the Essex Society had 9,315 members, the Wiltshire 7,130, and the Hampshire 6,322. The four largest county societies had a total membership of only 22,921 in 1871. This form of friendly society never proved very successful, largely because members from the working classes preferred to run their own affairs without middle-class intervention and supervision.

Meanwhile, after the end of the French Wars in 1815, the government passed further legislation affecting the societies. In 1817 the Savings Bank Act allowed registered societies to deposit their funds in savings banks at favourable rates of interest. In 1819 another act required JPs to register societies only when the rules and life-tables of the society had been given a certificate of approval by "two persons at least, known to be professional actuaries or persons skilled in calculations". Then in 1825 a Select Committee of the House of Commons was appointed on the laws respecting friendly societies. Its report was referred to a further Select Committee in 1827, which then produced a second report.

Generally speaking, the First Report is both discursive and largely descriptive and does not yield much to the researcher seeking information on the progress of the friendly society movement as a whole. At the same time, there are some interesting passages which merit consideration. First, the report has this to say on the subject of county societies:

County societies undoubtedly possess many advantages, for example, security is much greater ... Nevertheless, it is certain that the people themselves are disinclined to substitute a subscription to these general institutions for their contributions to clubs managed by themselves: and they have an undefined apprehension of an invasion of their funds by the government.

Secondly, the report fastens on the provisions of the 1819 Act regarding the certifying of the rules and tables submitted to the magistrates:

> Who are professional actuaries or persons skilled in calculation? And in what way are the Justices to satisfy themselves that the persons by whom the tables are signed , really answer to the description of skilled calculators? ... Your Committee are informed that in many counties, the Bench have been satisfied with the signature of petty schoolmasters and accountants, whose opinion upon the probability of sickness, and the duration of life, is not to be depended upon.

The report then goes on to comment that it is remarkable that until within a very few years, "no *data* was collected whereon a calculation of the average occurrence of sickness at the several ages of man, could be formed with tolerable accuracy".

This, of course, was a matter of the greatest importance, since the tables were the ultimate authority for the amount of weekly or monthly subscription, and of the benefit paid to the sick, and of the funeral benefit. It seemed that in many societies these rules were calculated in the most amateurish and unscientific way. As a consequence, societies might collapse, and members could find that all their subscriptions, sometimes paid in over many years, were lost completely. The First Report simply recommended that the Southwell Tables (compiled in the late eighteenth century by William Morgan, and based on the earlier Northampton Tables, drawn up by his uncle, Dr Richard Price) might be safely adopted, provided that a separate and sufficient provision be made for sickness or disability over the age of 65. The Second Report gives detailed consideration to the Southwell Society Tables together with six other tables. The last two of these tables were submitted by Mr Finlaison, the actuary to the Commissioners for Reducing the National Debt. Lastly, there was another set of tables, the Dorsetshire Tables, presented by the well-known Rev. Becher, the Southwell Poor Law reformer.

On the whole, the Committee thought that the Dorsetshire Tables might be safely adopted, subject to certain requirements. For example, women should be no more than a third of all members of any society; smaller societies (and all new societies) should make 70 rather than 65 the age of superannuation; and it was "imprudent" to establish societies with less than 200 members. Finally, the Committee suggested that the provision of the 1819 act regarding certifying by two actuaries should be repealed, that rules should be submitted to the Clerk of the Peace, and that returns showing the state of the societies should be made to the JPs at least every five years. These recommendations were largely implemented by the Friendly Societies Act, 1829, save for the further provision that the rules were first to be confirmed by the barrister appointed to certify the rules of savings banks before they were submitted to Quarter Sessions. This person was the famous and formidable John Tidd Pratt, who in effect became the first Registrar of Friendly Societies, although it was not until 1846 that he officially acquired this title.

By the 1830s then, the friendly society movement had spread to virtually all parts of the country, and was especially prominent in industrial areas. As we shall see in the next chapter, its success was to lead to the growth of great national bodies such as the Oddfellows and the Foresters. Meanwhile, we may examine a little more closely the general features of societies registered under the 1793, the 1819, and the 1829 acts. Each society was very much its own master, and prided itself on its independence. There was no standard set of rules laid down by authority. Consequently it is unsafe to generalize too widely about the rules made by so large a number of separate bodies, although, obviously, they did have some features in common. The best procedure seems to be to describe some of the most common characteristics, and then to provide some general comments, including reference to individual aspects.

All rules of registered societies naturally contained details of the office holders of the society. These officers could be surprisingly numerous. For example, the Castle Eden Friendly Society of Durham at the end of the eighteenth century had as officers, a steward, 12 directors, 12 committee men, a treasurer, two clerks, and a number of trustees. The Town Porters' Friendly Society of Edinburgh ("open to persons of different callings and employments" according to the printed rules) also had an array of officials in the early 1830s. The rules declared:

The Society shall always be under the direction of a Preses [President], Old Preses, Treasurer, Constable, and three Key-masters, who must be free members, and twelve assistants, who together shall form a standing committee for managing the affairs of the Society; but all their transactions shall be liable to the inspection and control of the society at large, at each ensuing meeting thereof: and the whole shall be chosen from the Members of the Society.

Next, age limits for membership would be specified. They would vary considerably from as low as 10 in the Castle Eden Society (but 20 or 21 was more common) to an upper limit in the mid-30s (although for Castle Eden it was 46). Applicants for admission had to be of good character, and in good health. The rules of the United Philanthropists of London in 1830, for example, laid down that:

No person who is employed in any pernicious trade should be a member of this society; nor shall any lapidary, colour grinder, looking-glass silverer, water gilder, painter, plumber, worker in white lead, fireman, tailor, plasterer, bricklayer, bricklayer's labourer, bailiff, or bailiff's follower, thief taker, or any danger-ous artificer, be admitted on any account whatever.

Other societies, such as the Friendly Society at the Angel Inn, Bed-ford (established 1826), would not admit anyone who was not in receipt of 15s a week. The applicant also had to be in sound health, free from hereditary disease or weakness, and of good moral character.

Would-be members might also have to pay an entrance fee – it could be 5s or even as much as £2 – and once elected, would be expected to attend the monthly, half-quarterly or quarterly meetings. This was often not a mere formality, for one of the most striking aspects of the printed rules of the seven societies under review in this chapter is the list of fines payable for breaches of the rules. The Edinburgh Town Porters Society, for example, lists 14 fines for different forms of absence from meetings: an ordinary member could be fined 6d for being absent at a quarterly meeting, and so could a committee mem-ber. A president absent one quarter of an hour after the time of a meet-ing had to pay 9d, and so did an absent treasurer. The list of fines is really quite astonishing. There are six penalties for different failures of duty by officials or members, then a further four fines for not accepting office; finally there are eight penalties as General Fines (for example, failing to attend funerals, 6d; calumniating office-bearers, or raising unjust reports, 2s 6d for the first offence, 5s for the second). Of course, the Edinburgh Society might have been unusually punctilious in its attempts to maintain good order, but a system of fines seems to have been a common enough way of attempting to enforce good order and discipline in all friendly societies. Naturally it was essential to maintain order at meetings. Thus, the rules of the London Society of Taylors provide:

> If any member shall curse or swear in club hours, he shall forfeit 2d for every oath or curse; and if any member lays wagers, or lessens a brother member, in regard to his trade, or comes into the club room disguised in liquor, or refuses to keep silence, after the stewards have called silence three different times, [he] shall forfeit 6d for each offence.

As for subscriptions, these would depend on how the society saw its commitments. The higher the benefits provided, the more the fees levied had to be. A subscription of 4s or 5s a quarter was common and in return for this members received an allowance of 6s or 7s a week, often dropping to a reduced amount after a stated number of weeks, and a funeral benefit of £4 or £5. Some societies aimed higher than this. The United Philanthropists of London (which sounds a rather grand body) had an entrance fee of £2 for members between 27 and 30, charged 2s 5d per month and paid out as sick pay 20s a week for 18 weeks, and then 10s for a further eight months. Pensions were paid at the rate of 4s a week (for those who had been members for less than 7 years), 5s a week (membership from 7 to 14 years), and 6s a week (membership longer than 14 years). Clearly this society, which was limited to 150 members, and excluded anyone engaged in a pernicious trade or earning less than 24s a week, aimed to supply superior benefits. It even allowed the secretary 12s a quarter "for his trouble", and members of the committee 1s a day for visiting the sick.

The administration of sick relief was one of the most important aspects of the running of any benefit society. It was essential for the society's monies to be kept in a safe place, and this usually took the form of a chest kept at the place of meeting, fitted with several locks. The Town Porters Society included three key-masters among their officials, while the Castle Eden Society specified that the keys to the three locks on their chest should be kept by the steward, the treasurer, and one of the committee. As soon as the fund amounted to £20, then £10 of this was to be put into the public funds, or placed out at interest on real or personal security. According to their auditors' report, the money in the chest and out at interest in January 1798 amounted to £567 19s, and the net savings in the previous year were £105 2s 11½d. In this society the treasurer obviously had considerable responsibility, and it is likely that he had to give a bond on entering into office (the society's rules give a specimen form for a treasurer providing a bond for £200). No doubt this society, too, was of a superior kind, and not typical of the average society. The extent and detail of its rules are very impressive. Indeed, the officials were probably middle class rather than working class – what working man could afford a bond for £200? But middle-class officials were not unusual, especially among the later affiliated societies, as we shall see. Nevertheless, the treasurer of even the most humble society often had to take responsibility for quite large sums of money.

Apart from the safe custody of the society's funds, there was the vital matter of their proper disbursement. All societies were concerned to see that claims for relief were *bona fide*, and some provided special forms for claimants to fill up. Some required a certificate from a surgeon or physician. All were quick to disallow any appeals for help from malingerers, or members who were to blame for their own misfortunes. Thus, the rules of John Bamford's Society in Barton, Nottinghamshire, provide:

> That if any member shall have the venereal disease, or shall fall sick or lame occasioned by any unlawful exercise whatever – as wrestling, fighting, boxing, jumping, etc., or through excess of drinking, he shall receive no benefit from the box.

Even then, the claimant would be visited by fellow members to check on his return to health. The Castle Eden Society reduced the allowance from 6s when confined to bed to 3s a week when able to walk. It was often said to be dangerous for a sick member to leave his sickbed even to mend the fire less his sick pay be reduced by the society. It was also common enough for societies to appoint their own physicians, surgeons or apothecaries to attend members.

So much for the major aspects of registered societies: they certainly had their own oddities and idiosyncrasies. One society stated in its rules that it would not accept as a member anyone who had *not* had the smallpox. Another was prepared to provide loans for the purchase of cows by members. The Castle Eden Society admitted women under 45, and would pay them annuities but not weekly allowances for sickness or infirmity; nor could they serve in any office. Some societies issued membership badges, which had to be returned when membership lapsed. Others kept their own stock of funeral apparel, lent out to members attending funerals. In fact, the rules of each society expressed the individual preferences of small, self-governing bodies. It is again emphasized that all the examples of rules quoted above are from registered societies. In the nature of things, they were likely to be the better-regulated societies that could afford to have their own rules printed, together with necessary stationery; but even then, we cannot tell how far their rules were observed in practice, and what proportion of the clubs survived over any length of time. Then again, it seems that there were as many non-registered societies in the first half of the nineteenth century as there were registered, and their history must remain largely unknown.

Apart from the watch clubs, breeches clubs and book clubs already mentioned, there were some clubs with distinctive characteristics that marked them out from the usual run of benefit societies. Dividing societies, for example, provided sick pay for their members, but periodically divided up their funds and distributed them to members, whereupon a new club would be started. In Birmingham, a more sedate form of society developed away from the public house, meeting in the vestries or schoolrooms of the churches or chapels to which they were attached. These so-called provident societies were regarded as more respectable than the societies meeting on licensed premises, and were described as being "more scientifically conducted" and "based in superior calculations". Another specialized type of Birmingham society is described in the 1809 edition of Hutton's well-known history of the town. According to Hutton, such societies might be started by a bricklayer, and aimed to build houses for working men on the basis of substantial contributions from members every month. Thus, according to Hutton:

> Every member perhaps subscribes two guineas per month, and each house, value about one hundred pounds, is balloted for as

soon as erected. As a house is a weighty concern, every member is obliged to provide two bondsmen for the performance of covenants.

Clearly, this kind of society was greatly superior to the humble benefit society. Relatively few workmen could afford subscriptions as high as two guineas a month to what were known as "terminating" building societies (as opposed to the "permanent" building societies which developed later). Yet such societies existed both in Birmingham, where they were especially well known, and in the Black Country. They also developed in Lancashire and Yorkshire in the late eighteenth century, and the historian of the building society movement, S. J. Price, has suggested that by 1825 well over 250 building societies had been founded; in Bradford, as many as seven societies were established between 1823 and 1835. It hardly needs to be emphasized that societies of this kind were very specialized and were generally out of the reach of the unskilled working man.

One further kind of friendly society requires attention: the local burial society. These societies were the result of a simple desire among even the poorest to avoid the degradation of a pauper burial in an unmarked grave. However mean and wretched their day-to-day existence, they wanted to be seen off this earth with some degree of simple dignity. Burial clubs were a way of achieving this. They were especially common in Lancashire and the adjacent counties – Preston, for example, had 108,120 members of burial societies later in the century in 1874 (the total population at the time was only 86,000, the discrepancy in all probability being accounted for by out-of-town and multiple membership). The simplest form of burial society was organized on the basis of an agreement by members to meet funeral costs by a levy every time a death occurred. In the West Riding, the societies were known as "funeral briefs". A small fund was maintained, and a levy was paid by members to keep up the level of the fund every time someone died and payment made from the fund. Children could be members as well as adults, and families could pay a special levy. In the course of time, some societies began to build up permanent funds and to collect regular subscriptions. Such clubs might grow into quite large-scale organizations, such as the Blackburn Philanthropic Burial Society, founded in 1839, which had a membership in 1872 of over 100,000. On the other hand, many societies were very much smaller than this. They could also be short-lived, as funds ran out and the society closed down. Sir George Young remarked in 1874 that "the burial club which survives a generation is an exception".

What can be said in conclusion about the development of friendly societies prior to 1830? The growth of these societies can certainly be seen as an integral part of the massive changes in British society associated with the Industrial Revolution, a process that involved an expanding population, urbanization and industrialization. Before these changes, as has already been pointed out, a still largely rural working class could always turn to the parish overseers of the poor, or else to the squire and parson, for help in times of distress. The help proffered might be minimal, but it would usually be within a community where everyone knew everyone else. It was otherwise in the anonymity of the new industrial towns, where self-help became an obvious necessity. The prevalence of disease in the towns was so marked that the level of mortality in urban districts in the period 1851–60 was a quarter as high again as in rural areas, while over the period 1833–44, child mortality in Manchester was three times higher than in Surrey. In these circumstances it became a matter of simple self-preservation for those who could insure themselves to do so.

Quite apart from the need to provide against ill health, there was also the problem of increasing fluctuations in employment as industry grew and trade entered into periods of booms and slumps. Many of the early trade unions, as will be seen in subsequent chapters, took the form of friendly societies and provided out-of-work benefits. Although the upper classes viewed trade combinations with suspicion, they nevertheless were prepared to acknowledge that problems could result from variations in trade. Thus, the Report of the Select Committee on Manufacturers' Employment, 1830 ("manufacturers" here refers to workmen engaged in manufacture) admitted that fluctuations in employment frequently occurred in industrial areas, and were "productive of great distress". Consequently they proposed that Unemployment Fund Societies should be set up, into which workmen would pay regularly, so that they might be helped over periods of slack trade. Nothing came of this remarkable proposal, and it was not until 1911 that a limited scheme of insurance against unemployment was introduced; but the proposal does show that there was an awareness at government level that some form of compulsory self-help might be desirable to meet the changed conditions of life in the new industrial towns.

When the whole spectrum of the various forms of friendly societies before 1830 is reviewed, it is apparent that self-help was an important part of working-class life at the time. Some of its manifestations were relatively trivial, like the watch and breeches clubs, but even so, they go against the view that is sometimes expressed that it was the middle classes rather than the working classes who saved in the nineteenth century. It is beyond dispute that where working people could save, they often did so. It is wrong to suppose that all industrial workers in the early nineteenth century worked such long hours for such low pay that there was never anything to spare for saving or leisure activities. This is manifestly untrue. Some (certainly not all) industrial workers did have a few pence to spare each week. Moreover, friendly societies met in public houses and spent money freely on refreshments. An essential aspect of their activities was conviviality and a sense of good fellowship (which is the reason, of course, for their being called "friendly societies"). So friendly society meetings provided the occasion for a night out, and sometimes, as William Hutton remarked, for a man spending more than he should.

Just what proportion of the population were actually members of friendly societies still remains unknown. Earlier in this chapter the figure is given as 8.5 per cent and since the membership of the societies was overwhelmingly male, and very largely of the working class, the proportion of male workers must have been much higher than this – probably at least double, and around one million by 1830. This constitutes something like a quarter of all male workers. Of course, this figure is speculative, and we have no further firm figures until those of the Royal Commission on Friendly Societies in 1874; but having said this, it seems clear that a very substantial section of the working classes insured themselves in case (as Defoe put it) "any disaster or distress fell upon them". It was a practice that was to continue and grow throughout the nineteenth century. Very many more working people were members of the societies than of trade unions, which were for the most part confined to skilled workers. Further, in the 1830s the trade union movement took a distinctly political turn, playing a part in the Chartist movement and later on, in the 1870s, securing their own representation in parliament. At no time did the friendly society movement go down this road. There was no reason why it should, and the need never arose for political action designed to achieve legislative improvements.

Finally, enough should have been said to indicate the range and strengths of friendly societies in the early nineteenth century. They certainly existed in a variety of forms, from the small, ephemeral local slate clubs to the well-established registered societies, the bigger burial clubs, and the terminating building societies. It is obvious that they met a need in the developing industrial society of the time, so much so that it was perhaps inevitable that larger, national societies should be established about 1830, with growing numbers of local branches affiliated to the national body. The friendly society movement therefore reached a turning point at this time with the establishment and growth of the affiliated societies that boosted powerfully the membership of the movement as a whole. This new development will be described and discussed in the next chapter.

Chapter Two

The growth of the affiliated and other societies

What happened to the friendly society movement after 1830 and in the middle decades of the nineteenth century must be seen against the economic and social development of those years. The growth of towns continued at an unparalleled rate; Bradford, Preston and Wolverhampton all more than doubled in population between 1831 and 1851. By the latter date, the average Englishman was just beginning to be more typically a town dweller than a countryman. The 1830s and 1840s were filled with political excitement, first with the passing of the great Reform Act in 1832, and then with the Chartist agitation resulting in the presentation of the three Chartist petitions in 1839, 1842 and 1848. Economic progress seemed to falter with the severe depression of the early 1840s, but the economy began to expand again with the railway boom of the mid-1840s. The middle decades of the century saw the development of the so-called Great Victorian Boom, or the Victorian Golden Age, a concept somewhat deflated by economic historians in recent years, but nevertheless a period of substantial advance, culminating in two years of great prosperity, 1870 and 1871. What is crucial to the growth of the friendly society movement is the change in the level of real wages between 1830 and the 1870s. Whatever happened to real wages in the earlier part of this period, there is little doubt that they rose from the mid-1840s onwards. This rise was not uniform in nature – for example, Lancashire cotton workers were badly hit by the American Civil War in the 1860s which interrupted supplies of raw cotton – but overall, the rise in real wages was unmistakable. Thus, those workers in steady employment had more to spare for subscriptions to friendly societies, whether they were of the small, local and traditional type, or a branch of the new affiliated orders.

These orders expanded rapidly from about 1830 onwards. By "affiliated order" is meant a friendly society having a central body with affiliated individual clubs or branches at a distance, such as the Manchester Unity of Oddfellows, and the Ancient Order of Foresters. These two orders were to become by far the largest of the affiliated orders by 1872, but there were others such as the Order of Druids, the Rechabites (a temperance society), and a number of splinter organizations such as the Grand United Order of Oddfellows, who had their origins in the Manchester Unity. By 1872, there were 34 affiliated societies with more than 1,000 members each, but only the Oddfellows and the Foresters had full national coverage. The smaller affiliated societies were strongest for the most part in Lancashire and in the West Riding of Yorkshire.

Why then did the affiliated orders grow so significantly after 1830? Why did so many working men join these societies rather than the small local societies that had preceded them? This is an interesting question that has not received as much attention as it deserves. Obviously enough, there is more than one possible explanation of the expansion that occurred. In particular, the Manchester Unity grew very rapidly in the period 1835 to 1845: of the 3,074 lodges active 30 years later, nearly half (1,470) were established in this decade alone. In fact, initially there is one very simple explanation for this period of growth. After some years of mounting criticism, the Old Poor Law was reformed and reorganized by the Poor Law Amendment Act, 1834. The result was that, henceforth, great efforts were made to stop all outdoor relief. In future, anyone seeking help from the new Poor Law guardians would be required to enter the workhouse, where conditions were deliberately made austere in order to deter idlers and scroungers. As a result, membership of friendly societies shot up as working people sought to guard against sickness and the threat of having to enter the dreaded workhouse.

Yet this in itself does not explain why working men flocked to the affiliated orders rather than to the small local society. The explanation would seem to lie in an increasing perception of the superior advantages of a larger-scale organization. As was pointed out by a witness to the 1872 Royal Commission on Friendly Societies, the cost of funeral benefit could be spread over a number of clubs in the same district rather than be confined to one small local society. Again, the affiliated societies usually provided tramping benefit for their members – that

Table 4 Cards issued to travelling members of the
Manchester Unity of Oddfellows, 1848–72.

Years	Cards issued	Amount paid (£)
1848–52	4,721	4,468
1853–57	2,500	1,619
1858–62	3,797	3,590
1863–67	2,864	2,406
1868–72	2,204	1,750
	16,086	13,833

is, when travelling in search of work, they would be issued with a card showing they were in benefit. This entitled them to an allowance from the local lodge or court, afterwards repayable from headquarters. This was a valuable privilege not available in the small local club. Furthermore, once a member had moved permanently to a new district, he could either be transferred to a new branch, or he could continue as a member of his old branch but pay his subscription locally. The importance of these travelling allowances can be shown by reference to the yearly number of cards issued and amounts paid to travellers in the Manchester Unity of Oddfellows for the period 1848 to 1872 (see Table 4).

One further advantage of membership of an affiliated order that deserves consideration is their social activities. Like the earlier local societies, the orders held monthly meetings, usually in public houses, and annual feasts. Their rituals could be elaborate, involving secret signs, passwords and handshakes, some of them copied from freemasonry. Initiation ceremonies were common, in the Foresters even involving what was presumably mock trial by combat until this was abolished in 1843. Special attire was necessary at meetings, including ceremonial aprons, while elaborate banners were carried in processions. Funeral clothing was also available for wearing at members' funerals. Some orders had a remarkable number of lodge officials. Thus, the Antediluvian Order of Buffaloes boasted the following officers: primo, city marshal, tyler, waiter, constable, physician, minstrel, toaster, scavenger, alderman of poverty, alderman of juniper and secretary. Even more striking are the officers of the Order of Cemented Bricks: grandmaster, sworn tormentor, venerable leech, grand usher, grand treasurer, elder, select guardian, master hodman, hodman, pantile and junior pantile.

All in all, the leading affiliated orders clearly proved more attractive to many working men than the small local club with its often inadequate financial resources and uncertain future. Benefits were also higher in the orders, although this could mean higher subscriptions, of course. Add the advantages of tramping allowances, transfers to other branches, and colourful social occasions, and the pulling power of the affiliated orders is readily apparent. The increase in the working-class population by over 60 per cent, coupled with the rise in real wages, completes the explanation of the growth of membership of the affiliated orders from the 1830s to the 1870s.

At this point it should be useful to provide a few details of the growth of the major affiliated bodies. The original, No. 1 Lodge of the Independent Order of Oddfellows, Manchester Unity, seems to have been the Abercrombie Lodge, founded in Manchester in 1810. By 1820, the movement had spread to the West Riding and to the Potteries. In 1816, the first corresponding general secretary was appointed, and in 1827 a Board of Directors was elected by delegates from the district committees who took the title of the Annual Moveable Committee. Thus, the organization of the Oddfellows was in three tiers – that of the individual lodge, then the district committees, and finally the Annual Moveable Committee, who appointed the directors. By 1838 there were said to be 1,200 lodges with 90,000 members.

The Royal Order of Foresters began somewhat later, about 1830, in Leeds. By 1834 there were over 350 courts in the West Riding, Lancashire and Cheshire. In that year, a splinter group was set up in Rochdale – the Ancient Order of Foresters – which within three months claimed to have 363 courts with 16,510 members. Thereafter the main body continued to grow, although remaining distinctly smaller than the Oddfellows up to 1850. The Foresters' system of central government was rather weaker than that of the Oddfellows. They had a High Chief Ranger and an Executive Council with an annual High Court meeting, but the actual executive offices moved physically each year – a remarkable example of the Victorian belief in rotating governing bodies to avoid any suggestion of local favouritism (a practice adopted by some of the smaller trade unions like the glassmakers who moved their secretarial offices periodically from branch to branch). This movement of the seat of government of the Foresters from year to year made for some inconvenience and inefficiency, and was actu-

Table 5   Membership of the Manchester Unity of
Oddfellows and of the Ancient Order of Foresters,
1850–70.

Year	Manchester Unity of Oddfellows	Ancient Order of Foresters
1850	224,878	80,089
1855	239,783	105,753
1860	305,241	168,576
1865	373,509	277,746
1870	434,100	361,735

ally criticized by the Royal Commission in 1874. The growth of the
two major affiliated orders during the period under consideration
may be seen from the figures taken from the records of the two societies (see Table 5).

Of the two orders, as already mentioned, the Oddfellows grew very
rapidly in the years 1835–45, but more slowly subsequently. While
their earlier growth was in Lancashire and the West Riding, by the
1870s there was more vigorous growth in the southern counties than
in the north. In fact, there was an actual decline in the number of
lodges in Lancashire from 737 in 1845 to 507 in 1875, and in the
West Riding from 600 down to 444 at the same dates. This seems to
have been caused by the efforts of the directors and the Annual Moveable Committee to tighten their control over the branches. There was
also a number of lodge collapses due to shortages of funds. However,
in 1853 the Annual Moveable Committee at last brought in a much
needed reform, the adoption of graduated scales of contributions
instead of flat-rate contributions, irrespective of age. This was a useful
financial reform, although it did not solve all problems of lodge sol-
vency, as will be seen later. Another improvement in the organization
of the Oddfellows was the growth in size of the average lodge, which
made for greater financial security. By 1875 the average number per
lodge had risen to 132 from about 70 in 1845.

The Foresters certainly grew more slowly in the early years than the
Oddfellows, although they were not far behind in membership by
1870. Generally speaking, they also lagged behind them in organization. As already noted, their central office changed location with the
annual High Court meeting, and the delegates to that meeting were
elected directly by the courts, not by district committees. Added to

8183

this weakness at the centre was the failure to adopt graduated scales for contributions until 1871, and even then this reform was largely ignored, and not enforced until 1885. There was one direction, however, in which the Foresters seemed to have made more progress than the Oddfellows, and this was in the recruitment of agricultural labourers in the southern counties. Here their success was due very largely to setting contribution rates at a low enough level for agricultural labourers to be able to join. Thus there were farm workers in Shropshire who were members of the Foresters in the early 1870s even though they were earning only 11s a week.

Understandably, attention is concentrated on the Oddfellows and the Foresters when the affiliated societies are discussed; they were far and away the largest of the orders. The membership of the Manchester Unity of Oddfellows, as given in the Fourth Report of the Royal Commission, 1874, stood at 426,663 on 1 January 1873, while that of the Ancient Order of Foresters on 31 December 1872 was 388,872 (in another place in the report, the figures are given as 470,043 and 421,988 respectively). But in addition to these two large orders there were others which, although admittedly much smaller, were still of some importance. They included the Grand United Order of Oddfellows (71,000 members), the Order of Druids (57,000), the Loyal Order of Ancient Shepherds, Ashton Unity (46,000), the National Independent Order of Oddfellows (35,000), and the Nottingham Ancient Imperial Order of Oddfellows (40,000). There were many smaller societies taking the title of Oddfellows (35 in all), and another five with the title of Forester. The total number of affiliated societies in 1877 was 163.

Among the lesser societies, two may be singled out for comment. The secretary of the Equalised Manchester and Salford District of the Order of Druids was interviewed at length by the Royal Commission, with particular emphasis on the need for gradualized contributions (which the Society had not yet adopted), and on the amount spent on drink at meetings. This the secretary sought to play down, claiming that they would not allow any man to remain who was strongly under the influence of liquor; but he went on, ". . . there is not the least doubt that many men occasionally do get what is usually termed a little top-heavy". Like the other smaller orders, the Druids with their 979 lodges were not organized on a national scale – "Lancashire and Yorkshire are our chief seat".

The Rechabites were different from other societies in being a temperance society. Any members indulging in strong drink were liable to dismissal from their ranks after three offences against the rules of temperance. Perhaps because they were more exclusive than other orders, they seemed to attract a superior class of working men. Their members were generally mechanics, and some were even from the middle classes – "we perhaps have some of the middle class". Indeed, their representative made much of this:

> The other day we counted, of persons of the mechanic class who used to wear the fustian jacket, 30 members who have done without the fustian jacket, and have placed themselves in a better class of society, and would not perhaps take the money if they were sick . . . yes, one-fourth of the members have left the working-class platform, and have said, "I will take my place higher", and they have got into a better position.

So much for social mobility through sobriety and the Rechabites. They were not founded until 1835, and their membership was only about 9,000 in 1872, but they were to increase greatly in numbers by the end of the century. In common with the other affiliated orders, they could not afford to offer superannuation benefits, but they were prepared to pay half sick pay for life.

The affiliated societies were not the only form of friendly society in the middle of the nineteenth century, of course, and other important forms will be considered shortly, but they certainly are the most striking development in the field of working-class self-help at the time. It has already been emphasized that the very poorest could hardly afford membership, and this view of them was stressed by a witness in 1872 who said that members of his Liverpool burial society were not generally members of the Druids: "No, not as a rule; the class of men who belong to friendly societies . . . are the thinking part of the working classes". But this could be misleading. The test was rather whether they could afford regular payments, bearing in mind, too, the liability to fines for falling into arrears and possible eventual loss of membership. So that although it is true that the majority of members were in better paid jobs, agricultural labourers, as we have seen, were not excluded. Indeed, an analysis of the membership of the Manchester Unity of Oddfellows contained in the 1874 Fourth Report of the

Table 6 Occupations of the largest groups of members, Manchester Unity of Oddfellows, 1866–70.

Agricultural labourers	107,760
Town labourers	85,774
Miners	77,161
Carpenters and joiners	74,760
Cordwainers	49,076

Royal Commission shows this very clearly. This survey is of occupations over the five years 1866–70, and it ranks 26 occupations in order, together with a very large "sundries" group. The five largest categories are shown in Table 6.

It is interesting to see that in these prosperous years, agricultural labourers had become the largest group of all, but in the aggregate, of course, they were heavily outnumbered by the handicraft trades. In passing, it should be noted that miners are included in the list, although some friendly societies excluded them as their occupation was too dangerous to make them welcome as members.

What then were the advantages of affiliated society membership? First and foremost, in return for weekly payments of a few pence, a sick allowance of 8s or 10s a week was paid, reducing after some months, together with attendance by a physician usually appointed by the society, and a funeral benefit (usually including the wife) of up to £10. Rates of contribution and of benefit varied from branch to branch, but in Liverpool in 1872 an Oddfellow aged 38 paid about 8½d per week, which entitled him to 12s a week sickness pay, and £10 on the death of his wife or himself. Sick pay came out of the lodge's funds, funeral benefit out of district funds. Both contributions and benefits were fixed by the local lodge or court, and not (originally, at least) defined by a national scale. The weekly subscriptions, generally payable at the monthly meeting, were obviously reckoned a sound enough investment by members of the societies, although occasionally lodges and courts had to close for lack of funds. Further, one of the shocks of the 1874 report was the revelation that many branches of the affiliated societies were insolvent in the sense that assets could not meet their liabilities – they were really living from hand to mouth. For example, only about one in ten of the Manchester Unity of Oddfellows' lodges was actually solvent (although this did not take account of possible secessions, which were numerous). Nevertheless, the affiliated orders were clearly far more popular than the older local societies.

The reasons for this are not far to seek, and some consideration has been given to them already. It seems likely that apart from the safeguards against sickness and mortality, one of the most attractive aspects must have been their conviviality. Those that met in public houses could offer a monthly night out with plenty to drink, mostly paid for out of the club funds – the so-called "liquid rent" that the publican expected as payment for the use of the club room. Then there was the dressing-up, the solemn rituals of the lodge or court, no doubt enjoyed by all as a piece of harmless nonsense, yet at the same time contributing to a sense of brotherhood and good fellowship, and a comforting feeling of togetherness.

It must be remembered, too, that the affiliated societies were working-class organizations run on a voluntary basis. Even by the 1870s, many secretaries were still unpaid, carrying out their duties in their spare time. Some still had difficulties in writing, which could cause problems in communicating with district or headquarters officials. Only when one comes to the senior officers of both the Oddfellows and Foresters – the Grand Masters, Directors, Chief Rangers, and so on – does one encounter middle-class figures such as manufacturers, managers, businessmen, retailers, and professional people who had more time to spare for society affairs, especially travelling from branch to branch. The rank and file were overwhelmingly working class. Moreover, it is worth remembering that such men had the courage and energy after a long day's work to organize the running of a lodge or court, and to take the responsibility for ordering its affairs. We know little of how a new branch of one of the orders was actually set up, but clearly it must have required initiative and enterprise on the part of its founder members. Much credit is due to the countless men (and women) who together created the affiliated orders. They provide a striking example of working-class self-help at a time of great economic and social change.

To turn to another and somewhat humbler form of friendly society, the burial societies. These were mentioned briefly in the previous chapter. They also expanded in the years after 1830. Such clubs existed principally, of course, to provide funeral benefit, although in a few cases they might offer sickness benefit as well. The Blackburn

Philanthropic Burial Society continued to be an impressive example of this kind of club. It was founded in 1839 by working men, and by the 1870s had 116,368 members and a capital of £14,545 11s 8d. Its president was paid £5 5s a quarter, the treasurer £2 10s a quarter, and the vice-president 10s 6d a quarter. A paid secretary was employed at £140 a year, with two assistants paid £1 2s 6d and £1 1s weekly. Committee members received £1 a year. A great majority of its members were factory workers employed in the local mills. This was a collecting society, that is, it employed 58 collectors who were paid 12.5 or 10 per cent of their takings, the best paid earning up to £1 17s 6d a fortnight. Subscriptions were paid fortnightly – a penny up to the age of 10 secured a burial payment of £4; over 10, the benefit was raised to £5. Over 10 it was also possible to pay an enhanced fee of 1½d, giving a funeral benefit of £7 10s. Many subscriptions were paid by housewives out of their housekeeping money and covered members of the family, so that it was often said that burial clubs were mostly for women and children. This was not necessarily so, although it is true that the male members of affiliated societies were usually covered for only their own deaths and their wives, rather than the family as a whole.

Some burial clubs had become large-scale commercial undertakings by the 1870s. The best example of this is perhaps the Royal Liver Society of Liverpool. Although founded in 1850 entirely by working men, by about 1872 (according to a witness before the Royal Commission) it had a membership of almost 550,000, based upon Liverpool and Glasgow. In Liverpool it employed a staff of 50 clerks. There were a thousand collectors throughout the country and a further 300 or more agents and sub-agents. The collectors retained 25 per cent of their takings for burials, 12.5 per cent on the sick branch, 12.5 per cent on endowments, and 5 per cent on medical aid – so that it was possible to subscribe for more than simple burial benefit. However, it is unlikely that many paid for extended benefits, for the witness remarked that members of the society were very poor.

Another collecting society of a rather more elevated type was the Liverpool Protective Burial Society, established in 1856. It had 42,700 members in 1869–70, and its secretary was paid £3 a week. It employed about 130 collectors, mostly working men, mechanics such as stonemasons, fitters and blacksmiths, who could earn £2, £2 10s or even (in one case) £3 a week. In the bigger commercial organizations, collectors' books could be bought and sold, and collectors often had some influence over the running of the society. The funeral benefit paid by this society was up to £7 10s.

The prevalence and growth of these burial societies is a testimony to the continued fear of the poorest among the working classes of not being able to afford a decent funeral. Yet the cost of this was not necessarily very great. The representative of the Liverpool Protective Burial Society was informative on this point before the Royal Commission:

– Will you tell us what they can be buried for?
– I buried a grown-up man out of the workhouse one day last week for £3 5s 0d employing a horse and coach, and I drove out in my own trap, as I always do to see the funeral properly carried out; that was not a case belonging to our society. I buried a woman belonging to our society for £2 18s 0d on one occasion.
– Should you say that would be a burial which the artisan class would call a fairly respectable burial?
– Yes; it would be in what they call the poor ground; it would not be in a grave set apart for that particular person, but merely where others were buried. The poor ground is considered to be cheaper than if you have to purchase a grave exclusively for the party.

Thus, the low costs quoted related only to burial in a common grave and without a headstone, which would be much more expensive. It is difficult to estimate the true cost to a family of a burial, and how far the society's death grant would cover it. All would depend on what the family thought necessary and could afford – how far they thought funeral attire desirable, the costs of the funeral meats and drink, and so on.

The small local burial societies served their communities reasonably well, since their officials were often part-time, and familiar local figures. The Chorley Family Funeral Society, for example, numbered 2,590 families among its membership out of a population of about 18,000. It was said in evidence before the Royal Commission that this represented about 80 per cent of the town's population; so that although the organization of the society seemed sketchy, and reliant on extra levies from time to time, at least it was a known neighbourhood institution. The large-scale collecting societies were a different proposition, especially in the big cities such as Liverpool, where there were many Irish immigrants, some illiterate, and open to fraud and exploitation by the collectors. According to Professor Gosden, "There can be little doubt that the large collecting societies were the weakest of the engines of thrift supposedly devoted to encouraging self-help in Victorian Britain". This seems a fair judgement, given their heavy management expenses, occasional instances of defalcations, and lack of any control by policyholders over the running of the societies.

At the other extreme, perhaps, are the building societies already touched upon in the last chapter, when it was pointed out that by 1825 more than 250 of these societies had been formed. It was also emphasized that although there was some working-class participation in these societies, the contributions required were often beyond the reach of the average workman. However, the great expansion of the urban areas throughout the century, and the rise in real wages in the middle decades, led to a further development of the building society movement. Terminating societies were still being established, and in particular a new type of terminating society, the Starr-Bowkett society, became well known, especially in the London area, involving interest-free loans and balloting for advances; but permanent societies gradually overtook terminating societies, as investors could get their money out any time. By the 1870s permanent societies had acquired the characteristics familiar at the present time, that is to say, they provided a safe place for investors to earn interest, at the same time lending money for house purchase secured by mortgage.

How far the societies really became middle-class institutions in the period since the 1830s is an interesting question. There was some difference of opinion among witnesses before the Royal Commission on this subject. One extreme view was put by a witness, Mr W. L. Harle, speaking of the permanent societies in the Newcastle area since 1851:

> . . . they are now large financial bodies, with a view to speculation in land and property of that nature . . . these institutions are no longer institutions representing workmen or small freeholders, who want a house to live in themselves, but simply speculators or gentlemen of the middle-class, who are anxious to buy property for purposes of general profit.

Another witness, a Mr J. S. Parker, an actuary of London, said that "few of the working classes can join permanent societies and buy their houses through them".

On the other hand, although the administration of the permanent building society was undeniably falling into middle-class professional hands, there is abundant evidence to show that members of the societies were very often working class. Mr Higham, secretary to the Fourth City Mutual Building Society, and a committee member of the Building Societies Protection Society, had some pertinent observations to make on this subject. For example, "I have more perhaps of what may be termed the tradesman class than many". Some of his members were above the working class, but "a large proportion belong to the working classes". He gave an example of one of his members:

> Tomorrow I have to settle an advance to a workman on the Metropolitan railway. We are to lend him £360; he has bought a house for £420, and is to pay £60 towards the purchase money . . . then he is going to occupy it; he is in permanent employment; he resides in a smaller house for which he pays rent; he will only have to pay us £5 or £6 per annum more than he now pays for his rent, and therefore we look on it as a judicious purchase, and lend him six-sevenths of the money.

This man was a skilled worker, a carpenter, and obviously a good risk from the society's point of view, even though he was paying well above average for a working-class house. The average advance of another society, the London Temperance Land and Building Society, was about £220. Of course, provincial house prices were distinctly cheaper. In Manchester, a good mechanic's house (three up, three down) cost £150.

In Birmingham, as was seen earlier, the building society movement was well established before 1830, and after that date the societies (all permanent by 1872) continued to flourish and expand. By the 1870s, nearly all the members were still working men, "certainly 95 out of every 100". A spokesman for the societies said that they had 13,000 houses in the town belonging to working men, and "streets more than a mile long, in which absolutely every house belongs to the working classes of Birmingham – Albert Road, Victoria Road, Gladstone Road, Cobden Street, Bright Terrace, and so on. . . . Bright Terrace has 28 houses in it, and they are all very nice houses" (to judge by the names, these were all recently erected streets). The building societies worked in conjunction with land societies, which bought the land and divided it. The purchaser of a plot then obtained an advance from the building society to build on it.

One Birmingham witness was anxious to point out the good social habits resulting from the building society activities there. He was asked,

> – You mean that such habits are increased by the possession by persons in that class of life of their own houses?
> – Yes, they save their money, and instead of spending it in public houses, they spend it upon property. They go home at night and cultivate their gardens, or read the newspaper to their wives, instead of being in public houses. We are the greatest social reformers of the day. . . .

This is a pleasant, if somewhat fanciful picture of sober working-class life, with the emphasis very much on the working-class nature of society membership. In fact, it was the well-paid workers who could afford the repayments, and this class was well represented in a town like Birmingham, which was famous for the range of its skilled trades. When asked what was the average wage of members of Birmingham building societies, the witness replied that the average was perhaps 30s a week:

> but there are others again, the clerks and respectable mechanics, who get their £100 or £120 a year. There are such members with us, but taking it altogether the average would perhaps be from 27/– or 28/– to 30/– a week.

As for the other large towns, in London the Starr-Bowkett societies were popular among the working classes, but were small-scale terminating societies. No doubt the high price of housing in the capital made house purchase difficult for all but the highest-paid working men. In Leeds, the bulk of the members of the Leeds Permanent Society – about four-fifths – were working class, including a great number of policemen, who visited the office on Fridays (their pay day), many of them depositing half-a-crown. There were also many customers of the higher classes, for example, merchants, tradesmen, professional

men, and persons retired from business. The society claimed to provide facilities for both house purchase and investment at a fair rate of
interest. In Manchester, there was a number of terminating societies,
with members who earned about 30s a week. These societies bor-
rowed money from time to time, although power to do so had been
struck from their rules by Tidd Pratt: "We never had any doubt about
it" (an earlier witness, Mr Higham, said of the late Tidd Pratt, the
greatly-feared Registrar, "Mr Tidd Pratt objected to many things
being in. He acted in a dictatorial and arbitrary manner. He was a gentleman we were always very pleased to meet, but I cannot say that we
respected his decisions").

In Liverpool, there was some division of opinion regarding the
extent of working-class membership of the building societies. One
witness said, "The working men in Liverpool do very little in the way
of buying through building societies; they are too migratory a character". But on another occasion, a witness said that members were
"with very few exceptions, artisans and all classes of labouring men,
small shopkeepers – in short, the humbler classes". One society was
almost altogether run by policemen, another by people in the Post
Office and Customs, and a third by shipwrights. In Oldham, they
were all terminating societies save one, shares being held by the
operative class or small shopkeepers, including many of the hands at
Platts, the famous makers of textile machinery. At Bradford, small
advances were made to operatives, overlookers, warehousemen and
clerks. They were 80 per cent of the investors, but not more than 50
per cent of the borrowers – "you get rather more into the middle class
when you come to the borrowers". Similarly in Sheffield, many of the
people advanced money were "above the working classes", while
most of the investors were working class.

To sum up, it is clear that large numbers of the better-paid working
men were members of building societies, and according to the Second
Report of the Royal Commission of 1872 the smaller terminating societies were often managed by the working classes "or persons very
near them in point of station". This, one might say, was one of the
simplest and most direct forms of self-help. On the other hand, the
larger permanent societies were almost invariably under middle-class
direction. This is really what one might expect; they had grown sufficiently large to require full-time professional management. Again,
membership might be for simple investment of small savings, or with

a view to house purchase. Sometimes, as in Oldham, investors joined with an advance already in mind. How far working-class men were potential house purchasers seemed to vary from place to place, dependent on the level of local wages, and the state of the local house market. In many towns, pre-eminently perhaps in Birmingham, they joined to buy their own houses, but apparently less so in London. Yet even there, in the Birkbeck Society, with 25,000 members, at least six out of ten advances were to the poorer classes, according to the evidence presented to the Commission.

How many building societies were there about 1870, and what was the total membership? This is a very difficult question to answer precisely. Professor Gosden, relying on some figures in the Second Report, which takes into account the unknown numbers of unregistered societies, suggests that there were probably about 2,000 societies in England and Wales, with an average membership of 400. This would give a total membership of about 800,000. At the same time, he points out that an estimate was made by E. J. Cleary in 1965 of about 1,500 societies, with a membership not greatly in excess of 300,000. However, Appendix A of the 1871 report gives an adjusted figure of 4,049 societies in England and Wales, with the four counties of Lancashire (1,428), Middlesex (927), Surrey (217) and Yorkshire (177) having the largest number of societies. Total membership of registered societies is shown in Table 7.

Table 7   Membership of registered building societies, c. 1870.

	Permanent	Terminating	Total
England	161,016	43,488	204,504
Wales	4,924	2,665	7,589
	165,940	46,153	212,093

These figures exclude Scotland and Ireland, and refer only to registered societies. The report stresses the fact that there are many known omissions, and says that the probable figure for membership is about one million.

With estimates varying as widely as this, it would be foolish to guess at the number of working men actually buying their houses, quite apart from those who had completed their purchase earlier on. Not only do we not know the breakdown between working-class members and middle-class members, but we do not know what proportion of the former were simple savers, and what proportion were buying their houses. All the same, it is worth noting that the working-class population in 1871 was about 20 million; that is, the male working-class population of all ages must have been about 10 million. This figure, of course, included the youngest children excluded by law from work and the number of men too old to work, which would reduce the 10 million considerably. Taking these facts into account, the figures quoted above, even the lowest numbers, are by no means insignificant or trivial; and it is clear enough that in some towns house purchase was an important aspect of the lives of skilled working men in steady employment.

Indeed, buying one's own house occupies a special place in the history of working-class self-help in the nineteenth century. It was not simply a matter of apeing the middle classes; most of the middle classes for much of the century lived in rented accommodation, which they found to be a convenient arrangement. Even in 1914, the proportion of all owner-occupied housing has been estimated to be about only 10 per cent. So house ownership seems to have been a significant aspect of the life of the better-paid working man, symbolizing a perceived need for independence, standing on one's own two feet, and being beholden to no-one. A man liked to have pride in himself, his skills, and the respect of his fellow workers. House ownership contributed powerfully to his sense of self-confidence and security in a changing world.

It remains to say something about other forms of friendly society apart from those already considered. In addition to the large-scale commercial burial societies such as the Royal Liver, there was also a group of commercial insurance companies specializing in insurance for the better-paid working classes. Their clientele was therefore different from that of the national burial societies which catered for the very poor, but they resembled them in having no club nights or social activities. Business was conducted through the post, both subscriptions and benefit being paid by postal orders. The biggest was the Hearts of Oak Society, which grew quickly in the 1860s. By 1874 it was reputed to have 32,837 members, and it provided superannuation, sickness, funeral, lying-in, and even fire benefits. No member was admitted unless he earned at least £1 2s a week (this would exclude labourers, of course), and there was a long list of excluded trades. The upper age limit was 36. According to the 1874 report, the Society apparently consisted of "picked members of a much more uniform age than usual". Contributions were 6s 6d a quarter, with an entrance fee dependent on age, ranging from 2s 6d to 3s 6d. The Commissioners regarded the Hearts of Oak as a well-run society, although there was no question of any direct control of the society by its policyholders, its affairs being managed by an elected Assembly of Delegates. Sometimes elections to this body were organized by clubs of members formed for this purpose, but all this was very different from the procedures of the affiliated societies.

Then again there were trade societies registered as friendly societies, which were very like the amalgamated trade unions. Such a society was the Locomotive Steam Engineers and Firemen's Society, established in Birmingham in 1839, and by the 1870s having 60 branches (one suspended) and a total membership of 6,887. Entrance fees (dependent on age) ranged from 5s to £2 16s 6d for those aged 35–40. Subscriptions were from 10d to 1s 2d per fortnight to the management fund, and 1s a quarter for pensions. Benefits were 10s per week for 52 weeks for sickness, pension 5s per week, and death benefit £10 to £18. There were also pit clubs, which provided what was called in the Black Country field insurance, that is, insurance against accidents. They were much disliked by the miners in the Lancashire and Staffordshire pits, because membership was compulsory, and the deductions from pay were regarded as a way of holding back pay. They were superseded in the 1860s by miners' permanent relief societies, the first being the Northumberland and Durham Miners Society, which was set up in 1862.

Another form of society disliked by its members was the railway friendly society. Membership of these societies was also virtually compulsory. They were organized by the larger railway companies for their employees, since, among railway men, inability to work due to sickness or injury was thought to be about 40 per cent higher than in other comparable occupations. Some companies had several societies – the Great Western Railway (GWR) had three. At their famous works in Swindon, there were as many as 7,000 employed. The GWR Sickness Fund Society provided sick pay of from 4s to 12s a week, and funeral benefit of £4 to £12 on the basis of contributions varying from 2d to 9d per week. There was also a pension of 6s a week for members aged 60 who had served 25 years. These benefits were not ungenerous, but the railway friendly societies were criticized in the 1874 Report. This was because of their compulsory nature, and also because the subsidies provided by the companies to their schemes were not legally binding. There was the further point of criticism that if a man aged, say, 40 left the company, he forfeited his benefits, and would be too old to join another company.

Two other, more unusual forms of society investigated by the Royal Commission were deposit societies and dividing societies. The former were confined very largely to the southeast of England. Each member of a deposit society paid money in and then withdrew it as sick pay when required, supplemented by a sum drawn from the general fund, the proportion between the two amounts being dependent on age; when the member's deposit was exhausted, his benefit came to an end. Basically such societies were savings banks, and the Fourth Report of 1874 suggested that they should really have been recognized as such from the start. Dividing societies were also known as tontines, and were commonly found in the agricultural districts of the southern and eastern counties. They also flourished in Liverpool, where it was said by Sir George Young, one of the commissioners, that the city was swarming with registered tontines; while in Bethnal Green and the East End of London they were known as Birmingham Societies. Contributions were paid in, and sick pay drawn as required, but as the name "dividing" implies, at the end of each year, the funds remaining were divided up among the members.

Two further kinds of society mentioned in the previous chapter were still in being in the 1870s. The county societies still had a considerable membership and were still run very largely under middle-class patronage. They provided sick pay and funeral benefit but without the regular club meetings that characterized the affiliated orders. The two largest, according to the Fourth Report, were the Essex Provident, with a membership of 9,315, and the Wiltshire County Society, which had 101 branches and 7,130 members. As for the other kind of society, the local village society, it was still in existence, but the report commented that it was impossible to count their number; in the southeast of England, there was hardly a village of 20 houses and a beershop that had not had its club. In the Midlands, for example, Ashby de la Zouch Poor Law union had a population of 31,544, and a total of 58 societies (28 unregistered), with a membership of 3,715. Another union in the south Midlands, at Stratford on Avon (population 22,374) had 21 societies, two of them unregistered, with 2,075 members. This was 9.27 per cent of the population. The 2,075 membership included members of affiliated orders, but they numbered only 922 of the total.

Lastly, the female societies, which were few. Victorian society was strongly masculine in character, and woman's place was thought to be in the home rather than in the workplace. The important thing was to safeguard the position of the breadwinner in the family, and that was nearly always the husband, not the wife who was customarily insured only for funeral benefit. As we saw in the last chapter, female societies did exist, some of them in the form of temperance societies, but their registered membership came to only 22,691 in 1874. The Chief Registrar actually believed that societies consisting of mixed membership were undesirable because of the difference between the sickness rates of men and women. The 1874 report devotes little space to women's societies, but does say that among registered societies were the following: Female Foresters, Female Druids, United Sisters, Female Gardeners, Female Rechabites, Odd Females, Odd Sisters, Loyal Orangewomen, Daughters of Temperance, Ancient Shepherdesses, Loyal Women, Comforting Sisters, and Alfred Sisters.

The 1874 report lists 11 major categories of friendly societies in all, together with a further group of six that could be called "miscellaneous". They include such societies as cattle insurance societies. One of the 11 categories is also really a miscellaneous group of societies established under the Friendly Society Act of 1855. It includes shipwreck societies, that is, societies insuring against shipwreck, a subject very much under public scrutiny in the 1870s as a result of Samuel Plimsoll's campaign against the deliberate overloading and sinking of ships to obtain the insurance money. Another kind of society in this group occupies an anomalous position, one might think. This was the working men's club, the Union of Workingmen's Clubs and Institutes (UWCI), which was formed in 1862. Apparently Tidd Pratt himself suggested that these clubs could be registered under the Friendly Society Acts. The leading protagonist of the club movement, the Rev. H. Solly, gave evidence himself before the Commission, explaining that the clubs were originally included as a social and recreational centre apart from the public house, but that beer was now served in many clubs. The amount consumed was very modest, according to Solly, because members were not constantly under pressure as they would be in a public house to refill their pots. It emerged that games were also played in the clubs, including card games, sometimes played for small stakes – an activity actually illegal in public houses. Solly had some difficulty in justifying this. Doubts were also raised as to the propriety in a game of billiards of the loser paying for the use of the table – it was solemnly asked, was this gambling? But the most difficult question of all for Solly was why the clubs should be registered as friendly societies at all. According to the secretary of the UWCI, about 200 were registered out of the 250 clubs in the Union (there were a further 175 or so clubs outside the Union). He also claimed that not more than 20 clubs sold beer.

Before drawing the threads of this chapter together, it would be as well to touch briefly on the legislation affecting friendly societies and the appointment of the Royal Commission in 1872. This legislation provided a more detailed framework for the operation of the societies without effecting any very profound changes in their practices. Thus, the 1834 Act abolished the previous need to submit rules and tables to the JPs; the rules were henceforth to go directly to the barrister appointed to certify the rules of savings banks (that is, to Tidd Pratt), with a copy to the clerk of the peace. Returns of sickness and mortality were also to go to Tidd Pratt, not the clerk of the peace. The scope of registered societies was also enlarged to include "any other purpose which is not illegal". Thus, the administration of the societies became more centralized, a move that was welcome to them.

Another act ten years later gave Tidd Pratt the title of Registrar, enabling him to file the rules himself without reference to the clerk of the peace. Societies were given certain additional powers of purchasing goods and materials, and for members to be paid dividends on the profits arising from the sales of such goods – this was to allow co-operative societies to register. The terms of the Corresponding Societies Act and of the Seditious Meetings Act were no longer to apply to friendly societies (they had not done so in practice for many years), but the affiliated societies were still not able to register as such because their annual meetings were not considered general meetings – another odd quirk of the law.

Two further acts were passed in the 1850s. The first, in 1850, was prompted by the embezzlement of the funds of the Manchester Unity by the secretary in 1848. In the resulting court case, it was held that the Unity was a mere partnership, and even an illegal organization.

The result was a campaign to allow the affiliated orders to register and so gain legal protection for their funds. The 1850 Act therefore permitted the registration of societies with branches – the Foresters registered their rules in 1850, and the Manchester Unity in 1851 – but the individual courts and lodges still had to register separately. This act was renewed annually until it was replaced by a permanent measure in 1855. The 1855 Act abolished all fees for registration (a valuable concession for the affiliated societies, with their many branches), and it allowed any friendly society merely to deposit its rules and by so doing gain the legal recognition that would allow it to sue and be sued.

This was the extent of legislation affecting friendly societies in the period 1830–72. On the whole, the law allowed them to go about their business without undue restrictions. Nevertheless, the branches of affiliated orders still had to register separately from the parent body (Tidd Pratt was very insistent on this), and in theory they still could not use their funds for social purposes. Then again, registration was still not compulsory, which makes any attempt to assess progress in the friendly society movement as a whole somewhat difficult. Many small societies still saw no need to register, and even in the affiliated orders, by the end of 1858, only 1,673 of the 3,198 Manchester Unity lodges had registered, and only 926 of the 1,876 courts of the Foresters.

No attempt has been made in this chapter to provide a complete list of all forms of friendly societies, as the intention has been to describe and comment on only the major forms. Thus, certain specialized forms of friendly society have been omitted, such as the Manchester Caledonian Society (150 members, all Scots, principally commercial travellers), the Warehousemen and Clerks Provident Society (1,500 members, providing out-of-work benefit as well as sick benefit, and on this ground refused registration by Tidd Pratt), and the small number of annuity societies (they had few working-class members). However, one last form of self-help still requires some comment, although not a friendly society at all, and not included in the list in the Fourth Report. This is the trustee savings bank.

Savings banks were different from most other self-help agencies in that in essence they were set up by members of the middle class to encourage working-class saving, and at the same time to keep them off the poor rates. Another characteristic which distinguished them from other working-class self-help bodies is that their depositors had no right to participate in the management. Small local banks of this kind existed in the early nineteenth century, and the Savings Bank Act, 1817, was a modest act designed to encourage their founding. In 1818, as many as 132 banks were set up, and a further 32 in the following year. An act in 1824 sought to discourage their use by the middle classes by putting a limit of £50 on deposits in the first year, and of £30 in subsequent years, with a maximum total of £200. The 1828 Savings Bank Act lowered the rate of interest payable, and required the rules to be submitted to a barrister – this was Tidd Pratt. Further regulations were issued under the Savings Bank Act, 1844.

In fact, trustee savings banks had a somewhat chequered career in the first half of the nineteenth century. Because they were established by authority of the state, it was erroneously believed that their funds were guaranteed by the government. A series of swindles and collapses in the 1840s and early 1850s made it clear that they were not. Moreover, it is not even certain that their clientele was exclusively working class; earlier beliefs were that only a minority of depositors were working class – perhaps a third – although more recent case studies in Glasgow and Aberdeen have disproved this, at least in Scotland. One new form of bank, starting in the late 1840s, certainly was for the working classes, and the poorest of them. The most famous was the Yorkshire Penny Bank, founded in 1859, and establishing 24 branches in its first year.

The full extent of the trustee bank movement before the 1860s is difficult to ascertain, although there seemed to be more depositors in rural areas than in industrial areas. For example, in Devonshire there were 10.33 depositors for every hundred of the population, while in Lancashire there were only 5.8, and in the West Riding only 4.77. It may be that in these industrial areas the affiliated societies had already taken a firm hold, so that the trustee savings banks had a good deal of competition.

At all events, the evident lack of security experienced by depositors in the crashes of the early 1850s led to the appointment of a Select Committee on Savings Banks in 1858. It was not only the safeguarding of the interests of the depositors that concerned the Committee, but also the question of the use under existing law to which the government could invest the banks' deposits. The new Chancellor of the Exchequer, Mr Gladstone, did not accept the Select Committee's report, but the bill he brought in was defeated in July 1860. A minor reform of the government's powers of investment was passed later in 1860, but the major matter of security for deposits was not tackled until the following year. In 1861 the government set up the Post Office Savings Bank (POSB) under the direct control of the government, which guaranteed the safety of the deposits. The attractions of the Post Office Savings Bank as compared with the trustee banks were very considerable; while most of the 600 savings banks were open only a few hours a week, the post offices operating the new bank numbered up to 3,000, and were open all day every working day in the week. Moreover, they could accept deposits as low as one shilling. The result is that by the end of 1862, 180,000 accounts had been opened in the POSB, with a total of £1.75m. deposits. Certainly they offered a better service to a poorer class of depositor than that of the trustee savings banks, along with the assurance of complete security.

The challenge thus presented to the savings bank movement resulted in nearly a hundred trustee banks closing by 1866, many of them transferring their business to the Post Office under the terms of a special act passed to facilitate this in 1863. Nevertheless, the larger trustee banks survived, opening for longer hours, paying higher rates of interest, sponsoring penny banks, setting up special investment departments, and in other ways fighting their corner. By 1870 some sort of equilibrium had been achieved. The trustee savings banks had 1,384,000 accounts, with £37.96 million on deposit and £316,000 in special investment. The Post Office Savings Bank had 1,183,000 accounts, with £15.1 million on deposit. Clearly, it had opened up new opportunities for small-scale, safe banking by depositors, probably more than half of them women and children. In an age of *laissez faire*, in which the free trade movement reached its highest point in Gladstone's "Crown and Summit" budget of 1860, the establishment of the Post Office Savings Bank in 1861 remains an outstanding example of government paternalism. It did not of itself create a new form of working-class self-help, but sought to encourage it among the poorest classes, and proved remarkably successful in doing so.

A final perspective may now be established on friendly society activity in the earlier years of Victoria's reign. The reasons for the great expansion in membership of friendly societies have already been examined at the beginning of this chapter, and all that needs to be said here is to reaffirm the importance of the rise in real wages of the time. Of course, this took place erratically, and there were periods such as the early 1840s when further progress was at least unsure; but even in downswings of the trade cycle, the effects of the Poor Law Amendment Act, 1834 seems to have been counteractive, and to have encouraged membership. This was even so although the official policy was to deduct any friendly society benefit payable from any outdoor relief that was paid. Strict adherence to this rule would have nullified the basic objective of membership, that is, to provide support in times of distress without recourse to the hated Poor Law. In practice, it seems to have been recognized that this would be a very harsh way to treat a man trying to maintain his independence; so whatever the official policy might be, it appears to have been customary to deduct only a proportion of sick benefit payable from outdoor relief. In Wales, the amount deducted in the 1870s was half the benefit payable, although disputes did take place over friendly society payments to members on indoor relief. It should perhaps be noted that benefit payments were usually only about a third of usual earnings, and that friendly society membership did not necessarily shield members in all cases from the Poor Law. In 1881, there were 11,304 adult male indoor paupers who had been society members, some 7,391 of whom had failed to keep up contributions, while the societies of the remainder had broken up.

Finally, as will be seen later in this book, it was no coincidence that the expansion of the friendly societies took place at the same time as a significant growth of both the trade union movement and the co-operative movement. These massive movements all occurred within the context of a vast expansion of the economy and in particular of the industrial sector. Naturally it would be helpful to be able to estimate numbers for the whole range of friendly societies. The figure of four million appears in the 1874 Fourth Report, and according to Professor F. M. L. Thompson, this implies that some 60 per cent of male adults were members. However, this includes membership of burial clubs. In 1880, the figure for friendly societies alone (affiliated and local) is about 2.2 million. This would mean about 30 per cent of adult males. If the membership of collecting societies and other industrial societies is added in, then Thompson's estimate of what he calls "the provident population" sails up to easily three-quarters, and possibly as much as 80 per cent of the total male population. These are impressive figures. However desperate the plight of the very poorest – and it must be remembered that the burial societies catered very largely for this class alone – it still seems reasonable to suppose that by the 1870s a substantial majority of the working classes sought to protect themselves through friendly societies against (to quote Defoe again) "any disaster or distress".

Chapter Three

Friendly societies after 1875

In the preceding chapters emphasis has been given to economic and social developments as determinants of the nature and growth of friendly society activity in the nineteenth century. Similar considerations apply to the period after 1875 and up to the outbreak of war in 1914. At first sight, the period from the early 1870s to the mid-1890s, often labelled the years of the Great Depression, might be seen as one in which friendly society growth was inhibited by the economic depression of the time. In fact, although there was some increase in unemployment, the depression was marked rather by a fall in prices and profits, while the imports of cheap food (principally of cheap corn from North America) meant that the cost of living fell, and real wages actually increased. For those who remained in employment, therefore, there was more money to spend, and more could afford friendly society contributions. This had been an important factor during the nineteenth century before 1875, and it continued to be a major cause of friendly society growth for the rest of the century. The Final Report of the Royal Commission on Labour in 1892 commented favourably on this aspect of working-class life. Under the heading "General condition of the working classes", it noted the "considerable and continuous progress" in the general improvement of conditions of life during the past half-century of the skilled workman, and of improvement among unskilled workmen also. It went on to remark that "the percentage of the total working population earning bare subsistence wages has been greatly reduced". Clearly then, there was more money available to insure against sickness and misfortune.

Yet at the same time, there was a change of attitude in some middle-class circles, at least, to the belief in encouraging self-help to the exclusion of all state assistance to the poor other than that provided by the deterrent Poor Law system. In the 1880s, as will be seen in more detail in a subsequent chapter, there was a revival of socialist thinking, with the founding of the Fabian Society, the Social Democratic Federation, and in 1893, the Independent Labour Party. There was an increasing awareness that in spite of the benefits of industrial capitalism, all was not well in the slums of the great cities where there existed an impoverished mass quite unable to afford normal friendly society benefits, and sometimes scarcely able to afford even payments to a burial club. In his investigation of working life in London, Charles Booth was shocked to find that a third of the working classes was existing below the poverty line. In spite of the optimistic note sounded in the passage just quoted from the Final Report of the Royal Commission on Labour, the Commissioners were obliged to refer in a further passage to this disturbing aspect of city life (although they sought to play down its significance):

> There is still a deplorably large residuum of the population, chiefly to be found in our large cities, who lead wretchedly poor lives, and are seldom far removed from the level of starvation; but it would seem that, not only the relative, but perhaps even the actual numbers of this class also are diminishing.

The plain fact is that although self-help had provided a powerful means of self-protection for the majority of the working classes in the nineteenth century, for an important minority – the so-called "residuum" – it provided no safeguards at all. This was particularly so in old age, when worn-out old people without any form of friendly society benefit might have no alternative but to spend their last days in the workhouse. According to Booth, old age in itself was the most important cause of poverty. Increasingly then, it was argued that the state must be prepared to come to the assistance of the very poorest classes who were too poor to drag themselves up from the depths; and the case for state assistance was made more and more not only by the socialists but also by progressive liberals. Moreover, the argument was not confined to old age pensions. It was also extended to some form of state health insurance, of a kind already existing in Germany by the end of the century. Thus, paradoxically, the period up to 1914 saw both the greatest development yet of the friendly society movement and, at the same time, significant events that were to supplement and ultimately in part to supplant it.

Against this background, we may now survey the major aspects of friendly society development as far as 1914. The Reports of the Royal Commission on Friendly Societies, 1872 were followed by the passing of the Friendly Society Act, 1875. This act contained a number of useful administrative reforms without making any very sweeping changes to the existing law. The affiliated orders could at last register as such, although registration was still not made compulsory. Dividing societies could register if they wished. The depositing of rules with the registrar without actual registration was abolished. Perhaps most important of all, registered societies were to supply annual returns of membership, have their accounts audited every year and submit five-yearly returns of sickness and mortality, and at the same time supply returns of their assets and liabilities. An amending act in 1876 cut down the costs of registration of the individual branches of affiliated societies, which cost had hitherto been considerable. In fact, much of the business of the Registry from 1875 to 1880 was taken up with the registration as branches of bodies previously registered as separate societies. Under the terms of the 1875 Act, assistant registrars were appointed for England and Wales, Scotland and Ireland.

The affiliated orders continued to have the largest numbers of members during the last quarter of the nineteenth century, and their growth continued, although at a slower pace. The monthly convivial meetings tended to decline as such, although subscriptions were still paid at them. Graduated contributions and better financial management meant that there was less money to spare for beer, but rival social activities were in any case diminishing the attractions of the old-style drinking meeting. Half-day Saturday working led to the growth of mass spectatorship at professional sport, new forms of urban entertainment developed (such as the music hall and, later, the cinema), railway excursions became a popular form of outing, while urban tramways made local trips and visits much more convenient. However, the individual lodges and courts continued to grow in size – for example, the average lodge of the Manchester Unity increased from 122 members in 1871 to 142 members in 1886 – while at the same time maintaining their financial independence. The one affiliated order showing really substantial growth by the turn of the century was the temperance society of the Rechabites. The membership figures for the major orders are shown in Table 8.

Table 8   Membership of the major affiliated orders in 1872, 1886 and 1899.

	1872	1886	1899
Manchester Unity of Oddfellows	427,000	597,000	713,000
Ancient Order of Foresters	394,000	572,000	666,000
Salford Unity of Rechabites	9,000	60,000	136,000
Ashton Unity of Shepherds	46,000	72,000	103,000
Grand United Oddfellows	71,000	83,000	70,000
Order of Druids	57,000	61,000	56,000

The building society movement, like the affiliated orders, had its origins in local working-class self-help, but although it continued to grow in the later decades of the nineteenth century, the building societies were increasingly managed by middle-class executives. They were affected to some extent by the fall in prices during the Great Depression, and by falling interest rates and the reduction in property values. Their rate of growth accordingly slowed down; the total assets of the Halifax Building Society, for example, amounted to £1,146,393 at the beginning of 1889. Ten years later, this figure had increased to only £1,209,312. There were also some major crashes – the Portsea Island Society in 1891 and the Liberator Society in 1892. A further act in 1894 helped to restore confidence in building societies. This act provided for a closer regulation of their affairs by the Chief Registrar, who could prescribe the form in which their accounts were presented; the act also gave him powers of inspection. Certainly building societies continued to meet the needs of the better-off working man, and the small terminating societies still provided a service at the end of the century. In 1896, the Chief Registrar estimated that at least a quarter of a million persons had gained ownership of their houses through building societies since 1836. The average size of a mortgage in 1896 was £300, there being 115,000 persons with such mortgages. According to the Royal Commission on Labour of 1892, there were 2,333 building societies in 1891, with 605,000 members (not all working class, of course), their total funds amounting to £58,582,000.

Savings banks also continued their useful services for the thrifty, although here again there were some failures. When the Cardiff Savings Bank collapsed in 1886, it was revealed that there had been many irregularities in its administration, and that its actuary had embezzled £30,000. Over a hundred savings banks closed down in the next five years, and a Select Committee was appointed in 1888. The result was the Savings Bank Act of 1891, which provided for regular inspections and prohibited the setting up of investment departments in the future. This was a severe blow to the trustee savings banks, who were also forbidden to make investment loans to school boards and local authorities. By 1897, only 74 banks still had investment accounts. However, in 1904 another Savings Bank Act allowed the larger trustee banks without investment accounts to reopen them, and to invest in any security issued under the Local Government Loans Act. This revived the fortunes of the trustee bank movement. Meanwhile, the Post Office Savings Bank continued to be a safe haven for small-scale working-class savings, and by 1900 the POSB had more accounts with greater funds than the trustee savings banks. See Table 9 for the figures for 1900.

Table 9   Accounts and deposits in trustee savings banks and the POSB, 1900.

Trustee Savings Banks		Post Office Savings Bank	
Accounts	1,625,000	Accounts	8,439,000
Ordinary Deposit Accounts	51,455,000	Deposits	£135,549,000
Special investment funds	4,530,000		
	£55,985,000		

The success achieved by the POSB in the last 40 years of the nineteenth century is an indication of the increasing amount of small savings among the working classes. The same may be said of the marked expansion of commercial insurance during the same period. Some of the insurance companies (which could also be collecting societies) became very large, such as the Prudential Insurance Company, and the Hearts of Oak. The latter company had 64,421 members in 1875, growing to a membership of 239,000 in 1899. Others were less well-run, in spite of rules in the Friendly Society Act of 1875, which sought to safeguard members' interests by, for example, excluding collectors from being members of a committee of management; the Act also required a period of 14 days for the payment of arrears (lapsed policies were a good source of income for unscrupulous companies). The insurance of any minor under the age of 3 was forbidden as well. Furthermore, children under 5 were not to be insured for more than £6, and children from 5 to 10, for not more than £10 (this was to allay suspicion that very young children were sometimes done to death or

57

simply allowed to die in order to collect the insurance money).

Yet in spite of the terms of the 1875 Act regarding collecting societies, some crashes still occurred, such as that of the United Assurance Company in 1883. A remarkable public enquiry into the affairs of the Royal Liver Friendly Society was held in 1884. According to a report made by E. Lymph Stanley to the Chief Registrar, published in 1886, an application had been made under the 1875 Act to appoint inspectors. A petition signed by more than 500 members made a number of serious allegations of misconduct, including the following charges:

(1) that there is now, and has been for a considerable time past, gross mismanagement and extravagance on the part of the Committee of Management of the Society.
(2) that whilst the collections during the past ten years have increased about 62 per cent, the expenditure has increased in the same period about 95 per cent.
(3) that in the past year (1884), out of an income of over £360,000, only the sum of £1,533 was saved, owing to the enormous salaries and commissions taken by the Committee of Management, quite disproportionate to the services rendered.
(4) that during the past ten years £124,595 was taken by the two secretaries and the other members of the Committee of Management.

It was further alleged that travelling expenses amounting to £5,600 had been incurred over the previous decade for which no vouchers had been produced, and that annual general meetings were packed by the Society's clerks, agents and collectors and their families. The inspector appointed, E. L. Stanley, reported that the petitioners had substantially proved the great bulk of their charges.

As a result of this enquiry, the two secretaries resigned, and a new secretary was appointed at a much reduced salary of £1,000 a year. A substantial reorganization of the company took place, more than a hundred clerks being dismissed. Further, a Select Committee on collecting societies was appointed in 1888 which still found much to criticize in the running of the societies, especially the near-exclusion of members from any say in their management. The recommendations of this Select Committee were followed by the passing of the 1896 Collecting Societies and Industrial Insurance Act. In fact, this act failed to adopt many of the reforms recommended by the Select Committee, and served merely to clarify the existing state of the law.

Ordinary members could still do little to challenge suspected mismanagement except by way of a petition for an enquiry to the Chief Registrar, which would usually require at least 500 signatures, as had happened in the case of the Royal Liver.

Nevertheless, the collecting societies clearly had something to offer
to the working classes, and this is to be seen in the continued growth
of the societies up to the end of the century. In 1903, there were 43
societies of this kind, with 6,973,136 members – membership had
nearly doubled since 1891. The three largest societies – the Royal
Liver, the Liverpool Victoria Legal, and the Royal London all had
membership of about two million each in 1905. They certainly provided a service for working people which permitted self-help, but in a
form that gave their members very little say in the matter. Membership of an affiliated society, on the other hand, at least gave the ordinary member the chance to play a part in the affairs of the lodge or
court, limited though that might be. But then, the clientele of the collecting societies was rather different from that of the affiliated societies in that, as we have seen, they catered for the needs of the very
poorest.

Meanwhile, the various forms of deposit and dividing societies
described in the last chapter all continued to grow, but at varying
rates. The Penny Bank movement grew steadily, and particularly the
Yorkshire Penny Bank. Small local societies still survived, many of
them of remarkable longevity, but on the whole they continued to suf-
fer from the competition of the large national affiliated societies.
Dividing societies (or tontines) still existed, while deposit societies
increased in size; the Surrey Deposit Society, founded in 1868,
changed its name to the National Deposit Society in 1872, and
expanded greatly by the end of the century. Another new form of society, the Holloway Society (named after its originator, George
Holloway), sought to provide allowances for old age by levying rather
larger contributions than usual, and converting the surplus in the
common fund into deferred savings accounts. These could then be
drawn on when a member retired. Two large societies were founded
on these principles – the Ideal Benefit Society in Birmingham, and the
Tunbridge Wells Equitable Friendly Society. The various pit, railway
and other friendly societies meeting the needs of specific trades were
also thriving at the end of the century. The Final Report of the Royal
Commission on Labour, 1892 supplies a lengthy list of specialized

friendly societies of this kind. The county societies also made quiet if unspectacular progress, as did the female societies.

How extensive was the friendly society movement as a whole at the end of the nineteenth century? As there is no official figure available for the number of small, unregistered local societies, it is impossible to give a precise figure for either 1900 or 1914. Furthermore, different authorities supply different figures for different years. Again, membership of a burial society at 2d a week was a rather different proposition from membership of an affiliated order at 4d to 8d a week, with its various benefits. When all these considerations are taken into account, it is clear that any estimate of membership totals must be highly approximate. One often quoted figure for the end of the century, and given by Professor Bentley Gilbert in 1966, is 4.25 million in registered societies. This Gilbert says represents about half the adult males in Great Britain. On the other hand, it was noted in the previous chapter that Professor Thompson suggests that even in the 1870s, the total in all forms of societies should be easily 75 per cent and even as much as 80 per cent of the total adult male population. However, when commenting on the situation in 1914, he appears to modify this number, suggesting that at least half the male workforce were in friendly societies, but adding that "it becomes hard to imagine that more than 10 per cent of the population can have been without some kind of protection". It is really impossible to give exact figures in this matter, although clearly all depends on what is meant by "protection" in this context – a simple penny or two for burial obviously gives less protection than a much larger payment for benefits from an affiliated society.

If precise membership figures are not available, it is also difficult to judge the financial health of the friendly societies at the end of the nineteenth century. Professor Gilbert asserts that as the Queen's reign neared its end, "a frightening number of societies were in financial trouble", and he quotes from a report made for the Rothschild Committee (1896) showing some societies in actual deficiency. Yet Gosden thinks that the societies "apparently flourished" until the 1940s and the coming of the welfare state. At the same time, he does acknowledge one increasing difficulty experienced by the societies by the end of the century. This is that the expectation of life was going up, and members were living to a greater age. They no longer suffered from the relatively speedy death resulting from typhoid fever and cholera that had prevailed earlier in the century, but were increasingly subject to lingering diseases such as tuberculosis and cancer. As a result, many members were on sick pay for longer and longer periods – first, on full sick pay, then on half, then on a quarter. Such benefit, however limited in amount at the end, virtually took the form of an old age pension, and as a result, funds were being seriously drained.

Given the actuarial deficiencies of the administration of even the major societies, it was not easy for them to know exactly what was happening, still less to know what to do about it. They remained in intense competition with each other, and were reluctant to make the first move, such as to limit sick pay in some way to a man's working life, say, up to the age of 65. As Brabrook, the Chief Registrar, put it in his 1898 book *Provident societies and industrial welfare*:

> At present the societies appear to be waiting for each other before effecting the reforms voluntarily, as the present system is still too attractive to the members for a society rejecting it to meet the competition of those which would maintain it.

In fact, the idea of some form of annuity scheme whereby contributions could be made and a deferred annuity paid had been under discussion for many years. Finlaison, the actuarial expert, was questioned about this by the Royal Commission on friendly societies in the mid-1870s. He thought that a man earning 30s a week might be able to afford to pay, but a payment to him of 5s a week from the age of 65 would require a monthly contribution of 1s 9½d at the age of 30. In short, any annuity would be too expensive for all but the highest paid to afford. In spite of this, the 1895 Royal Commission on the Aged Poor recommended that sick pay should cease at 65, and an annuity be paid. Both the Manchester Unity and the Ancient Order of Foresters introduced pension schemes to supplement sick pay (which continued after 65), but very few subscribed to the schemes.

Indeed, old age pensions presented a problem to social reformers from the 1870s onwards. The question was, who was going to pay for them? In 1878, Canon Blackley devised a plan for the compulsory purchase of pensions, but it was met with great hostility. The idea of compulsory contributions was strongly opposed by those who argued that it was wrong in principle to make compulsory deductions from a man's wages. A later scheme put forward by Joseph Chamberlain in

1891 was for a subsidized voluntary scheme to be administered through the Post Office. Thus, a man who could contribute an amount sufficient to buy an annuity of 2s 6d a week could have the sum doubled by the government. Again this scheme, although based on voluntary contributions, failed to win favour.

A third proposal was that put forward by Charles Booth, who could show that the percentage of old people over the age of 65 in receipt of poor relief was as high 38.4 per cent. His scheme was for a non-contributory pension paid by the government of 5s a week at the age of 65. Yet here the objections were twofold: first, it was thought wrong in principle to provide a straight hand-out by the state; secondly, the cost was thought likely to be astronomical and ruinous to the government's finances. In 1896 a Treasury committee (the Rothschild Committee) was appointed to consider schemes for providing for old age, but it broke up without reaching agreement. In 1899 a Select Committee known as the Chaplin Committee was set up with the same objective. It recommended a scheme for the payment of pensions of between 5s and 7s a week by the Poor Law authorities, payable through the Post Office, up to half the cost being refunded by the Treasury. It was to operate on a non-contributory basis. These recommendations were referred to a departmental committee to ascertain their cost.

There the matter rested at the turn of the century when the outbreak of the Boer War put an end to any prospect of immediate action. One stumbling block in the way of reform was undoubtedly the attitude of the friendly societies. They strongly opposed any contributory scheme on the grounds that it was wrong for the government to take any further contributions from the workmen's wages which were already paying friendly society subscriptions. In other words, they resented competition from the government for any part of the workman's wages, which were the main source of their income; and they made their opposition plain. Moreover, the societies were influential bodies. Joseph Chamberlain referred to this directly in giving evidence before the Royal Commission on the Aged Poor:

> They are in touch with the thriftily-minded section of the working class. Their criticism of any scheme would be very damaging: their opposition might be fatal. They have very great parliamentary influence and I should myself think twice before attempting

to proceed in face of hostility from so important and dangerous a quarter.

This was a very considerable compliment to the friendly societies. Yet by the beginning of the twentieth century, Germany and Denmark had been paying old age pensions since 1891, while New Zealand had become the first country in the British Empire to do so. The Trades Union Congress began to support the idea of pensions from 1896 onwards. Even the Charity Organisation Society, known for its fierce opposition to indiscriminate charity, was starting to support the idea of pensions, although characteristically the Society wanted them to be on a contributory basis. Finally it was borne in on the societies that a government non-contributory scheme would at least take the strain off their own sick funds, which were under ever-increasing pressure. In 1908 the Liberal government at last took action. The prime minister, Asquith, thought all forms of contributory schemes impractical, and of no assistance to the very poorest who needed help most. Besides, they would antagonize the friendly societies for reasons already indicated. He therefore introduced a scheme for the payment of 5s a week at the age of 70 on a non-contributory basis, and this became the law as the Old Age Pensions Act, 1908. The bill was piloted through the Commons by the new Chancellor of the Exchequer, David Lloyd George, and the weekly pension, which was paid through the Post Office in order to avoid the taint of charity had it been paid by the Poor Law Guardians, was soon nicknamed the "Lloyd George".

Two major points may be made about the coming of old age pensions. The first is that the amount given was very small, and was subject to reductions for those still earning. The justification for this was the claim that it was only intended to supplement and indeed to encourage savings. There was also a number of conditions attached to the grant of a pension – applicants were not to have been imprisoned at any time during the ten years before making a claim, were not to be foreigners or the wives of foreigners, were not to be guilty of "habitual failure to work", and were not to have received poor relief at any time after 1 January 1908. In effect, old age pensioners had to be good citizens who had been behaving themselves and had kept out of trouble. However, the disqualification for having claimed poor relief was dropped in 1911, while the clause relating to habitual failure to work in practice proved unworkable. Another objection to the scheme was that it did not take effect until the age of 70, although 65 had been put forward originally. Yet when all is said and done, old age pensions certainly came as a great relief to many of the aged poor who had been too proud to go to the guardians for help. According to Lloyd George, the numbers applying for pensions showed that there was:

> a mass of poverty and destitution in the country which is too proud to wear the badge of pauperism and which declines to pin that badge to its children. They would rather suffer from deprivation than do so . . .

The full cost of pensions in the first year 1909–10 was over £8 million, and Lord Rosebery, former Liberal prime minister, thought the cost excessive – "so prodigal of expenditure that it was likely to undermine the whole fabric of the Empire". Churchill commented in a rather different and characteristically colourful vein in a speech in Nottingham in 1909:

> Nearly eight millions of money are being sent circulating through unusual channels, long frozen by poverty, circulating in the homes of the poor, flowing through the little shops which cater to their needs, cementing again family unions which harsh fate was tearing asunder, uniting the wife to the husband and the parent to the children.

The second major point to be made is that the implementation of a non-contributory old age pension scheme shows up clearly the limitations of friendly society self-help. This kind of self-help had done much for the better-off working classes, especially in the second half of the nineteenth century, but the very poorest, as we have seen, could afford only the few pence necessary for burial expenses, if that. They certainly could not afford the contributions to the affiliated orders, let alone deferred annuities. For this reason it must be said again that caution must be exercised in estimating the proportion of the population covered by insurance at the end of the nineteenth century, and we must ask, "insurance for what?" For the residuum, the most they could afford would be burial benefit, and many could not afford even

that. The coming of the state old age pension scheme in 1908 is therefore a warning against too ready an assumption that the working
classes as a whole could provide for their own welfare in old age. Self-
help had been shown to have its limitations.

Almost inevitably the inauguration of the old age pension scheme in
1908 led the government to consider the provision of some sort of
state insurance scheme against ill-health. Undoubtedly there was
increasing alarm at the time at the state of the nation's health, and
already the Liberal government, in its concern for national efficiency
and the safeguarding of the British Empire, had authorized school
meals paid for out of the rates, and also medical inspections in
schools. The medical profession, too, was becoming interested in the
setting-up of some form of medical service for the "respectable"
working classes, that is, those not dependent on the Poor Law, and
those already obtaining sickness benefit through membership of
friendly societies. In fact, many general practitioners had contracts
with the societies for treatment of their members, and there was some
dissatisfaction with their rates of pay. In 1908 Lloyd George paid a
brief, five-day visit to Germany to investigate the Bismarckian insurance system. On his return, he was asked whether he was impressed
with the German pension system. He replied:

> I never realised on what a gigantic scale the pension scheme is
> concocted. Nor had I any idea how successfully it worked . . . It
> touches the German people in well-nigh every walk of life. Old
> age pensions form but a comparatively small part of the system:
> does the worker fall ill? State insurance comes to his aid. Is he per-
> manently invalidated from work? Again, he gets a regular grant
> whether he has reached the pension age or not.

From then on, Lloyd George began to plan for the setting up of a
state sickness insurance scheme.

His proposals were beset with difficulties. In the first place, there
was the question of whether it should be a contributory or non-
contributory scheme. After the controversies arising from the grant of
old age pensions, there was little doubt that it would have to be contributory in nature; the state could not possibly afford a fully contributory system (old age pensions had actually cost £2 million more
in their first year than originally estimated), quite apart from the fact

that a non-contributory scheme would be completely unacceptable to middle-class opinion. This did not preclude a limited contribution from the state, of course. A second and serious problem was how to persuade the friendly societies and the ever-expanding industrial insurance companies to accept a government rival in their field. As we have seen, the friendly societies had a long history of providing sickness benefit for their members.

More formidable still, the industrial insurance companies, although customarily offering death benefit only, had grown into what Professor Gilbert has called a gigantic industry with over 30 million funeral benefit policies outstanding, and a workforce of about 100,000 men, of whom about 70,000 were full-time, door-to-door collectors. Of the 75 industrial insurance organizations, twelve companies monopolized some 90 per cent of the business of collecting premiums. The largest of the twelve companies was the Prudential Insurance Company – an immense commercial giant that was the biggest private owner of freehold property in the kingdom, with about half a million pounds to invest each month. Lloyd George could hardly afford to antagonize such powerful bodies as these companies, especially as they had in their employ a collecting army of men in weekly contact with the majority of working-class homes in the United Kingdom. The political power that this implied is regarded by Professor Gilbert as most significant. Lastly, of course, Lloyd George and his civil servants faced the vast task of working out all the details of the proposed scheme, the rates of contribution, whether to include widows' and orphans' pensions, and so on.

It is not proposed here to trace the labyrinthine manoeuvres by which Lloyd George finally settled the details of what became Part I of the 1911 National Insurance Act. They are set out exhaustively in Professor Gilbert's standard work on the subject, *The evolution of National Insurance in Great Britain* (1966). More relevant to our purpose here is to examine the effect of the Act upon the friendly society movement. The Act itself may be described briefly as establishing an insurance fund to which all men and women earning less than £160 a year had compulsorily to contribute 4d a week, to be deducted from wages; the employer had to pay 3d a week, and the state 2d a week ("9d for 4d", as Lloyd George put it, rather misleadingly). This entitled the contributor to 10s a week sickness benefit, and to free medical treatment from a doctor chosen from a list or panel of local physicians. The administration of the scheme was entrusted to the insurance companies and the friendly societies, which were given the name of "approved societies". Thus, great emphasis was placed on the insurance principle, with the role of the state kept to the minimum. It was not a socialist measure, and indeed, emphasized the principle of self-help through the medium of insurance; contributors were entitled to relief through their payments, which were in no sense a dole.

Reaction to the scheme was very mixed. Not surprisingly, the Act came under heavy fire from the left – Keir Hardie attacked it bitterly (but somewhat unrealistically) as failing to get down to the roots of poverty, which was the capitalist system itself. He argued that the Liberals were merely supplying "a porous plaster to cover the disease which poverty causes". The Webbs also disliked the combination of contributions and of state aid – as Fabian socialists, they emphasized the need for the latter. The trade unions disliked the compulsory deductions from wages. On the right, the middle classes objected to licking stamps (the mode of collecting contributions was by the purchase and fixing of special stamps on cards); ladies in particular found it distasteful that they should have to lick stamps for their domestic servants, and the *Daily Mail* actually ran a campaign on the issue. A correspondent to the *Westminster Gazette* wrote:

> I have seen no reference in the course of this correspondence to the pathetic case of the nursery governess. Why should she – who has perhaps seen better days, who is perhaps a *lady* (think of it!) be dragged through the weekly ordeal of plastering nasty stamps on a grimy card? My blood boils when I think of the blush of shame, mantling her humble brow . . .

The doctors themselves ultimately benefited greatly, sometimes doubling their income from the capitation fees payable from panel patients. Nevertheless, they hotly disputed the amount and scale of fees proposed, and insisted on their professional independence; they had no wish to be considered state servants. The greatest opposition, however, probably came initially from the friendly societies and the industrial insurance companies.

For this reason, Lloyd George had to tread very carefully. In fact, it appeared at first that the friendly societies would be given special consideration in that work people would have a choice of contributing to the state scheme or joining a friendly society; but this option was soon dropped in favour of compulsory membership of the government scheme. Again, when it became apparent that the insurance companies were to become approved societies, the friendly societies fought unavailingly to require more democratic control of the companies. Moreover, Lloyd George was forced to drop his scheme for widows' and orphans' pensions in order to appease the insurance companies. All in all, it appears that victory in the struggle over the administration of the Act went to the big battalions of collectors with their influence over working-class households – that is, as Professor Fraser has put it, the friendly societies were sacrificed to the more powerful commercial interests. This may seems a severe verdict, but the friendly societies henceforth had to share the running of the new insurance service with the industrial insurance companies, who seemed to have got the utmost out of Lloyd George. Furthermore, the friendly societies also lost their contractual control over local general practitioners, which had been built up over years, as many of the doctors found they could exist very largely on the new capitation fees and no longer had to depend on the friendly societies for employment.

Nevertheless, before summing up the changed position of the friendly societies after the 1911 Act, it would be as well to point out how great an achievement the Act really was. Admittedly, it had its shortcomings: it applied only to the person insured, and not to his or her dependents. Additional benefits were limited to a small maternity grant, and free institutional treatment of tuberculosis. Otherwise nothing was done to provide the free hospital treatment which, for the most part, only poor law infirmaries supplied at the time. Against all this is the simple fact that Lloyd George carried out a superb feat of political legerdemain in the midst of the great constitutional struggle with the House of Lords over the Parliament Bill. He had to contend with the insurance companies, the friendly societies, the medical profession, and the Conservative opposition, not to mention the newly-formed Labour Party. Taking all these circumstances into account, he achieved a remarkable triumph. According to Dr Jones, Secretary to the Cabinet (and afterwards the author of a biography of Lloyd George) the National Insurance Act (which also contained in Part II a limited scheme for unemployment insurance) was the greatest Act of Parliament ever passed. The health scheme remains one of the foundation stones of the modern welfare state, although it should also be remembered that Lloyd George regarded it as only the first step towards further reform. Yet it constituted a substantial and irreversible setback for the friendly societies.

How did this come about? Before 1911 their position seemed secure. They had a well-organized system of treatment for sick members, based in some areas on local organized groups of branches and doctors. However, during the protracted negotiations leading to the passing of the act, they were constantly thwarted over administrative details by Lloyd George, ever anxious to placate the industrial insurance companies with their hoards of collectors (the force, according to Professor Gilbert, which won the industry its predominant place in health insurance). Early on, as already noted, their members had to pay compulsory contributions in spite of being members of friendly societies. Their efforts to enforce more democratic control in the insurance companies came to nothing, and so did their final efforts to gain some form of hospital benefit.

After 1911 they found themselves in strong competition with the insurance companies, which used their collectors to press the sale of life and other policies on state insurance customers. Two months after contributions began, the industrial insurance approved societies claimed a larger membership than that of the friendly societies, the membership of which tended to stagnate, in spite of an influx of new state members. The latter, of course, had no interest in the traditional, fraternal aspects of friendly society meetings. They were members because the law required them to join an approved society, and for no other reason. Some lodges of the Manchester Unity became composed entirely of state members; some of them were composed exclusively of women. Between the wars, friendly society membership remained static, and by 1938 there was a net loss of 4.8 per cent over the 1912 figures.

So 1911 was to prove something of a turning point in the history of the friendly society movement. The great age of expansion was over. There was no immediate fall in membership, of course. Indeed, as has just been noted, affiliated and other societies received an influx of new state members, but the government legislation was bound to have an effect on the traditional membership. It is true that the government scheme did not offer any grant on death, whereas the friendly societies did provide a funeral benefit; but the collecting societies also did this for a very small weekly contribution. So what really could the friendly societies offer to the young working man or woman faced with compulsory contributions to the state system? We have noted previously that the traditional monthly club night with its conviviality was already becoming less attractive as the opportunities widened for other social activities. The heyday of the friendly societies was over.

For deeper reasons than this, it seemed at the same time that the friendly society of the nineteenth century had served its purpose. Of necessity, its membership had been confined to the better paid worker, the only exception to this being the recruitment of agricultural labourers, especially in the southern counties. But the societies had nothing to offer the poorest classes in the cities, and when the state of the these deeply impoverished classes had become more and more painfully apparent toward the end of the century, then some form of state assistance became more or less inevitable. This was especially so after the introduction of old age pensions – that lifebelt, as Churchill called it, made available to the very poorest (he also talked of "spreading a net over the abyss" – he had a good turn of phrase). Of course, it was claimed that it was all a matter of insurance, that the worker was merely prudently guarding against the risk of illness, and in the event, drawing out against what he had paid in. The fact was that the state was to pay a proportion of the total weekly contribution, and after the First World War, all pretence that the insurance scheme was in any way self-supporting had to be abandoned.

We shall return to the necessity for state aid in the Conclusions. At the moment it is perhaps sufficient to suggest that the English working classes in the nineteenth century fought hard through the medium of the friendly society movement to protect themselves against illness, and to make provision for a decent and dignified burial; but the state of the residuum, especially in the towns, really meant that in the long run, a state system had to supplement and ultimately replace a movement that had served the majority of the working classes remarkably well.

Part Two

The trade unions

Chapter Four

The early days of trade unions 1780–1825

Employer/employee relations in the workshops of the eighteenth century tend to be obscure in nature, but the one form of self-help and of defence against an exploiting employer, when the need arose, was the trade combination or trade union. Before the nineteenth century, trade unions existed among the skilled trades in a variety of forms, often barely distinguishable from friendly societies. In a few cases their origins can be traced back to the craft guilds – for example, the journeymen printers seem to have emerged from the stationers' company – but most appear to have developed in more recent times, especially in the eighteenth century, as trade expanded. Some had a fleeting existence, coming and going with the changing fortunes of industry. Strictly speaking, these were excluded by the Webbs's definition of a trade union as "a continuous association of wage-earners for the purpose of maintaining or improving the conditions of their working lives", but although the Webbs have been criticized for providing too narrow a description, in practice they did take into consideration some more ephemeral forms of combination. Moreover, their definition does focus accurately on the prime function of the trade union – the maintaining or improving of working conditions, usually with reference to wages and to working hours. This was becoming increasingly important as the Industrial Revolution got under way, industry and trade expanded, and the workforce grew in numbers. However, it should be emphasized that combinations were by no means the creation of the Industrial Revolution, but rather that their development was a significant consequence of the great economic expansion of the second half of the eighteenth century.

About 1780 combinations were to be found in most of the major towns of England (the term "trade union" did not come into general use until the earlier part of the next century; in addition to "combinations", the expressions "trade clubs", or "trade societies" or even "confederations", were also employed). London was by far the largest centre of population, and the principal area for trade union activity. Combinations were usually confined to the skilled trades in which the higher wages paid permitted the collection of funds to be used for strike pay or sickness benefit. Public houses ("houses of call") became convenient local headquarters where subscriptions could be paid, vacancies made known, and the funds stored in money chests, often fitted with three locks and keys, as was the case with the friendly societies. In some societies, funds were sufficient to permit the financing of out-of-work members who went "on the tramp" – that is, travelled from town to town in search of work, as described in Chapter 1. Such members would be given a "blank" or ticket for identification purposes, and would be lodged overnight by members of their trade in the towns visited. According to John Rule, the system existed among the Tiverton woolcombers in the eighteenth century, while Eric Hobsbawm has also found it employed by compositors, paper makers and calico printers. Early in the nineteenth century, Francis Place said the system was in force among tailors, hatters, smiths, carpenters, boot and shoe makers, metal workers, bakers, plumbers and printers.

Combinations appear often to have been well-organized locally, usually having a chairman, secretary, treasurer and committee. Sometimes they had printed rules, otherwise they simply relied on oral tradition. Meetings were held regularly, and members might be fined for non-attendance and subsequently expelled. This could have serious consequences for members of the stronger unions where officials exercised a firm control over both the exclusion of defaulting members and of non-apprenticed labour; they also kept a close watch over the number of apprentices permitted in the trade. Generally speaking, only apprenticed labour was admitted; new members had to be proposed and seconded, and an entrance fee was usually payable. Sometimes there were exceptions to the rules regarding apprenticed labour, for example, for the sons of present members. Subscriptions were payable either weekly or monthly, usually a matter of a few pence a week. Efforts were made in most societies to conduct meetings in an orderly and civilized manner, and minutes were sometimes kept. Funds were used for strike pay (although this was illegal for a time after 1799), and also for sick pay and burial grants. Additionally, they might be used to support the members of other unions on strike. The strongest unions aimed to provide quite generous benefit for aged members. For example, the powerful shipwrights society in Liverpool had nearly 900 members in 1824, and levied a subscription of 1s 3d a month. They planned to build houses for members past labour (they had already bought the land), and to give them 5s a week and coal. Their burial grant was £7 for members, while £4 was given to members' widows.

However, there does not appear to have been anything like a national network of combinations in the skilled trades in the eighteenth century. As already indicated, combinations might come into existence and then disappear, dependent on the flow and ebb of trade; by no means all of them had a continuous existence – they could be formed to organize a particular strike, then afterwards fade into oblivion. Nevertheless, the tramping system was sufficiently widespread before the French Revolution for it to be a fair assumption that there were permanent organizations on a local basis among most of the older and well-established crafts. Rule has suggested that about 50 clubs or societies could be considered to be on a permanent footing. There is no doubt that some of these societies had a considerable influence in their towns. Thus, in 1792, the mayor of Liverpool wrote to William Pitt, the prime minister, regarding a particularly strong union:

> I am well-informed the journeymen carpenters of this town (who are a very powerful body of men) had a meeting of some of the heads of them on Saturday evening last, and were heard to say that if the abolition of the slave trade takes place, some houses in the town (which they had marked) should be pulled down . . . It is proper also to inform you that these men have it in agitation to leave their work for the purpose of advancing their wages, and it is daily expected, for it has been long threatened.

All the same, the lack of any form of national organization clearly set limits to the exercise of trade union power, and as we shall see later, efforts to set up national bodies in the 1830s were to prove failures. Furthermore, it must be reiterated that only a minority of workers, the skilled tradesmen who could not easily be replaced, were members of unions. The substantial majority of workers, male and female, were not to begin to be unionized for another hundred years. Agricultural workers, for example, were not at all organized in unions, and they were still the largest occupational group at the end of the eighteenth century. Miners were at first similarly unorganized, although by the 1790s, when their industry was subject to a vast expansion, they began to display concerted action. A Bristol correspondent, writing to the Home Secretary, Henry Dundas, in 1792, observed:

> I am just now informed that the Gloucester colliers to the amount of about 2,000 passed through the city this morning on their way to the pits at Bedminster, Ashton and Nailsea in Somersetshire to persuade or if necessary to compel the miners at these pits to leave off working and join their confederacy.

What were relationships like between employers and the combinations in the late eighteenth century? It is customary at this point to draw attention to the legal disabilities suffered by the combinations of the time. In the first place, there was a long-established tradition of the state's fixing wages, from the Statute of Labourers, 1349 onwards. This was considered to be the proper concern of the government, and no business of individual groups of workmen. The famous Statute of Artificers, 1563 not only laid down elaborate rules for the determining of wage rates by JPs, but also provided that all adult workers should be apprenticed. It also set penalties for leaving work unfinished. Moreover, by the eighteenth century, combinations had come to be regarded as conspiracies in restraint of trade and hence illegal at criminal law. Although an individual workman might properly withdraw his labour or seek an increase in wages, two or more workmen agreeing to do so could be accused of conspiracy. Thus, in 1721 a group of journeymen tailors in Cambridge was indicted for conspiracy to raise their wages. In the same year, "combination" entered the statute book as a legal name for labour organizations, earlier statutes having referred to "conspiracies" or "confederacies". The very word "combination" acquired a perjorative ring; Dr Johnson noted in his Dictionary that it was "generally used in an ill sense". In addition to these legal restrictions, combinations in trades such as tailoring and weaving were specifically forbidden by act of parliament during the course of the eighteenth century. By this time, industrial disputes had become increasingly common. Dr Dobson has drawn up a list of 333 recorded disputes between 1717 and 1800. On a first impression, therefore, it might seem that combinations were much disliked by employers, and were subject to severe legal disabilities by the end of the eighteenth century.

In fact, the situation was not as gloomy from the unions' point of view as it might at first seem to be. Although it is true that combinations were prohibited by statute in certain trades, four of the eighteenth-century acts applied only to London (two with reference to tailors, and two for silk weavers), and of the four acts having a national application, three were limited to weavers, hatters and paper makers. Only the Omnibus Act of 1749 applied to a number of trades, most of them concerned with textiles. Further, some of these acts provided procedures for the fixing of wages, and were not simply repressive in intention. As for prosecutions for conspiracy, Dr Dobson has listed 29 cases for the period 1720–1800 (although there may be more cases yet to be discovered). All the same, 29 cases is not a particularly impressive number, although of course it would be unwise to judge the severity of the threat of prosecution by this criterion alone. In any case, prosecution for conspiracy required a good deal of determination on the part of employers if they were to be successful. It was necessary to proceed on indictment, which made for a lengthy and expensive case at Quarter Sessions (as opposed to summary procedure at Petty Sessions), and during the progress of the case it was not unknown for the accused to leave town and be difficult to trace.

Indeed, many employers appear to have tolerated combinations as convenient organizations with which to negotiate wages, prices, and other matters, as in the London printing, coopering and brushmaking trades. Efficient production depended on a certain degree of goodwill on the part of both employer and workman, and employers were loath to interfere with the work processes of a smoothly running workshop. Hence such matters as the length of the working day, the number of apprentices, the severity or otherwise of the work discipline and so on, might be matters for mutual agreement. Local customary practices were also an important factor, of course. So that although disputes were bound to arise from time to time, the shrewd employer would be chary of threatening legal action, either because it would upset existing good relations, or because it might provoke intimidation and threats of violence.

There is also the point that combinations for trade purposes might evade legal action by setting up as friendly societies, which (as was seen in Chapter 1) were perfectly legal in the second half of the eighteenth century. All in all, the better-organized combinations in most skilled trades seemed to have led a more or less peaceful existence with the tacit consent of the employers. Only when relations had become bitter and inflamed would employers take legal action; and even then, the threat of prosecution might lead to a compromise settlement, and to a public apology by the workmen. It should perhaps be added that sometimes a local shortage of labour might make it difficult for an employer to refuse a wage demand. At other times, the numbers out on strike might make it impossible to take action against all involved, as when 4,000 or so Northumberland miners came out on strike in 1765. All in all, it would be wrong to depict labour relations and the role of trade unions in the 1780s as a battlefield over which war was continually waged. Both masters and men knew that the law frowned on combinations, but it suited both sides to ignore this for the most part in their day-to-day relationships.

Why then were the notorious Combination Acts passed in 1799 and 1800, acts described by the Webbs as a "new and momentous departure"? Moreover, according to another of the older authorities, the Hammonds, these acts "remain the most unqualified surrender of the state to the discretion of a class in the history of England". Francis Place, who subsequently led the campaign for the repeal of the acts, argued that the laws

> were considered as absolutely necessary to prevent ruinous extortions of workmen which, if not restrained, would destroy the whole of the Trade, Manufactures, Commerce and Agriculture of the Nation . . .

In other words, Place offered a simple explanation for the laws being passed. They were the result of the dislike of combinations by employers, and on this view, the parliament of the time was only too willing to oblige the masters. As Adam Smith had said, "Whenever the legislature attempts to regulate the differences between masters and their workmen, its councillors are always the masters". No doubt this is part of the explanation, but not the whole of it. Although the outbreak of the French Revolution was welcomed in England in 1789, middle-class opinion soon turned against it, especially after war broke out against the French in 1793. In 1797 two serious mutinies occurred in the Royal Navy, at Spithead and at the Nore, so that England's major defence against invasion by France seemed at risk. In the same year, the Illegal Oaths Act prohibited the swearing of oaths of association that were common in secret societies. In 1797 there was also a rebellion in Ireland, and in August 1798 the French actually landed in County Mayo. In these circumstances, it is not surprising that current fears of the spread of revolutionary ideas among working men were intensified and that political alarms strengthened middle-class dislike of combinations. When the prime minister, William Pitt, introduced the first Combination Bill, he referred to the "alarming growth of combinations"; but Lord Holland, in opposing the bill, probably put the case more accurately when he claimed that the masters had availed themselves of the contemporary fear of French revolutionary ideas. Certainly the prevailing fear of the spread of revolutionary doctrine played an important part in the passing of the combination laws.

The first bill was actually suggested by William Wilberforce, the great liberator of the slaves, who presumably saw no connection between negro slavery and the wage slavery of his own compatriots. The bill later introduced by Pitt was modelled on the Papermakers Act, 1796, with the wage regulations omitted. It passed rapidly through all its stages, receiving the Royal Assent in just 24 days. Its terms were relatively straightforward: it simply prohibited all combination in all trades aimed at raising wages:

> All contracts, covenants and agreements whatsoever . . . made or entered into by journeymen manufacturers . . . for obtaining an advance in wages . . . or for lessening or altering their or any of their usual hours or time of working or for decreasing the quality of work, or for preventing or hindering any person or persons from employing whomsoever he, she, or they shall think proper to employ . . . shall be and the same are hereby declared to be illegal, null and void.

Attendance at meetings, the collection of subscriptions, and the keeping of club funds all became punishable. So did preventing a workman from agreeing to work, or persuading him to leave work, or preventing a master from employing whomever he pleased; nor could a workman refuse to work with any other workman. Those convicted

79

of an offence against the act by a single magistrate could be sentenced to up to three months in the common gaol, or two months' hard labour in a house of correction.

The passing of this act led to a wave of protests and petitions from workmen all over the country. They complained especially of the loss of trial by jury, and of the right of appeal to a higher court. In 1800, an amending bill was brought in by the whig and tory members for Liverpool, General Tarleton and Colonel Gascogne (the Webbs comment shrewdly that the Liverpool shipwrights were freemen and parliamentary electors, and so not without political influence). This bill became the Combination Act, 1800. Under it, two magistrates were required instead of one, arbitration clauses were included, and JPs were disqualified from sitting when they were masters in the trade involved. Lastly, a new crime was created – combination by masters. They were forbidden to combine to reduce wages, increase or alter the usual hours of work, or increase the quantity of work. The penalty was a £20 fine.

To assess the significance of the Combination Acts as part of the history of the trade union movement presents an interesting challenge today. As we have seen, older authorities such as the Webbs regarded the acts as highly reactionary in nature, the Webbs heading their chapter on the period 1800–1824, "The Struggle for Existence"; but it was not long before Dorothy George in the 1920s challenged this view, pointing out that the acts hardly introduced a change in policy – there had been acts against combination before, and also prosecutions at common law against them for conspiracy. Furthermore, prosecutions under the combination laws were actually infrequent, and were often unsuccessful. According to George, this was because drafting an information was difficult, appeals to Quarter Sessions could be made and convictions were often quashed on technical grounds. She therefore concluded in 1935 that whatever the motive for the 1800 Act, "it was in practice a very negligible instrument of oppression".

Since the Second World War, leftwing historians have continued to emphasize the reactionary nature of the Combination Acts, though admitting for the most part the strength of George's arguments. E. P. Thompson, for example, has accepted the fact that the laws were not widely enforced, but has commented that "no-one familiar with these years can doubt that their general prohibitive influence was ever present". More recently John Orth has made the point that the Combination Acts created no new crime, and never aimed at doing so; they were simply designed to provide better procedures for punishing existing crimes already covered by statute and the law of conspiracy. The only novelty was the provision of arbitration clauses in the 1800 Act. However, Orth does suggest that there was one important change of policy implied in the acts, and this was the conscious abandonment of wage regulation. Henceforth, he argues, wages were no longer considered to be the business of the state, but were to be left to capital and labour to fight out for themselves. This is an interesting suggestion, although the wage clauses of the Statute of Artificers were not repealed until 1813, and wage regulations under specific Combination Acts could still take place until these acts were all repealed in 1824.

Any final judgement on the effect and significance of the Combination Acts must remain very general in nature. It seems clear enough that both the Hammonds and the Webbs over-emphasized their importance, and George has supplied a useful corrective. Successful strikes could and did take place following the passing of the Acts, for example, the strike of Manchester cotton workers in 1808 for a wage increase, the strike in 1809 by Tyne keelmen for increased piecework rates, and the ironworkers' strike in South Wales in 1816 against wage reductions. On the other hand, the acts remained on the statute book for nearly a quarter of a century, at a time of substantial industrial change and unrest, and to judge from the evidence given before the Committee on Artisans and Machinery, 1824, prosecutions certainly did take place from time to time. The problem here is that the evidence presented in 1824 was carefully tailored to present a strong case for repeal of the acts; so that it is hard to know how far it provides a fair picture. Whether the acts really exercised an all-pervasive, baleful influence is still not clear, but it seems reasonable to suppose that they at least posed a considerable potential threat to the freedom to form effective combinations.

The first quarter of the nineteenth century saw a brief period of peace from March 1802 to May 1803, and then a resumption of the war against France until the final victory at Waterloo in 1815. Towards the end of the war, the Statute of Artificers was repealed in two stages, the first act in 1813 abolishing the regulation of wages by JPs, and the second in 1814 repealing the apprenticeship clauses. There were strong protests against both acts of repeal from working-class bodies who wished to retain and revive the fixing of wages by the magistrates, but without effect. John Rule has argued that the attack on statutory apprenticeship was "an attempt to root out the very basis of existing and effective trade unions in the skilled trades". If so, it could not have been very effective, for apprenticeship certainly continued without noticeable signs of change in the skilled trades. The blanket provision in the 1563 Act that everyone, men and women, should be apprenticed had long fallen into disuse, and so had the regulation of wages by JPs.

By the early 1820s, more peaceful conditions had returned to industry, following the lifting of the post-war depression, and the end of a period marked by disturbances, such as the Spa Field riots (1816), the Pentrich Uprising (1817) and, above all, Peterloo (1819). The situation had therefore become more favourable to reform of the laws relating to combination, especially as Peel at the Home Office had begun his reforms of the criminal law and its administration. At the same time, Huskisson was introducing free trade reforms at the Board of Trade. The undoubted leader of the campaign for repeal of the Combination Acts was Francis Place, the radical tailor, whose shop in the Charing Cross Road became the centre of working-class political activity at the time (Place actually claimed to have begun work for repeal as early as 1814). His campaign brought in J. R. McCulloch, the famous economist, whose opinion was that "the laws to prevent combination are either unnecessary, or unjust and injurious"; and also Joseph Hume, MP, who in 1822 announced his intention of bringing in a bill against the combination laws. Before he could act, another MP, Peter Moore, introduced a bill for industrial regulation in 1823, but this was dropped after it was denounced by McCulloch. The way was now clear for Joseph Hume. A select committee had already been proposed on the export of machinery and the emigration of skilled workers. Huskisson was persuaded by Hume to add the combination laws to the terms of reference of this committee. It met early in 1824, issued six reports, and recommended that the combination laws be abolished.

These six reports make fascinating reading today. It is well known that Place drilled the working-class witnesses beforehand, and he supplied Hume with copies of the evidence to be given – Hume was in the chair throughout. Most of the witnesses appeared to have learned their lines very well (although one Samuel McCall, the vice-chairman of the Liverpool shipwrights, was twice warned to be careful in his answers, while the secretary of the society, John Cain, was also warned not to contradict himself). On the whole, they gave a very good account of themselves. Place was interviewed early on, and he spoke simply and strongly against the combination laws:

> I think the laws produce no good effects whatever; they appear to me wholly pernicious. They are a bond of union to the men. I know, practically, that the men have been kept together by them, when no combination would otherwise have existed.

This seems a somewhat dubious proposition, viewed at this distance of time; but his general argument was that the laws were unequal and unjust, and he was to claim later that if let alone, combinations would cease to exist. The majority of working-class witnesses argued similarly that the laws were unjust, that the men went in fear of prosecution, that the laws encouraged employers to keep wages down since the men feared to strike, and that everywhere masters were in tacit combination, although this was against the law. They also produced evidence to show that prosecutions had taken place for combination – although it appears that some of the prosecutions cited were for conspiracy rather than under the 1800 Act. On the whole, Place did his work so well that the workmen witnesses all told the same story.

The employers who gave evidence, on the other hand, were not so much under Place's control, of course, and their evidence is not always so predictable. Surprisingly, most were clearly sympathetic to repeal. In the First Report, Mr Taylor said that "the evils of the combination acts have been little felt, except that they have kept up a feeling of hostility between masters and men, which is always unfavourable to any reasonable settlement . . . ". Another employer, Mr Donkin, said that the Combination Acts had been entirely without effect, since employers were unwilling to disturb good understanding by a prosecution. These two London employers, together with the famous engineer Henry Maudslay, were asked, "What evil do you apprehend from the repeal of the combination laws?". They answered this question as follows:

Donkin: None whatever.

Taylor: I expect no evil, but much good.
Maudslay: I am of the same opinion.

Other middle-class witnesses spoke in the same vein. When the question was put to a Dublin solicitor, he replied, "No evil in the world; I think it would do much good and enable each man to obtain wages according to his ability as a workman". A London master printer, Mr Richard Taylor, said that the laws were of no use at all to the employers, and that repeal would certainly be no disadvantage to them. He also said that the London masters had resolved in 1816 not to enforce the laws, thinking them "abominable and unjust".

Other masters spoke against the acts, such as Ralph Burn, a London master bootmaker in Sackville Street, who said the law was unequal as against masters and men – he had never known any master prosecuted – and he had never found the men unreasonable, whereas some of the masters had been very unreasonable indeed. However, some employers were more qualified in their support for repeal, for example, Roger Fisher of Liverpool, a shipbuilder, who thought repeal would make no difference, for the same combinations would go on as before. Another employer, James Dunlop, a master spinner of Glasgow, declared that the acts were inefficient, creating dissatisfaction and irritation, and no advantage to masters. He had no objection to repeal, but could not predict the consequences.

Open hostility to repeal was very limited, but it was expressed from time to time. Two large-scale ironmasters from the Black Country, Samuel Walker and William Yates from Gospel Oak in Staffordshire, who employed 700 in their works and 1,000 colliers and ironstone miners, referred to their whole works standing still because of a strike by the colliers, the combination using violence at the pits, and the army having to be called in. Another group of employers, master shipwrights in Liverpool, complained that arson and violence (including murder) had taken place against blacklegs during strikes, yet the magistrates were unwilling to take action. The questioning continued:

– If you take it upon yourselves to dismiss any man for misconduct, would the others leave?
– They would.
– They do not allow you to judge whether the work is well-fin-

ished or not?
– No.
– When a man does do his work slovenly, are you allowed to find fault with him?
– We do it at our peril.

Later on, a further question was put to these employers:

– Are the committee to understand . . . that the association of the carpenters is such that they entirely rule the masters, and can work or strike whenever they please?
– That is our general opinion; we feel it so, there is not the least doubt of it.

Yet these employers actually supported repeal, provided that there was an efficient police force to suppress acts of aggression. They added, somewhat inconsequentially (but no doubt feelingly), "We conceive it would be very useful if the present club of the shipwrights could be annihilated". The worst examples of violence by combinations, however, seemed to have occurred in Dublin and in Glasgow. In Dublin, the Chief Constable testified to the beatings given to men victimized by the unions, and alleged that witnesses were intimidated and would not come forward. Mr Edward Carolan, a Dublin carpenter and builder employing an average of 168 men over the previous seven years, gave a lurid account of the violence of the carpenters' association against himself personally; he had actually wounded and killed a man during an altercation, and had been tried for murder, but had been acquitted. He was asked:

– In what state are the master carpenters with regard to the men; are they in dread?
– They [the men] are completely in command; the masters are not the masters; they are completely in command.

He claimed that he had got the better of the association, and he held them in defiance, but it had cost him £400. Obviously this witness was extremely hostile to the carpenters' union. He also said that very few workmen knew anything about the combination laws, while the masters thought the laws were of no use to them. Yet although Carolan might well have exaggerated the malign influence of the union – he seems literally to have been at daggers drawn with them – he was in fact the one employer who forecast accurately the consequences of repeal: he thought it would encourage the men to turn out – as indeed in the event it did.

In Glasgow, Mr Houldsworth, a master spinner, provided another striking account of violence towards blacklegs. For example, he referred to a man disfigured and losing an eye as a result of having a jug of vitriol dashed in his face. Houldsworth himself had been attacked, and pistols had been fired. He submitted a letter written to a spinner, warning him to stop work, and concluding – "This we swear by the living Good [sic], signed by Captain of the Blood-red Knights" (the drawing accompanying this warning included sketches of a skull and crossbones, a dripping heart on a dagger, a coffin, and crossed pistols). Another Glasgow cotton manufacturer referred to earlier, James Dunlop, complained strongly of women workers being beaten up, and of a mill set on fire. Violence had grown since 1816 or 1817, and vitriol throwing had occurred in 1823. However, in the last stages of the meetings of the committee, efforts were made by two workmen spinners to discredit the evidence of both Houldsworth and Dunlop. They were said to be "two particular masters who have had repeated disputes with their men", and it was claimed that "there are very few masters who have any disturbance with their workers". The first of these statements was probably true enough.

What are we to make of the six reports of the committee? The first thing that strikes the modern reader may well be that in certain towns the combinations appear to be very strong, for example, in London, among the tailors and hatters, in Liverpool among the shipwrights, and in Dublin, again among the shipwrights. In all these places their strength seemed to extend to a substantial control over their trade, that is, over decisions to strike or not to strike, over the number of apprentices, and over the exclusion of non-apprenticed labour. Strangers were kept out, and might be assaulted, tarred, run out of town, and their tools flung into the river. In other areas, as among the framework knitters of Leicester and Nottingham, the combinations were far weaker, and there was much less hostility between masters and men. If the existence and strength of combinations in the major towns are taken as an indication of the strength of the combination laws, then Dorothy George's verdict that they were a very negligible instrument of oppression seems acceptable enough, although prosecutions did take place under the acts, and might still be undertaken under the law of conspiracy. What seems lacking in the Webbs's account of the effect of the combination acts is any real emphasis on the strength of the unions in certain trades, which in itself shows how ineffectual the laws were in keeping them down. Presumably the Webbs did read the reports in full, but their footnotes refer only to a Digest of the Evidence published by George White in 1824.

Next, the attitudes displayed by both workmen and employers deserve comment. The opinions expressed by workmen witnesses are straightforward enough – after all they had been coached by Place. They all argued that the laws were unfair and oppressive, that masters were seldom prosecuted and never punished, and that the laws served only to sour relations between masters and men. The opinions expressed by the employers are far more puzzling: it may be assumed that on the whole they were not got at by Place, yet the majority appeared to believe that the repeal of the combination laws would have no ill effects and indeed be positively beneficial. This is quite remarkable. Why did hard-headed employers not anticipate the obvious consequences of repeal? In fact, as we have seen, only one employer, Edward Carolan, thought that repeal would encourage the men to go on strike. Yet Place, who gave evidence early on, seems to have expected that employers would be unfavourable to repeal, because they thought that wages would rise, and "the same absurd opinion is entertained by the men". Nearly all the employers who followed Place as witnesses proved to be in favour of repeal. Place then, the great contriver of repeal, appears to have got it doubly wrong, in expecting all the employers to be hostile and expecting combinations to end after repeal. In 1825 he actually wrote to Burdett, remarking that "Combinations will soon cease to exist . . . If let alone, combinations – excepting now and then, and for particular purposes under peculiar circumstances – will cease to exist". The mystery remains as to why so many employers supported repeal. Perhaps it is a tribute to the persuasive powers of the free trade ideas of the time that were being put into effect by Huskisson at the Board of Trade. Belief was certainly growing in the idea that trade would benefit if it could be completely untrammelled by any restrictions on the simple freedom of contract. At all events, and for whatever reasons, most employers giving evidence supported repeal.

One last comment on the 1824 evidence must be that some of the major and most powerful unions were obviously prepared to use violence to achieve their ends. Thus, the vitriol throwing and murder that so shocked the nation in the Sheffield Outrages later in the century in 1866 (see Chapter 6) were by no means new. Incidents of this kind had all occurred long before. In all probability, they were exceptional, but both employers and workmen certainly could be subject to intimidation. James Dunlop of Glasgow claimed that he had armed his workers with cutlasses and pistols so that they could defend themselves. Another employer, a Mr Roydon, when still a foreman, was said to have paid the shipwrights society in Liverpool the sum of £100, following a dispute for which he was held responsible, and as repayment of strike pay. Another employer, a Mr Grayson, also of Liverpool, was obliged to apologise to the society. According to the vice-chairman of the union, Mr Grayson "came down to No. 2 Graving Dock, and if they would work for him as they had used to, he would go down on his knees to them".

In contrast to all this, relations between masters and men in the declining framework knitting industry in Leicester appeared to be much more cordial, as was noted earlier. In Leicester, the employers claimed that much of the competition between employers was caused by the parish giving premiums (or subsidies) to manufacturers employing the poor. When the knitters went on strike in 1819, some action was taken under the combination laws, but no-one went to prison. Indeed, the combination was supported (or so it was claimed) by several of the nobility and gentry, and by the two Members for the borough, one of them (Mr Parry) blaming the laws for preventing the men from combining against the masters. One Nottingham framework knitter alleged that in the strike of 1819:

> Some of the manufacturers, who have been our friends at all times, wished us to make this stand. They considered that the wages were too low; they considered that if there was not this stand made, it never could be got up again, and on that account they persuaded us; and some of the manufacturers subscribed towards us to obtain it.

In a further strike in 1821, some 14,000 were out for nine weeks, the gentlemen of the county supporting the strikers, or so it was said.

In May 1821, when the organizing committee was prosecuted for combining, they were acquitted, but warned that it would be prison next time.

The Sixth Report of the committee began with a list of resolutions summing up the main points to emerge from the evidence. They included the statement that the combination laws had been inefficient, and tended to produce mutual irritation and distrust. As current opinion had it that both workmen and masters should be free of restrictions, the relevant statute laws should be repealed, and the common law regarding conspiracy should be amended. The arbitration laws should also be improved, and made applicable to all trades. Following these recommendations, a bill for repeal was introduced, and went through both Houses within a week, and without debate or division. It repealed 35 statutes by name, stopped prosecutions for leaving before the end of the contract, modified the crime of leaving work unfinished, abolished the crime of combination by masters, and also abolished the prosecution of combinations for conspiracy. The result of this sweeping and remarkable measure at a time of improving trade was the forming of many new combinations, and the outbreak of numerous strikes. It is said that in Sheffield the operatives had even to be warned that if they persist in demanding double their former wages for working only three days a week, the industry of the town would be ruined. In Glasgow, the master spinners sent a memorial to Robert Peel in April 1825:

> Sheweth . . . that the period since the passing of this Act [the 1824 Act] has been marked by a constant succession of intimidation, insult and outrage on the part of the operatives, and of alarm, anxiety and disturbance to the public peace of this populous manufacturing district.

There follows an account of a number of outrages, including incidents at the mills of Mr Houldsworth and of Mr Dunlop, the two evidently unpopular employers. In something of a panic, the shipowners of Liverpool persuaded Huskisson, still President of the Board of Trade, to appoint another committee, the Select Committee on the Combination Laws, 1825. The report of this committee started off with a most uncompromising statement:

... it appears that in almost every part of the United Kingdom in which large bodies of men are collected for the purpose of carrying on any craft or manufacture, Combination exists in a more or less objectionable form, and has been the subject of complaint and representation.

The evidence that follows is based on seven major geographical areas, and is almost uniformly hostile to the unions. This time Francis Place was unable to prime the witnesses as he had done before, though John Gast, the well-known secretary to the London shipwrights, put up a skilful defence of the practices of the shipwrights on the Thames. Otherwise there is much emphasis on matters unfavourable to the unions; for example, it was alleged that in the preceding few months, there had been increased violence on the streets of Dublin, with two deaths and 30 or 40 fractured skulls (evidence of a police officer). Again, it was said that the seamen of the Tyne and Wear would not sail unless the mate and the crew were in the union. The Yorkshire weavers obliged one master to indemnify them for money paid out to strikers in his works. The report therefore concludes by recommending the restoration of the combination laws, with an exception in favour of peaceful meetings of masters or workmen to consult on wage levels and working hours. The report ends with the observation that:

At the moment, the greater part of the manufacturing labour of the kingdom may be said to be under the domination of the committees of the respective Associations, which are themselves under the influence of agitators . . .

Although it appears that the original intention had been to call only employers as witnesses, and then to pass into law a highly repressive bill drawn up by the shipowners, in fact, some workmen witnesses were called; and although Joseph Hume was no longer in the chair, he was allowed to cross-examine employer witnesses. John Gast formed a committee of delegates from each trade in London, which kept up a persistent barrage of propaganda against any bringing back of the combination laws in their old form. Similar committees were formed in Manchester and Glasgow, in Sheffield and in Newcastle. As time went on, the shipowners' bill was dropped, and the bill that was eventually introduced (the Combination Laws Repeal Act, 1825) followed the report's recommendations in that it restored the law of conspiracy with an exception for peaceful consultation on wages and hours. Violence, threats and intimidation (including molestation and obstruction) were to be punishable by up to three months imprisonment, and offences included forcing a workman to join an association or to leave work unfinished, or forcing an employer to limit the number of his apprentices, or to employ a particular workman. Minor provisions were that the disqualification of JPs under the 1824 Act who were masters in any trade was changed to a disqualification of any JP who was a master in the particular trade concerned in the case. The 1825 Act also permitted an appeal to Quarter Sessions.

In this way, the combination laws were finally laid to rest. According to Karl Marx in 1867, "The barbarous laws against Trades Unions fell in 1825 before the threatening bearing of the proletariat". This is fanciful nonsense. Orth has commented that they fell not because of the bearing of the proletariat, but because of the machinations of clever intriguers who manipulated the select committee. Certainly the management of the first committee by Place was a triumph of political manoeuvring, although at the same time it is difficult to see how he could have influenced to any great extent the views of the employers. As suggested earlier, the favourable reaction of many of them to the idea of repeal was perhaps due to the prevalent and growing belief in free trade doctrine; only those employers who had been on the sharp end of trade union intimidation were doubtful about the benefits of repeal. As for the second committee, Place had little influence over either its composition or its proceedings, both being under the direction of the government, although he did as much as he could, in association with Gast, to bring pressure to bear from outside the House in the form of the press campaign and a flood of petitions to the committee.

Finally, what did the trade union movement really gain from the 1824 and 1825 legislation? There is no doubt that the 1824 Act represented a remarkable advance for the trade union movement, and the sweeping away of the law of conspiracy as it affected combinations, together with all the statutes forbidding them in specific trades, was an extraordinary achievement. The willing agreement of so many of the employer witnesses to repeal has already been commented on, and this must have been a major factor in the passing of the 1824 Act. (However, it should be noted in this connection that Lord Stanley claimed that many of the masters feared violence if they did speak against repeal.) On the other hand, the terms of the first Act were clearly in advance of public opinion. Both the prime minister, Lord Liverpool, and the Lord Chancellor, Lord Eldon, declared in parliament that they had been unaware of the passing of the act. It had certainly been rushed through without a debate. Given these circumstances, the 1825 Act undoubtedly represented a loss of the concessions in the first act. Prosecutions under the law of conspiracy again became possible, although the proceedings remained as lengthy and costly as before. However, the 1825 Act was still a distinct improvement on what had been the situation before. Prosecutions were no longer possible for the mere fact of association, and there was no longer the need for combinations to disguise themselves as friendly societies. Henceforth the danger lay in prosecutions for molestation or obstruction, and these offences were not defined in the act, but were a matter for interpretation by the courts.

All in all, the 1825 Act was still a substantial step forward, and the Webbs recognized this. They say that the manufacturers had not been wholly wrong in protesting that the act would make the workers the ultimate authority in industry: they assert that the 1825 Act was a real emancipation, and that the right of collective bargaining, involving the power to withhold labour, was for the first time expressly established. In fact, the right to strike does *not* seem to have been established, but their major point regarding the right of collective bargaining was certainly true. Another view is that although the 1825 Act represented an advance, it was a meagre one: trade unions had become legal, but it was a very limited and bare existence. Almost all the actions necessary to bring their collective might to bear could be construed as obstruction, or molestation, or intimidation. Yet it must be borne in mind that whatever the law, in some trades there were trade unions that operated very powerfully, both before 1824–5 and after, so that some employers in their own interests would try to avoid confrontation. Perhaps the final word should be allowed to John Orth, who has recently commented on the fact that for the trade unions, the 1825 Act remained their Magna Carta until the further legislation of the mid-years of the century. In 1871 the act was repealed and replaced. For nearly half a century "it set the ground rules", he says, "so to speak, for an economic contest that was fought over changing terrain".

It can be seen then that trade unions formed an often very effective mode of self-help for the skilled trades in the latter part of the eighteenth century and in the early years of the following century, and this was so in spite of the legal restrictions both before and after the 1799–1800 legislation. Its justification was the simple fact that the employing class as a whole had the power to offer or withdraw employment, and had all the resources relating to the possession of capital. In contrast to this, the only capital possessed by the working classes was their labour, and the freedom to withhold it, or to make conditions relating to its employment. On the whole, there are plenty of examples of amicable negotiations between employers and workmen over wages and conditions of work. Not all was friction and disharmony between the two sides; but, as might be expected, the employers raised objections to the violence and intimidation practised in some strikes, and to what they regarded in some instances as the tyranny of the unions. In both Dublin and Liverpool, in particular, the unions seem to have been very strong in the 1820s. Finally, it must be again emphasized that only a small proportion of working men were protected by unions, and very few women. The movement was still in its early stages of development in the first quarter of the nineteenth century, without national organization, and with its legal position still ill-defined and open to challenge in the courts. By and large, self-help operated only in the workplaces of the skilled worker, and then often on the sufferance of the employer, and within narrow parameters.

Chapter Five

Legal but under suspicion 1825–1850

Following the repeal of the Combination Acts in 1824–5, the further growth of trade unionism was at first limited by a severe trade depression lasting until 1828. In general terms, in the nineteenth century the unions tended to flourish and to be especially active during times of prosperity when trade was good and labour was in demand. A falling-off of trade was usually accompanied by the threat of wage reductions and restricted action by the unions, who were on the whole concerned to avoid wage cuts and maintain employment as far as possible. Put simply, unions were reluctant to take aggressive or provocative measures when more and more of their members were out of work, and their funds were depleted as a result. The development of trade unions in the first half of the nineteenth century must therefore be seen against the background of the evolving economy of the time. Moreover, it must also be seen in the context of the important technological advances in the cotton industry and the iron industry – the former leading to the factory system and the gathering together of large numbers of workers under one roof, thus facilitating the growth of unionism, and the latter to a great expansion of the iron industry and a corresponding increase in the number of both skilled and unskilled iron workers. At the same time, the coal industry expanded vastly in response to the demands of industry, and later, of the railways. If then at the beginning of the century the old craft unions formed the solid basis of trade unionism, the growth of industry ensured that as Britain became the first industrial nation, so the typical worker was becoming an industrial worker and so was increasingly a potential member of a trade union, dependent always on his ability to afford membership fees. In the remarkable and indeed unique circumstances of the Industrial Revolution in Britain, trade unionism developed as an essential form of protective self-help for the ordinary employed worker, at first in industry, then also later in the century in agriculture and the service industries.

The expansion of the cotton industry in Lancashire and in Scotland provides a good example of these changes. Cotton manufacture, of course, was a new industry, based on mechanized and eventually steam-driven spinning machinery, housed in factories. From the 1830s onwards, weaving also became mechanized with the advent of the power loom. Here was a new industry employing more and more semi-skilled workers, and ripe for unionization. It is not surprising that trade disputes and strikes became common in the cotton mills in the Manchester area, and that there was a strong spinners' union in Manchester itself in the late 1820s. According to a Home Office informant in 1827:

> In Manchester the combination is organised to perfection – many of the spinners pay as much as 5s or 6s a week to the general fund for supporting the "turnouts" and no master can turn off a workman, unless such be approved by the combination committee, without running a risque of all his work people turning out.

This may well have exaggerated the power of the union, but undoubtedly it was well-organized, having members in 91 firms and 106 mills. Its membership list in April 1829 contained well over 2,000 names, including 980 fine spinners, 967 coarse spinners, and 436 spinners "on pay", that is, on strike. In some mills, it operated virtually an all-union shop: for example, in Murray's New Mill in January 1829 it had 61 members out of 70 spinners. Contributions could be high – in the week ending 17 January 1829, income was £123 4s 6½d, averaging almost 1s 6d a member. The running of the society was in the hands of a Grand Lodge of 16–18 members who met weekly (each member was paid 6s 8d a meeting, often paid in liquor). It had one paid permanent official – the well known trade union figure, formerly an Irish spinner, John Doherty (also known as Doughty). He was paid £1 13s a week, out of which he had to pay 1s 4d subscription.

It was this spinners' union that embarked on a lengthy strike against proposed wage cuts in 1829, a strike that lasted six months. It began to crumble when the masters of the coarse spinning mills warned the workers of a reduction of five per cent in wages every fortnight unless they agreed not to support the striking fine spinners. In vain Doherty sought to find a solution by arbitration by the local JPs and church-wardens. After the strike, and the imposing of the threatened wage cuts, about 400 spinners were unable to obtain work. This strike, un-like the further strike that followed in 1830–31, seems to have been peaceful enough. Doherty was a vigorous leader both in words and deed, but was opposed to violence and advised the spinners accord-ingly:

> If unfortunately any disturbance should ensue in which you may be concerned, you will only be the sufferers. Submit cheerfully as we know you will, to the laws of the country. Obey the authorities of the town, who feel for and pity all your sufferings. Shun, we beseech you, all appearance of tumult.

One consequence of this strike was Doherty's determination to set up a national union of spinners in order to strengthen union support during strikes. This idea was not in itself new – for example, the first national union of carpenters was established in 1827, and in 1829 there was the first national union of bricklayers. Furthermore, there are earlier examples of some kind of federation of spinners aiming to equalize piece-rates as early as 1810 and 1818. Nevertheless, some-thing on an impressive scale was now attempted. A large five-day con-ference was held in December 1829 in the Isle of Man, attended by 17 delegates, representing 12,000 to 13,000 spinners, nearly all in the north of England and Glasgow. This new union – the Grand General Union of Cotton Spinners – aimed to support strikes where employers were underpaying the usual rates – a common occurrence in times of depressed trade. The strike levy was to be 1s a week, with 1d a week the normal subscription. The new union was soon put to the test by strikes in Bolton and later at Ashton under Lyne, both of which were unsuccessful. But the greatest test for the union was a large-scale Ashton–Stalybridge strike, which was the result of 52 firms agreeing to reduce wages in November 1830. Some 2,000 spinners turned out, but the Grand General Union's call for a general strike of spinners was very poorly supported, and the strike pay was all locally collected. There was a good deal of violence in this strike – knobsticks (black-legs) were attacked, the son of a prominent manufacturer was shot dead, another mill owner was wounded, and shots fired at still another master. In fact, the union seems to have lost control of the strikers. All attempts at conciliation failed, and by February 1831 the strike had collapsed. The employers then struck back. Three hundred of the strikers were refused re-employment, their names listed, printed in red ink, and circulated among the local employers. It was also the end of the union, in spite of the fact that according to Kirby & Musson, it was essentially defensive in nature. It had failed principally because of the spinners' fundamental sectionalism and lack of unity.

Meanwhile Doherty had resigned from both the Manchester spinners' union and the Grand General Union, and was devoting himself to a new and even more ambitious venture. This was a new organization aiming to incorporate unions in a number of different trades on a regional and even a national basis. This was the National Association for the Protection of Labour (NAPL), established in Manchester in 1829. Again there were precedents for associations of this kind, principally the Philanthropic Society, set up in Lancashire in 1818 and largely factory-based, and the Philanthropic Hercules, formed in London in the same year. Neither association lasted very long, but they do show an awareness at the time of the need for an association wider than that provided by purely local bodies. Indeed, John Doherty himself had earlier attempted to create some form of national union in 1825 – it was called the Grand Union of England – but this project was soon abandoned. The National Association for the Protection of Labour, by way of contrast, was to last about two years. Its basic principle was similar to that of the Grand General Union, the prevention of reductions in wages. The entrance fee was to be 1s and the subscription was 1d a week, with 10s a week strike allowance. In March 1830 the first issue of the union's journal appeared, the *United Trades and Co-operatives Journal*, edited by Doherty. According to Kirby & Musson, the word "co-operatives" in the title is misleading, since the union's leaders believed that it was essential to win economic power before making any attempt at co-operation, although, like other unions, there was general approval for producer co-operative schemes. Doherty's own viewpoint was that of a determined upholder of the rights of labour, though without spelling out any political implications. In his first editorial he wrote:

The main aim of our little work will be, to inspire the labouring classes with a sense of their own importance; to arouse them to a diligent and faithful performance of their duty to themselves, by a vigorous and determined resistance to any further encroachment that may be attempted, on their only real property, their labour, in the shape of reduction of wages.

The "little work" continued publication for seven months before being closed down under pressure from the government stamp commissioners, being replaced by the better known *The Voice of the People*, which Doherty also edited, at £3 a week, with Thomas Oates as reporter at £2 a week.

The NAPL got off to a good start, although most of the unions that joined were at first merely local. Later, branches were set up in Nottingham, Derby and Leicester, though only one nationally-organized trade ever joined, the National Associated Smiths. The different trades enrolled included fustian weavers, calico printers, spindle and fly makers, basket makers, jenny spinners, flannel weavers, ropemakers, coal miners, engineers, mule spinners, mechanics, tallow chandlers and sizers. In October 1830 the membership was estimated somewhat optimistically as about 80,000, and at the end of the next month, nearly 100,000. The general government of the union was in the hands of a Grand Committee, meeting every six months, while executive power was vested in a Provisional Council of seven members, also meeting every six months

However, in spite of this brisk start, the NAPL soon began to falter. The basic weakness was financial, and a consequent inability to support strikes by its members. An early failure came in October 1830, when the union was unable to support a proposed strike by the Rochdale weavers – it would have cost more than £2,000 a week to pay 7,000 strikers. Further, the failure of the union to give adequate support to the strikers in the Ashton–Stalybridge strike, combined with the absconding of the secretary, John Hynes, with £160 of the union's funds, dealt the union further blows. There were already criticisms of the administrative costs of the union; apart from the wages paid to Doherty and Oates at *The Voice*, Jonathon Hodgins was employed for a time as a full-time propagandist at £4 10s a week, plus travelling expenses. All this gave ammunition to enemies of the NAPL, especially to the *Manchester Guardian*, at this time a bitter opponent of the unions:

The fact is, the people have begun to discover the true value of the scheme of Messrs Doherty & Co: they have begun to say to themselves, What has the union done for me, or for anybody, except the individuals who have been working it? It has certainly emptied our pockets, and filled those of Mr Doughty and his assistants. But what did it do for the spinners at Ashton and Stalybridge, when they attempted to raise their wages, or for the spinners of Manchester, when their wages were reduced? It did nothing, it can do nothing; and we will have nothing to do with it.

Towards the end of 1831, Doherty seems to have become more radical in his views, and to have made further attempts to move into producer co-operation. He also proposed to reorganize the NAPL into "grand divisions", and to move the headquarters from Manchester to London. In November, there was a dispute between Doherty and the Committee over his plan to move *The Voice*, too, to the capital, and over the expenses of his recent visit there, and he thereupon resigned as editor. He did produce a new paper, the *Workman's Expositor*, while the Committee brought out a separate paper, the *Union Pilot and Co-operative Intelligencer*, but it closed in May 1832. It was really the end of the NAPL in Manchester.

Why did it fail? An easy answer would be that it was before its time, but the simple fact is that the time for one united union of all trades has still to come in this country – there has never yet been such a body. A more realistic answer would be that the NAPL was never a national body (membership was limited to Lancashire, which provided two-thirds of the subscriptions, and to Cheshire, Nottinghamshire, Leicestershire and Derbyshire), and members were predominantly textile workers. Hence, the true membership probably never exceeded 50,000 and, in particular, skilled workers never joined, having their own organizations and interests to consider. As a result, the NAPL was fatally weak financially, and what funds were available were never used directly on strike pay, the union relying on separate appeals. Furthermore, after the absconding of Hynes, the branches insisted on holding their own funds rather than letting them be held in Manchester. The financial weakness combined with the repeated failure to support strikes, especially the Ashton–Stalybridge strike, was to destroy the union. John Doherty himself deserves credit for his leadership and drive, but can be criticized on a number of counts, especially for failing to recognize that higher-paid and lower-paid workers required separate treatment, such as a sliding scale of payments and benefits. In summarizing the reasons for the failure of the NAPL, Kirby & Musson suggest that in some respects it was a glorious failure. It introduced the principle of federation and meeting of delegates, later copied by the builders' union and the Grand National Consolidated Trades Union (the GNCTU, to be discussed shortly). In fact, it lasted longer than the more famous GNCTU, and had more members. Kirby & Musson argue further that it also channelled workmen away from the ineffectual riots and machine breaking, which was their past, to the united and non-violent action, which was their future.

These views of Kirby & Musson command respect, and they have provided a massively detailed account of John Doherty's career and of the NAPL. Yet it has been suggested more recently that they have over-emphasized the class divisions among the working classes as a reason why so few of the skilled classes joined. The aims of the NAPL to stop reductions of wages, it is argued, had only a limited attraction for trades where wage reductions were not the critical issues. Furthermore, many trade unions were active only in boom periods, whereas the NAPL emerged during a slump. All this helps to explain the pattern of membership, rather than simple sectionalism. These points all deserve consideration, but the basic fact is surely the over-ambitious nature of the scheme, given the circumstances of the time – the state of the law, the hostility of the government (very marked at the end of 1830), the equal hostility of the employers, the problems of communication, and above all, the financial difficulties arising from the limited membership. One last comment on the views of Kirby & Musson: credit must certainly be given to the NAPL for trying to pursue peaceful negotiations, but it is questionable how far it channelled workmen away from ineffectual riots and machine breaking and into united and non-violent action. In the first place, not all union action in the past had been violent – some craft unions had a well-established history of non-violent negotiation. Secondly, although the union denied all responsibility, violent action by individual members *did* take place – knobsticks were assaulted, employers shot. The NAPL certainly did not put an end to all this. How far its leadership actually reduced the amount of violence practised is impossible to ascertain, but violence continued to feature in trade disputes in Glasgow and elsewhere in the late 1830s, in the Midlands during the Plug Plot of

1842, and in Sheffield and Manchester during the outrages of 1866. Lastly, perhaps it is provocative to ask, was rioting in any case always ineffectual in intimidating employers and the middle classes generally? It is an interesting question. Collective bargaining by riot, as it has been called, had often been effective in the eighteenth century.

Once the history of the NAPL has been dealt with and assessed, it is customary to discuss the rather better known Grand National Consolidated Trades Union, which also aimed at a nationwide trade union organization. Before doing this, it is as well to review what was happening to the trade union movement as a whole in the 1830s. This was a period of considerable conflict, much of it in textiles and in coal mining; not surprisingly, given the technological changes occurring in these industries at this time. In the textile industry, mechanical spinning was being speeded-up by the coupling-up of machines and by the introduction of the self-acting mule, while the hand loom was being replaced first in Lancashire, then later in the West Riding by the power loom. In mining, production was expanding, and conflict between mineowners and miners increased. In 1829 the hand loom weavers of Manchester and Rochdale went on strike and rioted. The flannel weavers' strike in Rochdale in 1830 has already been mentioned, while there were widespread strikes among bleachers in 1831–2, among calico printers in 1831, and among dyers in 1833–4. Miners were on strike in the winter of 1830–31; in 1833 there was a serious builders' strike in Lancashire, and in 1834 there were long tailors' strikes in Manchester and Bolton. The hatters were on strike in the Stockport area in 1834. In many of these strikes there was serious violence, and in the absence of local police forces, the authorities had often to bring in troops. It must also be remembered that in the national background to all this was the struggle over the Reform Bill, passed eventually in 1832. On the whole then, the early 1830s were years of substantial economic and political conflict.

The origins of the Grand National Consolidated Trade Union lie in the trade union conference of delegates meeting in London in February 1834 to discuss the great Derby strike and lock-out. This was a strike resulting from the refusal of unionists to give up their union membership as demanded by employers. The lead was taken by the London tailors, and a national body was set up, with a Grand Council meeting every six months and a full-time executive council of paid members. At district level, each district was to have a Central Committee of delegates from the various affiliated trades. There was also to be an organization for individual trades with a Grand Lodge in selected towns and cities, and then under them, district lodges, and under them, branch lodges. This elaborate organization was to be run by a permanent executive, elected by the Grand Council.

The name of Robert Owen, the famous advocate of co-operative communities, is always associated with the GNCTU, but in fact he took no part in its affairs until April, "watching and approving from a distance", as Dr Oliver has put it. It seems that it was the sentencing of the Tolpuddle agricultural labourers that brought Owen into active membership, and he at once set about shaping the ideas of the union to conform with his own beliefs. Owen is generally referred to as a socialist, but the better (if less convenient) word is really communitarian. His basic belief was in the creation of communities in which employers and workers co-operated in production; this had been the aim of the community he had set up in the New World. It is true that the tailors who dominated the GNCTU wanted the union's funds used for co-operative production, but their immediate aim was to finance strikes and cure unemployment. The views of James Morrison, the editor of the *Pioneer*, the official paper of the GNCTU, and of James Smith, the leading contributor, were uncompromisingly class-conscious and hostile to the employing classes. Indeed, Morrison was regarded by Max Beer as the originator of syndicalist ideas of the class war.

These views were very different from those expounded by Robert Owen. In fact, Owen had little interest in trade unions, seeing them merely as a means of propagating his own ideas of communitarianism. Moreover, he had little faith in working-class ability to organize. For him, community action, which included guidance from managers and entrepreneurs, was all-important. He even wanted to admit masters to the union in order to improve class relations. Thus, there was a fundamental division of opinion between Owen and leaders such as Morrison, which hardly augured well for the future of the union. In any case, the GNCTU had only just been launched when the trade union movement was confronted by the prosecution of the Tolpuddle labourers (the Tolpuddle Martyrs). These agricultural labourers from the village of Tolpuddle near Dorchester decided to form a branch of the GNCTU, and proceeded to swear in members, using an initiation ceremony of a simple kind. Such ceremonies were common enough, and were designed to impress new members with the seriousness of joining the union, whether they understood the ceremony or not. *The Times* reported the testimony of one witness in court as follows:

> Someone then read a paper, but I don't know what the meaning of it was. After that we were asked to kneel down, which we did. Then there was some more reading; I don't know what it was about. It seemed to be out of some part of the Bible. Then we got up, and took off the bandages from our eyes . . . Some one read again, but I don't know what it was, and then we were told to kiss the book, which looked like a little Bible . . .

These proceedings were entirely conventional, and harmless enough. Moreover, the aims of the society were specifically non-violent. Rule 23 stated:

> That the objects of the society can never be promoted by any act or acts of violence, but on the contrary, all such proceedings must tend to injure the cause and destroy the society itself. This order therefore will not countenance any violation of the laws.

In spite of the evident innocent intention of the labourers, the government decided to prosecute them for administering illegal oaths under the 1797 Act, passed at the time of the Nore and Spithead mutinies. The actual charge was for swearing illegal seditious oaths. Clearly there was no question of sedition, but the prosecution chose to ignore this. There had been considerable unrest in the area; local farmers had granted an increase in wages, then had taken it back. The new Poor Law abolishing outdoor relief and setting up new union workhouses was about to come into force. Memories of the agrarian Swing Riots were still fresh in the minds of the authorities, who must have considered the time ripe for making an example of the unfortunate labourers and crushing potential unrest. Their leaders, James and George Loveless together with four others, were sentenced to the maximum of seven years transportation in March 1834 and almost immediately were hurried off to Australia.

The case of the Tolpuddle Martyrs remains the classic example of government hostility to trade unionism. The verdict caused a great outcry, and a protest procession attended by 30,000 supporters was organized in London. A London Dorchester Committee was formed, and at length in 1836 the Tolpuddle Six were pardoned. They returned home in 1838. Five were settled on the land in Essex – only one went back to Tolpuddle. Their case was a setback for the GNCTU, but scarcely a cause of its decline; there were deeper reasons for its failure than this. In May 1834 the tailors went on strike and when their employers presented them with the "document" (a requirement that employees were not to be members of a union), the tailors seceded from the GNCTU. They were followed in late June by the cordwainers. Financial membership of the union seemed to have been limited to 16,000 members at maximum, with the London tailors numbering 4,600 and the London cordwainers 3,000. The loss of these two trades was therefore a severe blow to the GNCTU. The union was formally wound up at a delegate meeting in London in August, Owen being elected Grand Master, then resigning. The GNCTU was finally reorganized and transformed into the British and Foreign Consolidated Association, with Owen as governor, aiming to foster good relations between masters and men, and to diminish competition. It soon vanished into obscurity.

Two other bodies need to be mentioned: the first is the Builders Union, consisting of seven building trades, which was founded in 1832, and was organized on the basis of lodges and grand lodges, with an annual conference of delegates known as the Builders' Parliament. It spread through the Lancashire and Midland towns in 1832, and put up a spirited opposition in Liverpool to building employers' use of subcontractors or middlemen. It also brought its members out on strike in Birmingham, where the employers struck back with the use of the "document". Its annual conference in Manchester in 1833 lasted six days, cost over £3,000, and was attended by 270 delegates representing 30,000 members. At the conference it was decided to build a Guild Hall in Birmingham, where its journal, *The Pioneer*, was also published. But later in 1833, its two great strikes in Liverpool and Manchester were both unsuccessful and the union went into decline. The Guild Hall was never built, and *The Pioneer* was taken over by the GNCTU. The other body that must be mentioned is the National Regeneration Society – not a trade union at all, but for a brief time a somewhat unusual body that played a part in trade union affairs. This society had a basic plan, originally proposed by John Fielden, the fac-

105

tory reformer, which aimed to reduce the working day to eight hours, starting on 1 March 1834 but without any reduction in wages. This novel proposal was, of course, in conflict with the existing and well-established Ten Hour Movement. Furthermore, it was supposed to come about with the agreement of the employers. The Regeneration Society perhaps could not have made much impact on the industrial history of the early 1830s but for the fact that it was supported by Robert Owen, and also by John Doherty, who seems to have turned to it and tried to bring it trade union support in the last days of the NAPL. Its principal stronghold was Oldham, where working-class influence over affairs in the town was very strong, and where there was a prolonged spinners' strike in the first half of 1834. The idea of such a drastic reduction in hours, and in effect a great increase in wages, was grossly impractical, of course. The only serious attempt to implement the policy was in Oldham, where (it has been argued) the spinners' general strike was really political, its leaders being revolutionary radicals. However, this view of events has not found general acceptance, and the society collapsed very rapidly after June 1834.

Several questions arise out of the events of the first half of the 1830s: the first is, why did the GNCTU fail? Dr Oliver deals with this question very briefly, laying emphasis on its small membership, the incompetence displayed at the London headquarters, and the ideological differences between Owen and the other leaders. In fact, he provides a very different picture from that given by earlier historians such as the Webbs with their suggestions of half a million members, numerous lodges for women (they mention the Grand Lodge of Operative Bonnet Makers, the Lodge of Female Tailors, the Female Gardiners, and even the Ancient Virgins); and above all, according to the Webbs, there was the grand object of "a general expropriatory strike". According to Dr Oliver, when judged by membership and numbers, and effective power and cohesion, the GNCTU was "insignificant and fragmentary". In fact, this may be to go too far in the other direction, but the lack of documentary evidence makes it difficult to take the matter much further. It is self-evident that the GNCTU was enormously ambitious in conception, and the fate of the NAPL shows clearly enough how hard it was to organize such a vast national undertaking. To be successful, it would have required efficient administration and massive financial resources, which were simply not available. The union seems to have been very largely London-based, with only about 6,000 members outside London even when member-ship was at its peak. When first the tailors and then the cordwainers pulled out, it was the beginning of the end. It is possible to exaggerate the sectionalism of the trade unions of the time, but surely it would have called for a great burst of fraternal feeling in the provinces for such an enterprise to succeed, especially as the aims of the GNCTU were so ill-defined, and indeed self-contradictory, with Owenite communitarian idealism on the one hand, and on the other, James Smith's belief that workers should aim at changing their wages into a fair share of the profits of their employers. The fascinating question remains unanswered: why should hard-headed and experienced Lon don trade unionists ever think the Grand Union could achieve any-thing worthwhile?

One can only suppose that they were caught up in some sort of ideological fervour, and that following the disappointment over the Reform Act, 1832, which did relatively little for the working classes, they pinned their faith to action in the industrial field. Once upon a time it was fashionable to emphasize the pervasive influence of Owenite socialism, and the support it gave to reformist thinking, but it is now clear that Owenism was scarcely a coherent mass movement. Furthermore, it was based on class *collaboration*, not class conflict, and was really far removed from the realities of the day-to-day strug-gles in factory and workshop over rates of pay and similar matters. Hence the very different approaches of Owen, and of Smith and Morrison. It should be added that few historians today would accept the Webbs's description of the 1830s as the "revolutionary period". There was very little revolutionary thinking or action at this time, al-though there was probably a heightened class consciousness on the part of working-class leaders, a product in all likelihood of ongoing industrialization and of the Reform Bill agitation. Robert Fyson, writ-ing about the National Union of Potters in the 1830s, has pointed out that this union claimed that "we are the producers of all wealth – the capital of our employers is a dead weight without our labour"; yet at the same time they remarked somewhat submissively, "We only want our place". This seems a very fair description of radical trade union attitudes at the time. John Doherty, for example, was no revolution-ary. He simply believed strongly in justice for working people, declar-ing in 1831 that:

I want to better the condition of the people – to have them stand erect, and look boldly in the faces of their masters, and to tell them, "We are not your slaves; we are your equals. We are one side of the bargain, you are only the other. We give you an equivalent from what we get from you, and are therefore entitled to, at least, equal respect.'

A final comment on the significance of both the NAPL and the GNCTU would be that they each represented over-ambitious efforts to combine all trades into a massive single body capable of exerting the maximum pressure on employers. They failed in their aims for very obvious reasons – the magnitude of the tasks attempted, the problem of organizing funds to support members on strike, and in the case of the GNCTU, the deep ideological divisions between leaders. It was not really until the 1860s that any productive move was made to provide national consultation and collaboration between trades, but the Trades Union Congress of 1868 had very different aims from both the NAPL and the GNCTU. Nevertheless, both bodies had experience in organizing on a national scale, in arranging delegate meetings, and so on. All this experience was to be helpful in the continued growth of national bodies in individual trades, and something which was to be the pattern of future developments in trade unionism.

After the excitements of the GNCTU and of the Tolpuddle Martyrs, it was (in the words of one historian) business as usual for the trade union movement, inhibited only by the trade depression that developed in and after 1836, reaching a real intensity in 1841 and 1842. Nevertheless, growth continued, especially among engineers and ironworkers. For example, in 1838 the largest engineering unions in Lancashire and Yorkshire formed the Journeymen Steam Engine and Machine Makers Friendly Society, with a paid secretary from 1843. Minor schemes for co-operative production providing work for unemployed members also continued here and there – the Ropemakers of the Port of London had one such scheme in 1836. Large-scale strikes also occurred from time to time, as among the Preston spinners in 1836. The Potters' Union, which had been started in the potteries as the result of a visit from NAPL missionaries in 1831, was influential in local politics and staged a successful 15-week strike from November 1834 to March 1835. In 1836 the employers formed a chamber of commerce, and when in a further strike the union called out 14 factories, the employers retaliated by organizing a lock-out by its 64 members. In June 1837 the potters were forced back to work, and the union collapsed. It had been a national body, and in North Staffordshire it had included three-quarters of all the adult pottery workers, in 54 lodges, nine in each town; there had also been a separate women's lodge.

Also in 1837, a serious cotton spinners' strike broke out in Glasgow in which there was much violence, and five spinners were indicted on charges of conspiracy, violent intimidation and murder. Their trial excited a good deal of controversy, and in the Commons the Irish leader, Daniel O'Connell, attacked the practices of the trade unions in Dublin and Cork. The result was the appointment of a select committee on trade unions in 1838. This committee produced two very brief reports, each amounting to no more than a paragraph or so, simply reporting that evidence had been collected and printed. The evidence itself is of limited use to the historian since it is concerned very narrowly with the state of affairs in Glasgow and in Dublin. Only one prominent trade union witness was examined, John Doherty, and he was no longer a trade union official, having become a bookseller and printer in Manchester. He was really out of touch with trade union activity in that city (his estimate of 2,000 members for the Manchester spinners' union was corrected by their secretary, W. Arrowsmith, who said the total was about 1,060), but he did produce a moderate and effective statement explaining why men must be naturally adverse to striking:

> In the first place, there is the loss of employment for a time at any rate, there is the probable consequence of their ultimate discharge, and their entire loss of employment, and if they take an active part, of endless unceasing persecution . . . and there is a great reluctance on their part from the fear of what it brings upon their wives and families at home whenever there is a strike.

This was well said. The 20 pages of his evidence are distinctly low-key, as compared with the 102 pages of evidence by Archibald Alison, who had been the judge in the trial of the spinners. This witness was clearly intensely hostile to the unions, and accused them of employing "intimidation and violence without any reserve" in order to gain their ends. Apparently after the trial he wrote a violent article anonymously in *Blackwoods* accusing all the men who had been acquitted of all the same serious offences yet again. This must have made an unfavourable impression, as he was asked by the chairman whether this action was consistent with his conduct and character as a judge.

It would be tedious to dwell at too great a length on the evidence of the employers, nearly all of whom were highly critical of the unions, but two extreme examples are quoted. Mr Edward Murray, a Dublin architect and builder, said his firm had been burned out five months previously. His men had been persecuted by the union, and he himself had been assaulted; for two years he had carried pistols and a dirk. He produced three threatening letters, the second half of the third reading as follows:

> We are not yet satisfied with your house being burnt, nor won't be satisfied till we kick the guts out of you. We don't think it worth our while to tell you for what. But we think you can think yourself. All we are sorry for is that you were not burnt yourself: You Bloody hangman Beware – Prepare – take care – Do if you dare – you bloody old bear – we will give you your fare, will make you run like a hare – For you we will tare – Your Bloody flesh we will Pair – you may think it very Quare – For your old clothes we will wear – so take care and beware, for we are determined to doctor you.

This remarkable epistle concluded with a skull and crossbones, an outline of a coffin with the words superimposed "Bloody old Murray", and the final words, "It's now all over with you. Amen." All Murray was asked was whether he thought men in their senses would write such a letter, but his reply was not recorded.

The other extremely hostile employer was Mr Edward Carolan of Dublin, referred to in the previous chapter when giving evidence before the 1824 Committee. He described four outrages, the last being a vitriol attack on himself, which burned all the clothes off his back; he had also been beaten. Since 1826 he had employed only Scotsmen, between a hundred and two hundred in number, all non-union men. He thought the former laws (those before 1824) were better than those of the present: "they were a terror over them". The present law, he thought, had increased breaches of the law, and there had been more violence, although the number of combinations in Dublin had remained the same. Only one employer, Mr Benjamin Eaton, a Dublin architect, spoke favourably of body-men (members of unions). He said that he had always employed them, and got on well with them; he had no complaints. He admitted that violence did take place – "No man deplores it more than I do" – but he spoke very warmly of his 45 workers.

The only trade union witness other than Doherty to be examined at any length was James Kavanagh, secretary of the powerful Dublin society of carpenters. He said he was paid £25 a year, they had 500 members, the ordinary committees met twice a week, and were elected four times a year by ballot. Violence was never authorized by the society, which was building a meeting house with a room large enough for public meetings. The room had so far cost £700, and would cost another £200 or £300 to finish it. The levy for unemployed men was 1s a week (who themselves received 5s a week). He admitted that the union really determined the men's rates of pay, so that the inferior workman was paid the same as the good workman, but that employers could pay above the standard if they wished. The last 20 or so pages of the second volume of evidence contain a detailed examination of the rules of the carpenters. Again, the use of violence was denied, but the witness did admit that he knew of the existence of the *welters*, a kind of secret society of intimidators in Dublin. There are several previous references by witnesses to this gang of thugs and hitmen.

To sum up: the evidence collected by the 1838 Select Committee, as noted earlier, is not very helpful to the labour historian. In some ways it was the same mixture as in the 1824 and 1825 reports. According to the Webbs, "the Parliamentary Committee proved both perfunctory and inconclusive". They think the government evidently had no intention of taking any action on the subject, and that it was generally expected that the Committee would be reappointed to complete its task; but when the next session came, the matter was quietly dropped. So the modern reader is left with little information regarding the unions that is new, and with the customary and familiar complaints by employers of trade union tyranny and violence. As to their tyranny, it appears that some unions in Dublin still retained a firm control over the workings of their trade, and as for violence, although its extent may have been exaggerated, it seems likely that it did take place. The

Webbs, in the 1920 edition of their work, make some interesting comments on the violence displayed in the Glasgow spinners' strike. First, they admit that the evidence given in court and repeated before the 1838 Committee "leaves no reasonable doubt that the Cotton Spinners' Union in its corporate capacity had initiated a reign of terror extending over twenty years, and that some of the incriminated members had been personally guilty not of instigation alone, but of actual violence, if not murder". They then go on to say:

> The use of violence by working men, either against obnoxious employers, or against traitors in their own ranks, was regarded in much the same way as the political offences of a subject race under foreign domination. Such deeds did not, in fact, necessarily indicate any moral turpitude on the part of the perpetrators. No-one accused the five Glasgow cotton spinners of bad private character or conduct, and at least four out of the five were men of acknowledged integrity and devotedness.

The Webbs add in a footnote, "The five prisoners were pardoned in 1840, in consequence of their exemplary conduct". It is not often that one encounters such direct justification by historians of violence during strikes. Most simply refrain from comment, and politely look the other way.

The Glasgow cotton spinners' strike, and the Select Committee that followed it in 1838, occurred just before the first petition of the Chartists was presented to the House of Commons in 1839. By the time the second petition was presented in 1842, Chartism appears to have become much more aggressively class-conscious in outlook, and the rejection of the petition was followed by widespread industrial unrest and rioting. This used to be called the Plug Plot (since plugs were removed from boilers to prevent their functioning), but is now more generally called the General Strike of 1842. This title is somewhat misleading in that it was hardly a general strike in the modern sense of participation by all trades, while the strike was limited geographically for the most part to the Midland manufacturing areas and parts of the textile industry in Lancashire and Yorkshire. Nevertheless, it was a very serious outbreak of industrial protest, leading to 1,500 arrests, and 79 transported to Australia. Professor Mather has even referred to the Plug Plot as a "semi-revolutionary" strike movement, and as the most intense threat to public order in the early industrial period. Two questions therefore arise: how far did trade unions participate in Chartist activity, and how far did they co-operate with Chartists in the Plug Plot?

As regards the first question, the former view was that trade unions as a whole held aloof from Chartism, having their own interests (including their funds, of course) to preserve. The rule books of many societies forbade the discussion of political matters. Although the rule could be broken, it is a significant indication of the desire of most societies to confine themselves to trade affairs. Certainly most of the craft unions gave no official support to Chartism, and branches of the Steam Engine Makers Society were suspended by the society for placing funds in the Chartist Land Bank, and there were strong protests against two branches of the Stonemakers Society which proposed to do the same. In addition, the Manchester printers actually attacked the "futility" of aggressive Chartism, and also criticized Feargus O'Connor, the Chartist leader, as an unfair employer. In turn O'Connor criticized the craft unions in the famous phrase, "the pompous trades and proud mechanics". There is still much to be said for the earlier view that well-established unions in thriving trades showed no desire to commit their membership and their funds to the National Charter Association – why should they? This view must be modified to some extent, however, for although the trade union movement as a whole failed to support Chartism, this is not to say that individual members were not active Chartists – many obviously were. More recent research has shown that in London in and after 1840, older trades such as the tailors, the shoemakers (whom even the Webbs said were "thoroughly permeated with Chartism"), cabinet makers, and the building craftsmen (who were faced with the development of middlemen known as "general contractors") all gave support to Chartism, since they were all threatened with the coming into their trades of sweated or "dishonourable" labour. All these found the political advances promised by the Charter attractive.

The second question, regarding union participation in the Plug Plot, is perhaps more difficult to answer. Undoubtedly the very severe trade depression of the early 1840s was the basic reason for what happened. The grievances of the strikers were at root economic not political, and although the Chartists appear to have been active from the start and not merely joining in later and dominating the strike for their own ends, there were often divisions between the politically motivated Chartists and the strikers, who were concerned more with wages and jobs than with the political aims of the Charter. The fact remains, however, that the strikes were not begun by Chartists as a means of gaining the Charter – O'Connor actually declared at first that the strikes were orchestrated by the Anti-Corn Law League. It may be that further research might provide more details of the involvement of local trade union leaders in Chartist activities. This in itself would not be at all surprising, giving that many of them were of a radical turn of mind. The point remains that very few unions gave official support to Chartism. Exceptions to this can be found in Scotland, where contributions were made to Chartist funds, and fleetingly in 1842 during the Plug Plot when a meeting of trade delegates representing trades in the Manchester area called on all workers to stop work until the Charter had become the law of the land; but the moment passed. No doubt local Charter organizations gained much from the administrative experience and the expertise of trade union leaders, but there can be little question of the trade unions themselves becoming fronts for Chartism. They were not taken over, although many trade unionists contributed to the Chartist cause. When the smoke had cleared at the end of the 1840s, Chartism was at low ebb, whereas the trade unions continued to move ahead, arguably stronger than before.

It remains to put the general development of trade unions in the 1840s into some sort of perspective. With the lifting of the depression from 1842 onwards, new groups and federations were formed. In 1842 itself there was a new federation of Lancashire cotton spinners, and in 1844 the National Association of Printers was established. There was even a last attempt at a national union of all trades in the shape of the National Association of United Trades for the Protection of Labour, set up in Sheffield in 1845, which aimed at conciliation and arbitration in disputes, and at co-operative production. A surviving circular of this body is full of high-flown sentiment and dubious declarations, as in the following extract:

It is the only Institution in this country which is capable of providing for the wants and necessities of the Industrious Classes upon the principle of self-support.

In the first place, a ready market is found for the labour of the

Mechanic and Artisan by the strongest of human ties – the Bond of Union – unity is strength, and in no instance can be seen so powerfully and with advantage as in an Association of this nature. Every member of the Association determinedly combines with his Fellow man for the protection of industry, and not, as is erroneously supposed, for opposing the Employer.

The funds of this noble association were dissipated in legal action and, not surprisingly, it faded away within two or three years. Another move towards federation was taken by miners on a county basis in 1842, when the Miners Association of Great Britain and Ireland was set up. W. P. Roberts, the well known Chartist solicitor, was appointed to defend miners in court. The association was successful in having the miners' yearly bond abolished in Durham and Northumberland, but was gravely weakened by the four-month miners' strike in the northeast in 1844, and finally collapsed during a depression in the coal trade in the years 1847–8. In 1851 the powerful Amalgamated Society of Engineers was formed – an event of considerable significance in trade union history, which will be discussed in the next chapter. Undoubtedly the 1840s were to see a further development of the trade union movement in terms of the national organization of important trades leading to the growth and stability of the 1850s.

If the period 1825–50 is taken as a whole, it would be easier to assess progress made if firm statistical evidence were available to show the growth of trade unionism. Unfortunately this is not the case. In 1834 membership was inflated by the existence of the GNCTU, but even then, the total trade union membership was estimated by G. D. H. Cole at only a million or so, less than 20 per cent of the workforce. Much of this membership must have been only temporary in nature. In 1842, admittedly a very bad year for trade, the Webbs put the figure at under 100,000, that is, about 1.5 per cent of the labour force. So membership varied from year to year. It is a fair assumption, nevertheless, that trade unionism was stronger in numerical terms in 1850 than in 1825, and its legal position had improved to some extent by the legislation of 1824–5; but it remained a movement for the protection of only a minority of workers, the skilled and semi-skilled.

How far trade unionism had become more acceptable to employers in these 25 years is also a difficult question to answer. It is easy, of course, to cite examples of extreme employer hostility in the reports of the 1838 Committee. Hostility clearly existed among some employers in Dublin and Glasgow (the latter still a very important centre for cotton manufacture), and violence was commonplace. Violence during strikes continued well into the 1860s, as was made plain by the Sheffield outrages of 1866. In contrast, some employers certainly wished to co-operate with their unions as far as possible – indeed, they were useful allies in regulating trade matters, including the all-important question of wages (such employers, understandably enough, were considered to be "good" or "honourable" employers by the unions). In towns such as Birmingham, where labour relations were generally thought to be good, some of the larger employers ran their own sick clubs, and sought to foster good relations by annual works trips and jaunts, annual dinners, and excursions to local beauty spots (known as "gipsy parties"). One firm actually sent a party of workmen to witness the opening of the Liverpool–Manchester railway in 1830. Similar activities took place in the Black Country; in 1851 a prominent Stourbridge iron works dispatched a 400 strong contingent of workmen to visit the Great Exhibition. However, violence might still occur even in such poorly-organized trades as Black Country nailing, where wage disputes might result in visits to workshops accepting lower rates by what was known locally as "the flying horse" who slashed workshop bellows as a reprisal.

On the whole, it seems safe to say that, especially as concerns the older craft unions, labour relations had probably improved by 1850. Throughout the whole period, of course, the government had been more sympathetic to employers than to the unions. By the 1840s, certain economic and social developments had made it easier to maintain law and order, and militated against the forms of collective bargaining by riot thathad been common in the eighteenth century (often in the form of food riots), and had continued even in the earlier years of the nineteenth century. The best example of this is the "Scotch Cattle" activities of bands of miners and iron workers in South Wales in the 1820s and early 1830s, designed to intimidate both employers and recalcitrant workers. The coming of the railways in the 1830s, however, made it much easier for the government to move both troops and police to sensitive areas. In 1839, for example, a party of officers from the Metropolitan Police were sent by train to Birmingham to keep order when the Chartist Convention moved there from London (they were given a warm welcome). Another development was the creation of county police forces in and after 1839. Thus, any wide-spread collective bargaining by riot was made much more difficult after 1840, although of course rioting in itself did not entirely cease.

Lastly, the 1830s have always been an extremely important period for study by labour historians. In particular, E. P. Thompson singled out this period as one in which working-class consciousness rose to new heights, and the English working class was "made" (Harold Perkin has asserted that "it was between 1815 and 1820 that the working class was born" – a most remarkably precise pinpointing of the time of its creation). Both assertions remain unproven, in the nature of things, although it is true enough that working-class con-sciousness probably increased – a reasonable enough assumption, given the class-conscious statements of leaders such as Doherty, Smith and Morrison. What remains very dubious is Thompson's conclu-sions that in the early 1830s, "the battle for the minds of English trade unionists, between a capitalist and a *socialist* political economy, had been (at least temporarily) won". One is bound to ask, what battle? What socialist political economy? The major form of socialism on offer at the time was Owenism, which rejected the class struggle and was based on co-operation between capitalist and labour. Thus, there is very little to show that trade union leaders aimed ultimately at political revolution; and such co-operative schemes as were initiated by the unions were aimed at providing employment for out-of-work members, not at communities planned on Owenite lines.

None of this denies the importance of the 1830s and early 1840s for the working classes. Indeed, the 1830s provide a fascinating mix-ture of political and industrial action, starting with the agitation for political reform, culminating in the passing of the Reform Act, 1832. (Some working-class voters lost their vote under the act, but others gained, depending on the rating system in individual towns; after 1832, 26 per cent of borough voters were working class, and in Cov-entry, an exceptional 70 per cent had the vote in 1866.) Then there was the movement towards general unionism, followed by a swing back to political action represented by the Chartist movement. This alternation of emphasis between political action and economic action has often been represented as a pendulum movement of working-class interest, but this is clearly an over-simplification, for trade union and political activity obviously continued side by side throughout, especially during the Chartist period.

So what final significance can be attached to trade union development in the period 1825–50? It is safe to say that it was a period of growth, based on a marginally more secure legal basis, and fed by an expanding industrialization. General unionism, especially in the form of the GNCTU, owed something to the support of Robert Owen, and was indicative of the need to explore ways of increasing pressure on employers during trade disputes; but it proved a chimera – in more mundane terms, the organizational difficulties were too great. Chartism provided another outlet for the reforming enthusiasms of trade unionists. But when Chartism died, trade unionism went marching on into the new era of the 1850s.

Chapter Six

Model unionism and respectability 1850–1880

In January 1851 a landmark in trade union history was reached with the establishment of a new amalgamated trade union, the Amalgamated Societies of Engineers (ASE), based upon the Journeyman Steam Engine and Machine Makers and Millwrights Society. According to the Webbs, the creation of this new union marked a turning point in the history of the trade union movement. Other engineering unions soon joined, such as the Smiths Society of London; the one union still remaining apart was the Steam Engine Makers Society, which did not join until much later in 1919. By October 1851 the ASE had 11,000 members, each paying a subscription of 1s week, with substantial out-of-work, sickness and funeral benefits. For the Webbs, the ASE became a New Model union, providing a model for other unions with its high subscription rates, its careful organization, its conciliatory attitudes, and its ample financial resources. In addition, it was a national organization, with a paid secretary. As such, it looked to the future; gone were the days of what the Webbs called "the revolutionary period", and their chapter on the period 1843 to 1860 is headed "The New Spirit and the New Model".

The Webbs published their pioneering history of trade unionism in 1894, with a new edition in 1920. Perhaps no part of their survey has come in for more criticism since the Second World War than their assessment of the significance of the creation of the ASE. In the first place, it has frequently been pointed out that there was nothing new in its being national, or in having a paid secretary – there are numerous precedents for these features earlier in the century – nor was it new in being a union of skilled workers; nearly all unions up to the mid-century were of this kind. Then again, lacking the resources of the ASE, relatively few unions were able to model themselves on the society, so the notion that model unionism became the accepted form of most unions is quite misleading. Many unions, such as those in the textile industry, remained regional if not local in operation. Nor did the ASE exhibit any novel characteristics; it simply retained the attitudes of the traditional craft unions, enforcing apprenticeship where it could, and imposing high rates of subscription, thereby permitting ample out-of-work and sickness benefits. For all these reasons, Professor Musson has suggested that "what occurred in the fifties and sixties was not the creation of a 'New Model' but the strengthening of the old". In addition to these criticisms it should be added that the ASE was not always conciliatory in approach. A year after it was established, a serious strike broke out in the engineering trades, and there was a lock-out in every large engineering works in Lancashire and London. The ASE supported not only 3,500 of its own members, but also 1,500 mechanics and 10,000 labourers. The strike, collapsed by April 1852, under threat of "the document", but the Society survived, with £700 still in hand.

On a number of counts, therefore, "New Model Unionism" must be treated with reserve, if not actual suspicion. One historian has even described it as "a piece of historical fiction". It really seems that in their efforts to provide a contrast with the earlier so-called "revolutionary period", the Webbs over-emphasized the novel aspects of the more powerful unions created in and after 1851, and were unduly influenced by the more conciliatory attitudes of the unions in the 1850s and 1860s. On the other hand, the Webbs did give prominence to the ASE strike in 1852, and to subsequent strikes such as the great builders' strike in London in 1859, so there is no suggestion on their part that model unions never went on strike. Clearly, the establishment of the ASE was an important event in trade union history, and this must be acknowledged. Unlike earlier efforts at amalgamation, it survived, its membership and resources multiplied, and it was increasingly accepted by employers. According to its secretary, William Allen, by the mid-1860s its membership was increasing by 2,000 to 3,000 members a year, and included up to three-quarters of all those employed in engineering. Total membership was about 33,600, based on 308 branches, with 11 branches in the USA. Funds amounted to about £140,000, and the annual income in 1865 was £86,885. This was obviously success on a considerable scale. More recently it has been suggested by W. Hamish Fraser that reaction to the Webbs's views has been excessive, and that the real significance of the ASE was as a symbol of its survival, growth, large funds, and so on. This seems a fair verdict, although when Fraser goes on to say that its progress was something to be emulated, this appears to be taking us back to the idea of a "model". Perhaps the Webbs's use of the word was not so inappropriate after all.

How then was the ASE organized? Each branch of the society elected its own officers, retained its own funds, and administered its own benefits, but all this was subject to strict rules laid down by the Executive. Branch funds were the property of the whole society, but balances were equalized at the end of each year by an elaborate system of remittances from branch to branch, so that each branch started the year with the same amount per member. Strike decisions were taken by District Committees, who advised the Executive Council of their decisions. The holding of local office brought considerable responsibility. Branch secretaries were paid up to £10 4s a year, although the branch had to have at least 300 members for this payment to be made. Branch committee members were paid 6d a night for attendance, while executive committee members received 1s 6d per night. For meetings during the day, they were paid their wages plus 5s 6d. This was raised to 7s for travel beyond seven miles, together with 1s for fares. Thus, the society was strictly organized at both local level and centrally, William Allen's office being famous for its mountains of paperwork.

Undoubtedly trade unionism spread in the relatively prosperous years of the 1850s, 1860s and the early 1870s. Yet it must be stressed again that still only a minority of the working classes were members of a union. Henry Mayhew, for instance, thought that only about 10 per cent of the average London craft was unionized in the 1860s. This is only a rough approximation, of course, and may indeed be misleading, since figures varied from trade to trade. In 1867, for example, it was estimated that nationally 25 per cent of cabinet makers were in unions, 90 per cent of cotton spinners, 90 per cent of provincial printers, and 85 per cent of London bookbinders. However, overall growth appears to have been well-established. In 1859, the total number of trade union members has been estimated at about 600,000; in 1865 at about half a million, while George Potter put the figure at 800,000 in 1867.

If membership varied from trade to trade, so did organization.

Again, it must be said that very few trade unions could conform to the ASE pattern in this respect. Of these, the Amalgamated Society of Carpenters was the most prominent. In 1867 it had 190 branches with 8,261 members paying 1s a week, and with a net income in 1865 of £10,487 15s. Benefits were quite generous: donation benefit (strike pay) 10s for 12 weeks, then 6s for the following 12 weeks; out-of-work benefit 15s a week; sick benefit 12s for 26 weeks, then 6s for as long as sickness persisted; funeral benefit £12; accident benefit up to £100; superannuation for life 8s a week for membership of 25 years, 7s for 18 years, and 5s for 12 years; emigration grant £6. All this was much beyond the means of the smaller unions, and only a few unions adopted such extensive friendly society benefits as the ASE, the Amalgamated Carpenters, the Ironfounders and the Boilermakers. Many kept their sickness and their trade funds separate, while most societies offered little beyond out-of-work and funeral benefits. Even the powerful Brickmakers Society of London (about 5,700 members, 96 branches) had no sickness fund. When sickness benefit was provided, it was often on the basis of a special levy on members rather than payment out of funds as of right. The rank and file membership often opposed friendly society benefits as opposed to strike and unemployment pay, which was considered the essential thing.

Certain other features of the earlier trade unions remained evident. Hostility to the unskilled workmen among the skilled members was still very marked, and continued well into the 1870s. One working-class author observed in 1873:

Between the artisan and the unskilled labourer a gulf is fixed. While the former resents the spirit in which he believes the followers of genteel occupations look down upon him, he in turn looks down upon the labourer. The artisan creed with regard to the labourer is, that they are an inferior class, and that they should be made to know, and kept in their place.

So much for brotherly feeling. A second working-class writer remarked in 1879 that labourers were grateful to be spoken to "like as if we was the same flesh and blood as other people", and he continued:

There is no place in which class distinctions are more sharply defined, or if need be, violently maintained, than in the work-shop. Evil would certainly befall any labourer who *acted upon* even the tacit assumption that he was the social equal of the arti-san . . .

Unionism itself became identified with the skilled workman, and helped to perpetuate the division between the skilled and unskilled.

One noticeable new characteristic of the unions in the middle dec-ades of the nineteenth century was certainly an increasing respectabil-ity, itself the consequence of a new emphasis on moderation and conciliation. Back in the 1830s, trade union leaders often spoke of employers and indeed of the whole capitalist system in highly critical terms – the speeches of John Doherty provide many examples of this, let alone the views of radicals like James Morrison and James Smith. By the 1860s there is a remarkable change of tone. The reasons for this are not difficult to discover: prosperity had brought a kinder eco-nomic climate in which to negotiate wage increases, and employers were making good profits. In addition, experience had taught that continued clashes with employers often failed to achieve their pur-pose, and were attended by hardship, short commons and sometimes violent struggles with blackleg labour, or even the introduction of new machinery designed to save labour. As noted in the previous chapter, Doherty spoke feelingly in 1838 of the difficulties of going on strike, and of the strains it imposed on both striker and his family. Increased prosperity brought increased employment, and increased trade union membership, allowing the unions to build up their funds, which in fact they were reluctant to dissipate unnecessarily on strike pay. As a result, far greater emphasis than formerly was laid on nego-tiation, and on the avoidance of strikes if at all possible.

Nowhere is this change of attitude seen more clearly than in state-ments made at this time by trade union leaders regarding strike action. For example, the editor of the *Flint Glass Makers Magazine* wrote in 1855, "We believe that strikes have been the bane of Trade Unions", while according to George Odger, the radical leader of a small ladies shoe union and the secretary of the London Trades Coun-cil, "Strikes are to the social world what wars are to the political world. They become crimes unless promoted by absolute necessity". Alexander MacDonald, the Scottish miners' leader, declared before a Select Committee of the House of Commons in 1873:

I look upon strikes as a barbaric relic of a period of unfortunate relations between capital and labour, and the sooner we get rid of it by the more rational means of employer meeting the employed, and talking the matter over, the better.

Of course, such declarations need not necessarily be taken at their face value, but they were not confined to trade union leaders seeking to butter up their employers. The Majority Report of the Royal Commission on Trade Unions, 1867 stated that:

It does not appear to be borne out by the evidence that the disposition to strike on the part of workmen is in itself the creation of unionism, or that the frequency of strikes increases in proportion to the strength of the union. It is indeed affirmed by the leaders of unions that the effect of the established societies is to diminish the frequency, and certainly the disorder, of strikes, and to guarantee a regularity of wages and hours rather than to engage in constant endeavours to improve them.

Once more, it could be said that the last sentence in this statement might perhaps be taken with a pinch of salt, but it is certainly true that the union witnesses made a good impression on the Commission, and it is also true that at times unions performed a valuable service in restraining their more unruly members from undisciplined and violent strike action, and also helped to preserve order when strikes did take place.

Another noteworthy development after 1850 was the creation of numerous local boards for conciliation and arbitration. The word "arbitration" in this context means consultation and negotiation rather than the umpiring of a dispute, but this in itself was not excluded from wage negotiations from time to time. The Nottingham Board of Arbitration for the Hosiery Trade, 1860 is one of the best-known examples of a wages board, and a parliamentary bill for local councils of conciliation became law in 1867, to be followed by A. J. Mundella's Arbitration (Master and Workmen) Act, 1872 (although neither proved very effective). There were other boards of arbitration in the 1860s and 1870s, for example, in the Wolverhampton building trades in 1865, in the Teeside iron industry in 1869, in the Staffordshire iron trade in 1872, and in the Leicester boot and shoe industry in

1875. In some cases, sliding scales of wages were adopted by such boards, for example, in the Midlands Iron and Steel Wages Board wages were determined by the movement of trade prices in the commodity concerned. In theory, these scales made bargaining by the unions superfluous, and they were understandably regarded with suspicion by some unions, although not by all. On the whole, the scales were acceptable enough to unions when prices were rising, and wages went up appropriately (even though employers refused to allow rising profits to be taken into account), but they were criticized strongly when prices fell with the onset of the Great Depression after 1872. A variation on the wages board system was provided later by the alliance system in Birmingham, whereby employers would come to an agreement with the unions on wages and conditions, subject to the exclusive employment of union labour.

Trades councils are another development of the period. At first sight, these local organizations of trade union officials might seem to represent a move away from conciliation and a strengthening of the trade union front against the employers. In practice, this was not necessarily so. Trades councils met to discuss issues of more than local interest, such as affairs in parliament, labour legislation, foreign policy as it affected workers abroad, and the like. Such matters were of particular interest to the London Trades Council, which dates from 1860, and was said by William Allen, secretary of the ASE, "to look after parliamentary affairs". This council was described by the Webbs as being dominated by the group of leading trade union officials they called the Junta (Allen, ASE; Applegarth, Carpenters; Guile, Ironfounders; Coulson, London Brickmakers; and Odger, secretary of the London Trades Council). The Webbs also claimed that in some years the Engineers and the Carpenters supplied half the income of the Council. Thus the London Trades Council became, in effect, a joint committee of the officers of the large national societies – the beginnings of an informal cabinet (as the Webbs put it) of the trade union world.

This view of the influence of the Junta has been disputed by W. Hamish Fraser, who has argued that never at any time were all the members of the Junta on the London Trades Council, and that the Council *never* functioned in the way described by the Webbs. Indeed, the ASE disaffiliated from the Council in 1874. It is true, of course, that trades councils sprang up in a number of cities and towns – in 1860 there were permanent trades councils in Glasgow, Sheffield,

Liverpool and Edinburgh, about a dozen being established between 1858 and 1867, this number doubling again in the period 1870–73; but Fraser argues that trades councils had no executive powers, and were weak organizations. In any case, he says that they depended on the smaller craft societies, and were vulnerable to economic fluctuations. All this may be so, but there is still a good deal to be said for the earlier views of the influence of the Junta on political affairs, whether exercised through the London Trades Council or otherwise. They certainly actively promoted agitation for an extension of the franchise, for an amendment of the Master and Servant law, for further mines regulation acts, for popular education, and finally for the trade union legislation of the 1870s. In particular, Odger, Applegarth and Coulson were all leading members of the Reform League, pledged to franchise reform; and after the passing of the Franchise Act, 1867 the London leaders, including Applegarth, founded the Labour Representation League in 1869, to work for the return of working men to parliament.

Thus, the trade union movement was beginning to exert an influence on national affairs, scoring its first positive success in the field of legislation when, after lobbying MPs and securing the appointment of a Select Committee in 1866, the Master and Servant Act, 1867 was passed. Under this act, the law was modified so that workmen could only be sent to prison for aggravated breach of contract – previously, workmen were imprisoned as a matter of course for breaking their contracts, while, for the same "crime", masters were only subject to a fine.

If the industrial scene in the mid-1860s is surveyed, it is clear that a considerable change had come over trade union organization and attitudes. The largest unions had become more conciliatory in attitude, and more prepared to accept the current economic system. This applied especially to trades most deeply affected by the new industrial system – the engineers, ironfounders, boiler makers (all engaged in the booming iron industry), workers in cotton (another great and flourishing industry) and, later, the miners and building workers. Yet this adoption of more peaceful approaches, and the avoidance of strikes where possible, does not mean that strikes did not take place; one of the most important and widespread strikes of the time broke out among the London building workers in 1859 and continued into the next year. The strike had its origins in a demand for a nine-hour day in the London building trades, and began in the first place at Trollope's, the great London building firm. It led to a general lock-out in London, with 24,000 workmen thrown out of work. The employers finally broke the strike by the use of "the document". The men were forced back to work, and the shops re-opened, without any reduction of hours. However, the employers did withdraw the document, so that the unions were able to claim it was a drawn battle. During its course, the strikers received much support from sympathetic unions, the ASE providing three successive weekly donations of £1,000 each. One important consequence of the strike was the formation of the London Trades Council, and the establishing of another "model union", the Amalgamated Society of Carpenters, led by Robert Applegarth. So it would be wrong to suppose that the newer, more conciliatory attitudes necessarily brought a cessation of strikes, nor did the more peaceful settlement of disputes end completely the occasional use of violence against both blacklegs and hostile employers.

This last fact was dramatically illustrated in 1866 by the so-called Sheffield Outrages. In October 1866 a keg of gunpowder was thrown down a workman's chimney in Sheffield, causing a serious explosion, and a series of press reports followed, revealing instances of physical violence by the Sheffield unions. There had been examples of this kind of thing before in Sheffield, where it was the common practice for trade union rules to be enforced by "rattening", that is, removing the wheelbands or tools of offending workmen until they obeyed the union; failure to do so would lead to more serious action, such as the use of gunpowder. The Sheffield unions themselves supported the Town Council and the employers in demanding a government enquiry, while the London Trades Council and the ASE sent a deputation to investigate the original crime. Robert Applegarth himself saw the Home Secretary, and suggested a Commission of Enquiry; it was increasingly urgent for the unions to clear their name. Finally in February 1867 a Royal Commission was appointed, to enquire into the organization and rules of trade unions and other associations. At the same time, a body of Examiners was set up, to enquire into all outrages in Sheffield and elsewhere over the previous ten years, with the power to indemnify all witnesses from prosecution (a rather remarkable provision). The commission proved to be very middle class in composition, but at least two of its members were friends of the union movement – Thomas Hughes, the Christian socialist, and Frederic Harrison, the Positivist.

It so happened that just at the time when it was vital for the trade union movement as a whole to disassociate itself from the violence of the smaller Sheffield unions, the legal position of the unions was also brought into question. In the first to place, the right to picket and its legal limitations had been the subject of different interpretations in the courts ever since 1825. The fundamental problem was what constituted "molestation", "obstruction" and the like; in 1847, Baron Rolfe had ruled that a threat of physical violence was necessary to constitute illegal action, but later in 1851, Judge Earl considered that even the peaceful persuasion of men to leave work was actionable. Finally, in 1859 the Molestation of Workmen Act appeared to settle the matter, since it allowed workmen "peacefully" and "in a reasonable manner" to persuade others to strike. Yet even then, in 1862 Baron Bramwell declared that even watching men not on strike, and giving them "black looks" was intimidation. So picketing was still a hazardous business.

Of more immediate seriousness than this, however, was the *Hornby* v. *Close* case decided in 1867. In this case the Boiler Makers Society sued their Bradford branch secretary for the sum of £24, which he was withholding from the society. The society had deposited its rules with the Registrar of Friendly Societies under the generally held assumption that this entitled it to bring an action under the terms of the Friendly Society Act, 1855. In fact, the court ruled that the Society was not entitled to bring such an action because although not positively illegal, trade unions had no defined legal status, and might still be considered to be in restraint of trade. Thus, trade union funds were quite unprotected at law. For a number of reasons, therefore, the newfound acceptance of trade unions as respectable and prosperous bodies was put in jeopardy: there was a need to establish themselves yet again as essentially law-abiding, and there was a need to put their legal position beyond question, at the same time putting the vexed legal position of picketing beyond doubt.

For a time they faced an uphill task. The Report of the Examiners, dated 2 August 1867, began by asserting that rattening, a means of enforcing the payment of subscriptions or enforcing union rules, was admitted to take place by the unions, although they had at first denied it. The report then went on to give details of acts of violence committed by members of a dozen or so Sheffield unions during the past ten years, declaring that of about 60 unions in Sheffield, 12 had promoted or encouraged outrages. These outrages were set out in detail, union by union, amounting to 35 incidents in all. The saw grinders had the worst record, having been involved in ten cases where gunpowder had been employed, and three cases of attempted shooting, one of which proved fatal. The most sensational case involved the murder of an employer, James Lindley, as he sat in a public house in Scotland Street, by one Samuel Crook. This man, together with an accomplice Hallam, had tracked Lindley from house to house nearly every day for five weeks, intending to shoot him. In evidence, Hallam admitted that he had obtained the pistol to shoot Lindley, while Crook freely confessed that he had fired the fatal shot from the back yard and through the window of the pub. According to a dramatic newspaper report, Broadhead, secretary of the Saw Grinders Union, sat in court with bowed head, calling through the fingers of his hands, "Tell the truth, Sam – everything . . . ". Crook then said that he had been paid £20 by Broadhead for the shooting – although he had not meant to kill Lindley, only wound him in the shoulder. Another remarkable outrage concerned a gunpowder attack on the house of a non-union man, George Wastnidge, who lived in Acorn Street together with his wife, child and lodger, Bridget O'Rourke. According to the Examiner's Report:

About one o'clock in the morning of 23rd November [1861], a can of gunpowder was thrown through the chamber window. Mrs Wastnidge, hearing a noise, ran down into Mrs O'Rourke room and found her holding in her hand a parcel emitting sparks. She seized it in order to throw it through the window, but it exploded in her hands, setting fire to her nightdress, and seriously injuring her. She ran upstairs, her husband stripped off her burning clothes, and in her fear she threw herself through the garret window into the street. Wastnidge dropped his little boy to persons who were below in the street, and by means of a ladder, which was brought, escaped from the house. Mrs O'Rourke was found in the cellar, shockingly burnt.

Mrs Wastnidge never fully recovered. Mrs O'Rourke died a fortnight later. The can of gunpowder was thrown by one Robert Renshaw, who was paid £6 by the union acting secretary, who then falsified the union books to conceal the payment.

Fortunately for the unions, these sensational revelations were soon countered by the sober and impressive evidence given by the leading members of the Junta to the commissioners – Applegarth, Newton, and Coulson all gave evidence, Applegarth at some length. All spoke freely of the membership, organization, financial resources and reluctance to strike of their unions. As for the employers, some of whom spoke at inordinate length, their arguments were often hostile to the unions although without departing from familiar ground. In particular they criticized the opposition of many unions to piecework, their dislike of higher wages being paid to better-than-average work-men, and their prohibition of what was termed "chasing". The unions were in effect accused of slowing the pace of work down to that of the slowest workman. The employers also tried in some instances to challenge the financial soundness of the funds of the bigger unions, bringing actuarial evidence to bear to show that their benefit schemes were actually unsafe. Restrictions on the number of apprentices, the banning of overtime, intimidatory picketing – any modern enquirer wishing to know what objections employers still had to trade union practices in the mid-nineteenth century need look no further than the reports of 1867; although he needs to be of a patient disposition, since there are no less than eleven reports, extending to some thousands of pages.

To all these objections the trade union witnesses replied patiently and well. They undoubtedly made a good impression, being helped from time to time by judiciously worded questions from Frederic Harrison. Here and there they were on weak ground: Applegarth was uncharacteristically evasive when answering a question on why the better workman should not get better wages, arguing that the union was always interested in obtaining a minimum wage for all, although he did not oppose a good man being paid above that amount. Again, Richard Harnott of the masons was pressed on "chasing", defined as "setting too high a pace of work", and forbidden by Rule 11 of his union. He defended this by saying that the rule prevented scamping of work, and avoided "over-exertion". The rule therefore "cultivated efficiency". In common with other witnesses, Edwin Coulson was questioned on the unions' opposition to piece work. He argued that piece work made for rushed work; it was injurious to the men, who became slovenly and careless. It also encouraged employers to use inferior quality materials (in fact, it should be said that some trade

unions had always accepted piece work, notably miners, cotton spinners, iron workers, tailors and shoemakers). One odd question
regarding bricklaying was put to several witnesses: was it true that unions forbade the laying of bricks with both hands? It had to be pointed
out patiently that bricks were normally laid with a brick in one hand,
and a trowel in the other, so that the question made little or no sense.
Inevitably, one of the most important topics to be raised was that of
picketing, peaceful or otherwise. On this subject, Applegarth made a
memorable reply, as recorded in the Fourth Report:

> I *do* justify picketing . . . I say that it is perfectly justifiable for men
> to appoint other men to wait at a shop door and say to those who
> come, "The men were dissatisfied with the terms upon which
> they were working at that place, and if you go in, you will go in
> and undersell us; now we beg you that you will not do that". This
> is as far as I would justify men in going . . . If they use threats or
> coerce or intimidate, that is beyond the instructions, and which
> the laws of the society give them; and no-one more than myself
> would wish to bring them under the laws of the country for so
> doing. If they did not do what I have justified, it would be abso-
> lute folly to strike in many instances . . .

Understandably, Applegarth was pressed on this remarkable statement, which might be regarded today as being somewhat economical
with the truth and a little remote from reality. In reply, he instanced a
strike in Cardiff, where the pickets behaved with the greatest propriety. Evidently the Commission remained sceptical, for Applegarth
was asked whether he thought the Cardiff case was not an exceptional
instance of moderation in picketing. He was obliged, of course, to
deny that it was at all unusual.

On the whole, the evidence given by the members of the Junta was
very favourably received, and they deserved much credit for the way
in which they presented the case for the unions. Weekly meetings had
been held in London by the Junta to agree on tactics; they met under
the title of the Conference of the Amalgamated Trades. Harrison
proved a good friend in his influence over the Final Report, although
he and Hughes refused to sign it, and produced their own Minority
Report. The Majority Report recommended that trade unions should
be given a clear legal status, and that their rules could be registered

with the Registrar of Friendly Societies, provided they did not permit restrictive practices, such as the limitation of the number of apprentices. The Minority Report prepared by Harrison and Hughes emphasized the peaceful nature of trade unionism, pointing out that with the exception of recent events in Sheffield and Manchester:

> instances of actual attempts on life and limb rarely occur. The peculiarly atrocious crime of vitriol throwing, with which the former Reports are full, has not been mentioned here. Nothing has been heard of either incendiarism or machine-breaking. There has not been given in evidence, outside the two areas mentioned, any single case of taking life, and few definite acts of injury to the person.

This was true enough, except that the Examiners' enquiries had been confined to Sheffield and Manchester, where in both places the use of vitriol had obviously been replaced by the use of gunpowder. The Minority Report also recommended the legalization of trade unions, but without the restrictions suggested by the Majority Report. As a temporary measure, the Trades Unions Funds Protection Act, 1869 gave legal protection to trade union funds against embezzlement by their officials. There the matter rested while further legislation was prepared by the new Gladstone ministry which had come into office in 1868.

Meanwhile, interesting developments were taking place in what was to become the political field of action for the trade union movement. As we have seen, in the earlier years of the century trade unions in their corporate capacity had avoided direct participation in politics. However, in 1868 the Manchester Trades Council organized a Congress of Trade Unions at which there could be discussion of matters affecting trade unions generally. At one time it had been thought that the Conference of the National Social Science Association could provide a suitable forum for such discussion, but their proceedings had become more and more hostile to the trade union movement. Only 24 delegates attended the Manchester meeting, most of them from trades councils, but none from the London Trades Council. The Second Congress, held in Birmingham in the following year, was rather better attended by 40 delegates, while at the Third Congress, held in London in 1871, a Parliamentary Committee was appointed.

Since the 1867 Reform Act, working-men householders in the towns had obtained the vote, and as we have seen, the Labour Representation League was founded in 1869 to elect working men to parliament. Thus, a movement was growing not only to bring pressure to bear so as to influence proposed trade union legislation, but also to obtain direct trade union representation in parliament. In the 1874 general election, 14 Labour candidates stood for election, and of these, two were elected – Alexander MacDonald at Stafford, and Thomas Burt at Morpeth. They were the first working-class MPs. During the election, the Parliamentary Committee of the TUC presented candidates with test questions on their attitudes to trade unions, and union members were advised accordingly on how best to vote.

In the last years of the Gladstone administration, pressure on the government to introduce trade union legislation had increased. A bill introduced in 1871 proved a great disappointment to the unions. True, it at last placed the legal position of the trade unions beyond doubt, making it possible for the unions to register with the Registrar of Friendly Societies as recommended earlier. Yet at the same time it in effect prohibited picketing, in spite of the previous legalization of picketing in 1859. The best that the unions could do was to persuade the government to divide its proposals into two bills, one containing the beneficial changes to the status of unions (the Trade Union Act, 1871), and one forbidding picketing (the Criminal Law Amendment Act, 1871). In this way they could concentrate on getting the second act repealed. The need for this soon became urgent. The government certainly intended the latter act to be enforced, and later in 1871 seven women were imprisoned in South Wales for saying "Bah, bah" to a blackleg. In December 1872 some London gas strikers were given 12 months' imprisonment under the act for conspiracy to coerce their employers by merely preparing to strike (this preparation was interpreted as intimidation with "a view to coerce").

Yet another Royal Commission was appointed in 1874, this time on the Labour Laws. Burt refused to sit on it, although MacDonald and Hughes agreed to be members. The Webbs called the investigation "perfunctory", and the Report "inconclusive". The Commission was boycotted by the Parliamentary Committee. Nevertheless, in 1875 Disraeli's government introduced and passed the Conspiracy and Protection of Property Act, which confirmed that trade unions were not conspiracies, and once more legalized peaceful picketing. In the

same year, the Employers and Workmen Act abolished the imprisonment of workmen altogether for breach of contract, and made
employers and workmen – a significant change from "master" and
"servant" – equal partners in a contract of employment. A further
Trade Union Act in 1876 redefined "trade union", and generally
tidied up minor legal loose ends.

These were remarkable gains indeed, and the Parliamentary Committee considered the "work of emancipation" to be "full and complete". Its secretary, George Howell, even thought that the Committee could be disbanded. In fact, the early years of the 1870s saw a
high tide in union affairs. These years were so prosperous that membership grew to an extraordinary degree. In 1872 the TUC claimed
that it represented 375,000 members, a figure that grew by 1874 to
1,191,922. Even the agricultural labourers became unionized with
the founding of the Agricultural Labourers Union by Joseph Arch in
1872. Trade unionism began to spread further into the ranks of the
semi-skilled and the unskilled with the establishing of unions such as
the Amalgamated Society of Railway Servants in 1871, and the London gas workers' union in 1872. A striking tribute to the power and
influence of the trade union movement by this time was paid in a
statement by the newly-formed National Federation of Associated
Employers of Labour in 1873. After referring to their "enormous
funds", their "well-paid and ample staff of leaders", their literary resources, and their frequent public meetings, the statement goes on:

> They have a standing Parliamentary Committee, and a pro-
> gramme; and active members of parliament are energetic in their
> service. They have the attentive ear of the Ministry of the day;
> and their communications are received with instant and respect-
> ful attention. They have a large representation of their own body
> in London whenever Parliament is likely to be engaged in the dis-
> cussion of the proposals they have caused to be brought to it.
> Thus, untrammelled by pecuniary considerations, and specially
> set apart for this peculiar work, without other clashing occupa-
> tions, they resemble the staff of a well-organised, well pro-
> visioned army . . .

Understandably flattered by this fulsome appraisal, the Parliamentary Committee had it reprinted and distributed to union members.

A further success for the movement was the gaining of the Nine Hour Day in the engineering and building trades. This was the result of the campaign waged by the Nine Hours League, organized by both unionists and non-unionists (perhaps two out of three men in engineering were still not unionized). After a five months' strike, a week of 54 hours was achieved. It should also be noted that at this time of growth for the unions, further attempts were made to establish unions for women workers, and what the Webbs call "the oldest durable union for women workers only" was set up in 1872 – the Edinburgh Upholsterers' Sewers' Society. Yet another development within the movement took the form of further attempts by some unions to establish producer co-operatives, but none of them survived for long, whereas the consumer co-operatives on the Rochdale pattern continued to thrive and indeed to expand in the prosperity of the early 1870s.

However, from 1873 onwards trade became increasingly depressed; it was the onset of that period of reduced prices and profits that so alarmed middle-class observers that the expression "the Great Depression" was employed at the time. For some time now, modern economic historians have been at pains to explain that this is misleading, and have freely referred to the "myth of the Great Depression". In fact, there was a very real falling-off of trade in some parts of the country between 1873 and 1896. In the Black Country, for example, there was a permanent decline in the iron and coal industries as local supplies of iron and coal ran out. Nationally, the unions had to face wage cuts. In January 1875 miners in South Wales came out over a threatened reduction of 10 per cent, returning at the end of May to accept an even bigger cut of 12.5 per cent. In 1877 there were unsuccessful strikes by the Manchester carpenters and by the Clyde shipwrights, and in 1878 by the Lancashire cotton spinners. During the Lancashire strike, an employer's house was looted and burned out.

It is true that during the Great Depression real wages actually rose, so that for those who stayed in work, the standard of living actually improved. But unemployment did increase, and this is shown in the union membership of the time. For example, the societies of ironfounders and boilermakers, which had less than one per cent on their books in 1872–3, had more than 20 per cent unemployed in 1879. In the years 1878–80, the ASE paid out £287,596 to its unemployed members. The Operative Plumbers had to exclude nearly a third of their members in the years 1880–82 for non-payment of contributions. In 1873, the National Union of Ironworkers had 35,000 members; in 1879, membership was down to 1,400, mostly in the north of England. The National Union of Mineworkers also lost members heavily, and survived for the most part only in Northumberland, Durham and Yorkshire. As for the Agricultural Workers Union, which had claimed a membership of 100,000 in 1872, it was reduced to only 15,000 in 1881, and to 4,254 in 1889.

The traditional picture of trade union history after 1875 and during the Great Depression, therefore, has been one of setbacks in membership and in influence, and also of a sharp check to the spread of unionism among semi-skilled and unskilled workers. Progress was resumed in the 1880s, but the early 1870s represent a kind of false dawn. The later 1870s, it is thought, showed an increased sectionalism, division between unions over wages policy, and demarcation disputes, for example, between engineers and boilermakers. More recent views, however, emphasize that although nationally the craft societies appear pacific enough, at the local level they continued to defend their members' interests energetically. One historian even goes so far as to argue that during the period 1875–88, the major craft industries actually expanded and were continually effective (this seems difficult to reconcile with falling membership figures). Again, there has been a difference of opinion over sliding scales. One school of thought suggests that as a result of sliding scales "trade unionism was contained and disarmed at a significant stage of its growth", while others have argued that on the contrary the acceptance of sliding scales in the northeast iron and coal trades was actually of benefit to the trade unions, being a sensible acceptance of the realities of the situation. On the whole, this would be true of the Midlands Iron and Steel Wages Board, where many accepted the scales as a worthwhile alternative to continual strikes, as will be noted later. One last issue relating to the 1870s is that of "closed unionism", that is, the continued exclusion of the unskilled from the craft unions. As we have seen, unionism had begun to spread to the unskilled trades in the early 1870s, but many "new" unions of this kind withered and perished in the colder clime of the later 1870s. The problem of the unionization of unskilled workers was to revive and indeed produce problems of industrial strategy in the 1880s.

136

To sum up at this point, it is probably unwise to see the late 1870s purely as a period of sectionalism in trade union history, as did the Webbs, marked by inter-union disputes, falling membership, and the loss of leadership by the Junta (Applegarth resigned in 1871, Odger went more into general politics from 1870, Allen died in 1874). It would seem that the loss of membership cannot be disputed, although membership figures were to pick up and increase again later. On the other hand, not all "new" unions collapsed – they were to be a marked feature of the industrial scene in the 1880s, as will be seen in the next chapter – and the Webbs rightly emphasize that unionism survived the Great Depression without loss of its major characteristics. As for sliding scales, clearly trade union attitudes were divided. In 1892, William Auscott, the operatives' secretary on the Midlands Iron and Steel Board, remarked that he had been in all the strikes between 1847 and 1872 till he had become sick of striking, and prepared for any machinery (that is, any system of arbitration or conciliation) and to take any trouble to prevent a reoccurrence of strikes. Lastly, the unionism of the unskilled remained a problem: it must be remembered that even in the iron trade, membership was usually confined to master puddlers and master rollers, underhands not being admitted. Even in the mines, in the Midlands the butties were union men, but not the men in their teams. Subcontracting could still inhibit the growth of trade union membership in the Midlands in more than one trade.

In conclusion, it might be helpful to step back from the detail, and to weigh up the significance of the 30-year period, 1850–80, as a whole. Certainly there has been a good deal of reinterpretation in recent years of the detailed events of this era. Nevertheless, its character is clearly profoundly different from that of the previous quarter of a century. Before 1850, and especially in the 1830s, trade unions were regarded with suspicion. Although legal, the open attacks of some of their leaders on the capitalist system upset employers and provoked counter-attacks. Blackleg labour was often used to break strikes, and acts of violence were commonplace. After 1850, great changes took place. The model unions established new standards of organization, and collective bargaining became the accepted practice in many industries. As already noted, many union leaders came to see this as the pattern of the future, and wanted to avoid strikes as far as possible. For employers, this made sense. Agreement on wage rates with the unions avoided the price cutting indulged in by some of the smaller

137

firms. Furthermore, trade union leaders were usually better informed than their rank and file, could restrain them from intemperate action, and could calculate tricky piece work rates – very important in the cotton industry, as seen in the well-known Blackburn List of weavers' piece rates (this industry probably showed the biggest advances in collective bargaining in the period). After 1850, therefore, many employers saw that unionism had come to stay, and that it had its advantages for them. Old prejudices died hard, of course. Some employers were still hostile – witness Thomas Garnett, a Clitheroe manufacturer, who said in 1859, "The real question is whether an employer is to be ruled by an irresponsible committee sitting he knew not where and composed of he knew not whom". Hostile views lurking beneath the surface certainly found open expression in the evidence given before the Royal Commission of 1867, but on the whole, the conciliatory views of the Junta were acceptable to many employers.

The 30 years from 1850 to 1880 constitute perhaps one of the most significant periods in trade union history. Their legal position was at last fully established – or so it appeared. The Sheffield Outrages had caused alarm, but had been shown to be exceptional, and certainly not characteristic of the larger unions. The Parliamentary Committee of the TUC was an important advance, and in 1874 Burt and MacDonald spoke for the trade unions in the House of Commons, taking the Liberal Party whip as "Lib-Labs". Trade unionism had begun to spread to the unskilled trades. The scene was set for a further advance in this direction, but as the Great Depression showed that the prosperity of the early 1870s would not continue indefinitely, political questions were revived as to the acceptability and vitality of industrial capitalism. It was increasingly asked whether the self-help that protected the working man in his employment might not usefully be extended to procuring changes in the social and economic system itself. Thus, old questions were asked anew after 1880 about the proper place and value of the working man and woman in an industrial society.

Chapter Seven

New unionism and new outlooks 1880–1900

In the previous chapter reference was made to the Great Depression that lasted from 1873 to 1896. This was a depression not so much of production but of prices and profits, and it alarmed the employing classes to such an extent that two Royal Commissions were appointed to enquire into its causes, one in 1879 on the depression in agriculture, and one in 1886 on the depression in trade and industry. Such a prolonged depression inevitably had an effect on the craft unions and, as we have already seen, some suffered a considerable loss of members. Moreover, some of the new unions of unskilled workers, which had been established in the boom years of the early 1870s, also lost members heavily. Yet in spite of this, in the years 1889–91 total trade union membership actually shot up, even doubling in these three years – a remarkable achievement. A major reason for this apparent paradox is that not all the 20 odd years from 1873 to 1896 were gloomy – in fact, the earlier period 1880–82 saw a temporary revival of trade, and then a further return to prosperity in 1889–91. This last period in particular witnessed the creation of numerous new unions, and heralded the beginning of a new phase in trade union history. According to the Webbs, this change was the biggest event in trade union history before 1900; it was the rise of new unionism.

Why did new unionism develop in the 1880s? Of course, the temporary improvement in trade was not the only reason for its growth. Younger members of the trade union movement were becoming increasingly dissatisfied with what they saw as the complacency and inertia of the old unionism. The programme of the Parliamentary Committee remained very mild and limited; admittedly it demanded further franchise reform, but it also included such backward-looking proposals as peasant proprietorship. This was hardly good enough for younger socialist members such as Tom Mann, who in a pamphlet in 1886 asked his trade union colleagues:

> How long, how long will you be content with the present half-hearted policy of your unions? I readily grant that good work has been done in the past by the unions; but in Heaven's name, what good purpose are they serving now? All of them have large numbers out of employment even when their particular trade is busy. None of the important societies have any policy other than that of endeavouring to keep wages from falling. The true trade union policy of *aggression* seems entirely lost sight of: in fact, the average unionist of today is a man with a fossilised intellect, either hopelessly apathetic, or supporting a policy which plays into the hands of the capitalist exploiter . . .

Mann and others like him had learned the lesson that the Great Depression showed clearly enough, that industrial capitalism did not automatically bring ever-increasing prosperity to the working classes. Trade unionists, he argued, must be prepared to act more aggressively to stamp out poverty. Following the Franchise Acts of 1867 and 1885, male unionists who were householders now had the vote. Illiteracy was fast decreasing, and trade unionists were better-educated. Because of the fall in prices during the Great Depression (especially food prices), the rise in real wages enabled some unskilled workers to afford union subscriptions for the first time. For all these reasons, the time was ripe for the spread of unionism to the unskilled and semi-skilled, not it is true for the first time, but on a far wider scale than in the early 1870s.

Undoubtedly the revival of socialist thinking also played an important part in motivating younger trade unionists in the 1880s, and in promoting a more vigorous policy generally. Socialism was not new in England, of course, and socialist ideas were current in the 1830s among leaders of the NAPL and the GNCTU – John Doherty and Robert Owen readily come to mind. However, the increasing prosperity of the middle decades of the nineteenth century seemed to make socialism less relevant, and it had little influence over trade union leaders at this time. Karl Marx's major work *Das Kapital* was published in 1867, but did not appear in English until 1887. Yet by the 1880s socialist ideas were spreading again, especially among the middle classes, some of whom, at least, were uncomfortably aware of the extent of poverty revealed in London by such works as Charles Booth's *Life and labour of the people of London* (17 volumes, 1889–1903), Mearn's *Bitter cry of outcast London* (1883), and William Booth's *In darkest England and the way out* (1890). All this was at a time when the Liberal government led by Gladstone was increasingly occupied with the issue of Home Rule for Ireland, and paying only limited attention to the need for social reform in England.

The field was therefore open for the development of socialist thinking, and for the emergence of socialist bodies such as the Social Democratic Federation (SDF). This association started life as the Democratic Federation in 1881, then moved to the left and became the SDF in 1884. Its leader was H. M. Hyndman, educated at Eton and Cambridge, and of impeccable middle-class background (a contemporary remarked on his essentially bourgeois appearance at meetings of working men, with his tall hat, frock coat and long beard). His views were strongly Marxist; he had read *Das Kapital* in a French translation in 1881. Hyndman had his eccentricities: he is said to have attempted to convert Disraeli, the Conservative prime minister from 1874 to 1880, to Marxism. Although the SDF had only a tiny membership, among its members were unionists such as John Burns and Tom Mann who were to acquire national reputations. Another member was William Morris, the well-to-do Pre-Raphaelite art designer and poet, who soon left the group at the end of 1884 to form the Socialist League, an organization that became dominated by anarchists.

Another body established in 1884 became the most famous socialist organization of all – the Fabian Society. It was far more middle-class than the SDF, and its leading members included intellectuals such as Sidney and Beatrice Webb, George Bernard Shaw, Graham Wallis, H. G. Wells, and journalists and activists such as Annie Besant. The society was named after the Roman general Fabius Cunctator ("Fabius the Delayer"), who won his battles not by direct full-scale attack but by wearing down the enemy with constant pressure. The Fabian belief was in the converting of all political parties by rational argument. Socialism was to be achieved not by revolution, nor by a sudden and violent seizing of political power, but slowly, peacefully and democratically, as socialism permeated the thinking of men and women of all parties. The frequently-used phrase, "the inevitability of gradualism" sums up this process very well. Sidney Webb summarized Fabian beliefs in *Fabian essays*, published in 1889, as follows:

> Socialists as well as Individualists realise that important organic changes can only be (1) democratic, and thus acceptable to a majority of the people, and prepared for in the minds of all; (2) gradual, and thus causing no dislocation, however rapid may be the rate of progress; (3) not regarded as immoral by the mass of the people, and thus not subjectively demoralising to them; and (4) in this country at any rate, constitutional and peaceful.

This was a creed readily acceptable to middle-class intellectuals of tender conscience, concerned and disturbed by the evidence of poverty and unemployment which they saw around them, especially in London, the richest capital in the world.

Since the main idea of Fabianism was to influence the thinking of men and women of all parties or none, there was no need for the creation of any new party. All that was required was a steady flow of convincing, rational argument directed to "making thinking persons socialist", as Beatrice Webb put it. As a result, some three-quarters of a million tracts were circulated by the Fabians between 1887 and 1893, and several thousand lectures a year were delivered in London and other industrial centres, all intended (in the words of the Webbs) "to substitute a practical and constitutional policy of collectivist reform for the earlier revolutionary propaganda". Of course, there is always the danger of exaggerating the influence of the Fabian Society in the late Victorian period because it had such powerful middle-class backing; its leading members were well known in London society. On the other hand, the society membership also included Tom Mann, Ben Tillett and other trade union leaders, and the 90 independent local Fabian Societies in the provinces usually included many members of local trades councils. Moreover, since the Fabians believed in all forms of state enterprise and collectivism, they could readily claim that socialism was already advancing in local government in the form of municipal schemes for waterworks, gasworks, tramways and so on – a development soon termed "gas and water socialism", and made much of in a famous passage in Shaw's *Intelligent woman's guide to socialism* (which has a businessman boasting about various forms of municipal enterprise without realizing that for the Fabians they were all socialist in nature).

How far the Fabian Society and the SDF actually influenced trade union thinking at the time is difficult to say. Older trade unionists were loyal Lib-Labs, and were certainly hostile to SDF Marxist ideas. Yet some of the most prominent leaders among the new unions were or had been members of the SDF. Some of them were members of both the Fabian Society and the SDF, such as Tom Mann. It seems safe to say, however, that both bodies, numerically minuscule as they were when compared with the trade unions, and without any direct connections with them, nevertheless supplied a drive and determination to younger unionists who wanted more from their unions than simple bargaining over wages and working conditions. Certainly socialism supplied a cutting edge to unionists increasingly concerned at the unemployment of the mid-1880s.

This was clearly demonstrated from 1886 onwards. During a march of unemployed men in London in January 1886, windows were broken in Pall Mall, the police intervened, and Hyndman and Burns were arrested. In 1887, much more serious violence erupted. A meeting was organized for Trafalgar Square, but the square was closed by the police. John Burns and Cunningham Graham, MP broke through the police lines, and heavy fighting occurred, many being injured. This episode became known as "Bloody Sunday". Burns and Graham were sentenced to six weeks' imprisonment. In the next year, 1888, London had its first taste of new unionism with the famous strike of the match girls working at Bryant & Mays. Their strike was organized by Annie Besant, who had written about their working conditions in her weekly, *The Link*, and had accused their employers of treating them as white wage slaves. The women came out on strike, and appealed to Mrs Besant for help. They succeeded in gaining higher wages, and then set about organizing a union of their own.

The next year 1889 was to witness two of the best-known successes of the new unionism. The first was the setting-up of a union among the London gasworkers by Will Thorne, a Birmingham Irishman and member of the SDF, assisted by Eleanor Marx, the daughter of Karl Marx. This new union, the National Union of Gas Workers and General Labourers, immediately demanded a change in their working hours from their employers, the South Metropolitan Gas Company, and were successful without even having to go on strike. Two 12-hour shifts were replaced by three 8-hour shifts. Later in the year, Ben Tillett brought his small union of tea warehousemen in the London

143

docks out on strike for an increase in pay from 5d to 6d an hour (the "dockers' tanner"), and for a minimum engagement of four hours. It was the beginning of what proved to be the most famous strike of late Victorian times.

Tillett's union was soon joined by the stevedores and other dock workers. Some of London's best-known socialists added their support – Tom Mann, John Burns, Eleanor Marx, Annie Besant, and numerous members of the SDF, especially followers of the SDF secretary, H. H. Chapman, who acted as public relations officer. After a fortnight the strike began to weaken, but was saved by a donation of more than £30,000 from Australian unionists. What was remarkable about the strike was the extent of public support. John Burns organized dockers' marches through the City, and made sure of their orderly conduct and good behaviour. Tom Mann controlled the pickets, insisting on good order and peaceful persuasion. For their part, the police showed remarkable restraint. Cardinal Manning was especially prominent in his support and influence over both the leaders and the rank and file – many of whom were Roman Catholics. Finally a special Mansion House Committee of conciliation was set up, and the strike came to an end after five weeks. The dockers gained their "tanner", and new working rules were agreed. Tillett organized a new union for dockers named the Dock, Wharf, Riverside and General Labourers Union. It had recruited 30,000 members by November 1889.

The year of 1889 was undoubtedly one of triumph for new unionism and its socialist supporters, some of whom were fast becoming well known to the general public. When the Royal Commission on Labour was appointed in 1891, Tom Mann was one of those serving on the Commission, while Ben Tillett gave evidence on working conditions in the docks, and Keir Hardie on work in the Ayrshire pits (he also took the opportunity of advocating the nationalization of the mines, a minimum wage, and a national insurance scheme for miners). The Fifth and Final Report of this Commission, published in 1894, is generally held to be inconclusive, but it nevertheless contains some interesting material regarding trade unions. For example, in one place it lists the allegedly injurious effects of trade unions, such as giving workmen a false sense of confidence in their bargaining power with employers, bringing an undesirable uniformity of hours and wages, discouraging individual effort, and refusing to work with non-unionists; but all this is balanced by a list of the beneficial effects of trade unions that were thought to be essential to protect workmen in the workplace – unions improved wages and conditions, did *not* insist on equality of wages, and at the same time prevented employers destroying each other through unlimited competition.

This Final Report was signed by Tom Mann, but he and three other commissioners then insisted on producing a Minority Report. The introduction to this dwells on the state of the working classes, claiming that five million working people were "unable to obtain a subsistence compatible with health or efficiency", that there were probably two million every day seeking Poor Law relief, that in London 32 per cent were below the poverty line, and of all surviving to the age of 70, one in three was receiving poor relief. It was also claimed that in London in some districts, a half, or even three-fifths were below the poverty line. After this great blast against the workings of industrial capitalism, and after further passages on the sweated trades, hours of labour, and other matters, the Minority Report concludes:

> To sum up: we regard the unsatisfactory relations between employers and employed as but one inevitable incident of the present industrial anarchy. The only complete solution of the problem is, in our opinion, to be found in the progress of industrial evolution, which will assign to the "captains of industry" as well as to the manual workers, their proper position as servants of the community.

This might well be thought to be the voice of the new unionism. Yet new unionism as a new and militant form of unionism had already passed its peak by 1894. Although it had spread on the south bank of the Thames with the creation of the South Side Labour League, and also in the docks of Glasgow and Merseyside, as well as in Ireland and on Tyneside, there were setbacks as early as 1890. The gasworkers in London suffered defeat in a further dispute with the South Metropolitan Gas Company, and lost members heavily as a result. In Hull, the dock unions were also defeated. The Webbs ascribed all these reverses to economic depression, but Clegg, Fox and Thompson point out that actually they were the result of a counter-attack by employers that came at the height of a boom and not in a period of depression. In fact, the new unions lost thousands of members in the early 1890s. In 1890, the new unions had a maximum strength of over 350,000; by

1900, this number was reduced to about 204,000, which was less than a tenth of the total trade union membership. Some individual figures will illustrate the decline: gas workers in the union numbered 60,000 in 1890, but only 47,979 in 1900. Ben Tillett's union had 56,000 members in 1890, but only 13,839 in 1900. The National Amalgamated Union of Sailors and Firemen had 58,780 members in 1890, but had collapsed completely by 1894.

So far from supplanting the older forms of unionism, new unionism became numerically only a minor part of the trade union movement as a whole. At this point we may pause to consider in more detail its basic nature and importance. Hitherto it has been portrayed as a movement by mostly younger unionists, influenced by socialist thinking, to bring into trade unionism the large numbers of unskilled workers who could afford only low subscriptions. Consequently their funds were for strike pay only, not friendly society benefits, and the major purpose of the new unions was to achieve success through militancy, being fully prepared to use coercion against blacklegs and non-unionists. All this still holds good in general terms, and John Burns's description of the new unionists at the 1890 TUC still makes a significant point:

> Physically, the "old" unionists were much bigger than the new . . .
> A great number of them looked like respectable city gentlemen;
> wore very good coats, large watch chains, and high hats . . .
> Among the new delegates not a single one wore a tall hat. They
> looked workmen; they were workmen.

However, closer investigation will show considerable variety in the nature of the new unions. In the first place, some were confined to single industries, others straddled a number of industries. Not all included large numbers of unskilled, general labourers – where these were an important element, as in the gasworkers' union, they had been recruited almost accidentally, as ancillary workers seeking to join the main body. Nor were all new unionists unskilled and poorly paid – this did not apply to the seamen, or to the London gas stokers – and some provided friendly society benefits from the beginning, for example, the seamen, gasworkers, and the National Amalgamated Union of Labour. Again, not all were led by socialists, not all wanted a "closed shop", not all even agreed on the Eight Hour Day. Clegg, Fox and Thompson narrow down their major characteristics to four: (a) they were all new creations; (b) they all spent heavily on administration; (c) they favoured general unionism; (d) they adopted militant and coercive tactics, as in the water front strikes, and in some of the gas strikes.

It is evident from this discussion that there was great variation among the different forms of new unionism, and these unions certainly did not all come from the same simple mould. In fact, new unionism represented not an entirely new departure but rather an expansion of unionism into new fields, led by young and vigorous leaders, often of a socialist turn of mind. They did not turn the movement as a whole towards socialism, and their attacks on the older craft unions as being too concerned with the interests of craftsmen, hoarding funds to pay friendly benefits (which they argued should have been paid by the state under a national scheme), eschewing militancy, and hopelessly imbued with old-fashioned liberalism, were often unfair. In the course of time, new unionism was assimilated into the main stream of trade unionism. More new unions began to provide benefits other than strike pay. Older unions, for example, the engineers, began to recruit less skilled members. Old and new unions settled down to work amicably together. However, one of the most important legacies of new unionism remains its emphasis on the need for political change, and this is reflected in the number of socialist resolutions passed at the TUC in 1890; in 1894 Keir Hardie actually had a motion passed at the TUC by 219 votes to 61 approving of the nationalization of the means of production, distribution and exchange, and also of the land. This hardly represented the outlook of the movement as a whole. In supporting Hardie's motion, Havelock Wilson, the seamen's leader, said that "it must not be supposed that it would be put into force twenty-four hours later on . . . ", and said he did not believe that he would live to see it carried into effect, but it does indicate the influence of socialist beliefs at the time. Indeed, in the same year, the Parliamentary Committee of the TUC changed the system of voting at Congress, which hitherto had been on an individual basis. As trades councils were represented separately, often by socialists, the old system was to the advantage of the new unions, which could benefit from double representation. Henceforth trades councils were no longer to be represented, union delegates were to have one vote per thousand members, and every delegate had either

147

to work at his trade or be a paid trade union official (this effectively excluded Keir Hardie as a journalist). So socialist influence was cut back at the TUC, but this did not affect its influence over the movement as a whole, or in the country at large.

At this point it must be recalled that in 1890 the trade unions were still represented in the House of Commons by union representatives who took the Liberal whip – the Lib-Labs. In the parliament elected in 1892 there were eight Lib-Labs, in 1894 there were eleven, and the same number again in 1898. Although as a group the individual members seemed to have co-operated well with each other, they did not always make much of an impression on their fellow parliamentarians. In 1894 Joseph Chamberlain, by then a liberal unionist, spoke contemptuously of them as "mere fetchers and carriers of the Gladstonian party", and in 1900 declared that

> when they come into parliament they are like fish out of water, their only use is as an item in the voting machine . . . not one of these gentlemen has ever initiated or carried through legislation for the benefit of the working classes, though occasionally they have hindered such legislation.

This unflattering remark was scarcely just, for the very small group of trade union MPs had few if any opportunities to take independent action; and on the whole, both Gladstone and his successor Rosebery were well-enough disposed towards their Lib-Lab colleagues. Nevertheless, the record of the group during the years since 1889 when their numbers had increased from eight to eleven (in which time trade union membership had moved from three-quarters of a million to more than two million) was hardly impressive (and in the 1900 khaki election, held during the Boer War, they lost four seats). It seemed, therefore, that the time was ripe for new initiatives in the political field.

The first such initiative came in 1892 with the election to parliament of working men who claimed to stand as independents. Two of them, John Burns and Havelock Wilson, soon joined the Lib-Labs, but the third, Keir Hardie, refused to take the Liberal whip, and at the 1892 TUC spoke in favour of setting-up a separate labour party (he had already established a small independent society in Scotland in 1888, the Scottish Labour Party). Keir Hardie was perhaps the most

148

striking and appealing of the Labour leaders of his time. He had gone down the pit in Lanarkshire at the age of ten, been blacklisted for his trade union activities, and then had become a journalist and organizer of the Ayrshire miners. Originally a Liberal, he became a socialist of a humanitarian if not actually romantic kind, never becoming a member of the SDF, or ever a Marxist, although he often employed Marxist terminology. His socialism was based on a simple belief that the capitalist system was unfair and unjust to the ordinary working man. Yet he himself whatever his upbringing was scarcely an ordinary working man; in spite of his belief in comradeship, he was an intense individualist, who went his own, often self-contradictory way, as seen in his famous arrival to take up his seat at Westminster in 1892. He deliberately dressed informally in loud yellow tweed trousers, a serge jacket, and a tweed cap, with a rosette in his buttonhole. He was transported to the House from his constituency in West Ham in a two-horse brake, accompanied by a cornet player who contributed to the proceedings by playing the *Marseillaise*. It was his dress, however, that caused the greatest comment: John Burns said it was the kind of thing you saw going to Epping Forest, his trousers having a check so loud that draughts could have been played on them. George Lambert, a Liberal backbencher, in comparing Burns with Hardie, said, "Here is a Labour man dressed like a gentleman, but look at that bugger . . ."

Hardie, then, was the first independent Labour member of parliament, and as such his early days in the House were not easy since he insisted on his independence from both the Liberals and the Lib-Labs. Yet he still persisted with his idea of creating a separate Labour Party to give direct representation at Westminster for the working classes – an idea that, as we have seen, he had put before the TUC in 1892. The situation seemed not unpromising in the country generally, where local Labour representation was improving. Between 1882 and 1892 Labour representatives on local bodies increased from 12 to 200. In 1895, there were 600 Labour members of borough councils, and they achieved a majority in West Ham in 1898. They also shared nine seats with the Progressive Party on the London County Council.

In Bradford the outlook seemed particularly promising – there were already 23 Labour clubs in the city. Here Hardie helped to organize a conference in January 1893, attended by 120 delegates, representing the Labour clubs, the Scottish Labour Party, the SDF, the Fabian Society, and a small number of trade unions. At this conference a new political party was formed – the Independent Labour Party (ILP), in-dependent of the Liberal Party and of Lib-Labism, and having as its objectives the public ownership of the means of production. Thus it was an avowedly socialist body. At last it appeared that in the course of time a truly socialist policy could be developed and implemented at Westminster. Yet the early years of the ILP were to prove disappoint-ing. Both the Fabians and the SDF gave only limited support, while the Liberal Party was understandably hostile. The TUC was scarcely more welcoming; the Parliamentary Committee was satisfied with the Lib–Lab system, and could not be expected to greet the creation of a new socialist organization with much enthusiasm. The ILP had con-siderable local support, setting up 400 branches within a year with a membership of about 50,000, but it was relatively unknown nation-ally. So it was no great surprise that all the candidates put up by the new party in the 1895 general election were defeated, including Keir Hardie himself (he was afterwards returned to parliament as member for Merthyr Tydfil in 1900). Nevertheless, the ILP survived its difficult early years, and was to play an extremely important role in the key year in Labour history, 1900.

The early years of the 1890s, therefore, were to see the creation of a new labour body with a specifically socialist programme, but one disappointingly unsuccessful in its immediate aims. Meanwhile, as we have seen, new unionism was being assimilated into the main body of trade unionism, and socialist leaders were supplying an edge to TUC proceedings. But they had no marked impact on either the growth of the movement, or on its industrial policy. As regards the former, Clegg, Fox & Thompson point out that the major increase in membership took place in unions where socialist influence was small. As regards the latter point, the major change in industrial policy of the time was in the growth of collective bargaining, which again owed little to socialist thinking. However, it seems undeniable that the socialists constantly raised social and economic issues that put in doubt what the true objec-tives of trade unionism should be. In other words, they raised political questions that demanded answers. In fact, a number of developments towards the end of the nineteenth century brought a sense of urgency into the discussion of the future of trade unionism, and indeed how far it was to survive in its existing form at all.

The first of these developments was a series of adverse legal deci-sions that, taken together, seemed to question the firm legal position of the trade unions that had been established (or so it had seemed) by the legislation of the mid-1870s. In the case of *Temperton* v. *Russell* (1893) a local committee of building trade unions in Hull had imposed a boycott on a firm of builders whose men were on strike, and on another firm supplying materials to the first firm. The second firm then sued for damages, and the union officers were found guilty of "maliciously procuring and coercing others to break contracts with the plaintiff", and of forming a conspiracy to injure him. In *Trollope* v. *London Building Trades Federation* (1895), union officers had to pay damages to Trollope, the London builders, for including their name on a blacklist of non-union firms. Most serious of all, in the case of *Lyons* v. *Wilkins* (1897), the plaintiff, Lyons, a leather goods manufacturer, obtained an injunction restraining the union from picketing both his firm and another working for him on sub-contract. Although the picketing was entirely peaceful, Lyons was not only granted his injunction but was also successful in suing Wilkins, the secretary of the Amalgamated Society of Fancy Leather Workers, in a subsequent action. In the course of this action, it was declared in court that picketing was lawful only to communicate information, while picketing to persuade to strike, for example, was unlawful. The decision against Wilkins was confirmed in the Court of Appeal, when one judge even declared that "you cannot make a strike effective without doing more than what is lawful". Lastly, in *Charnock* v. *Court* (1899), a Halifax union sent two members to the port of Fleetwood to persuade two workmen from Ireland not to break a strike at a firm in Halifax, and to offer them their fare back home. The trade unionists were accused of watching and besetting, and found guilty. The cumulative effect of all these decisions, therefore, was not only to throw into doubt the right to boycott or blacklist employers, but also the right to picket peacefully, or even (it could be) to go on strike.

Towards the end of the century, a development of a different kind was the renewed hostility of employers in the industrial field. In 1890 the shipowners formed the Shipping Federation, which compiled its own list of seamen whom they would employ only if they were prepared to work with non-union men. This federation then proceeded to supply blackleg labour at the ports, leading to a violent strike at Hull in 1893, where scab labour was imported under army protection. A further supply of blackleg labour was provided by the National Free Labour Association, established in 1893 by William

Collison, the blacklegs being employed mostly in the docks and on the railways. Collison described his organization very frankly in a book entitled *The apostle of free labour* (1913):

> If the situation is ominous, the Chief Office is communicated with by telephone – for quick action is the first requisite in our business – our objective being either to avert a strike, or to prevent the strikers from obtaining too strong a position . . . A contract is then made with the employing company or firm, at a rate of so much a day for each man's services . . . the ordinary man in the street would naturally ask whether a sufficient number of competent and fearless men, as they must be to brave the pickets, could be obtained at such short notice. Under our Free Labour Exchanges system it is easy. Each has a live register of competent men, averaging eighty thousand, embracing 150 different trades, in all parts of the country.

Obviously, this labour could be engaged for the most part only when unskilled labour was engaged, but even skilled labour was affected by the determined resistance of employers. In 1897 the ASE brought its members out on strike over the Eight Hour Day, and their members were then locked out for six months between July 1897 and January 1898. The employers were organized by the Employers Federation of Engineering Associations, deliberately formed in 1896 to challenge the strength of the ASE. The struggle was hard and bitter: it has been called the first national strike or lock-out in British history. It cost the ASE £489,000, an additional amount of about £169,000 being raised by voluntary subscription by other sympathetic unions. It ended in the defeat of the ASE, who had to abandon the demand for the Eight Hour Day – something of a humiliation for the foremost union in the country. One last counter-action by the employers must be mentioned: in the year of their triumph over the ASE, they set up the Employers Parliamentary Council as a rival to the Parliamentary Committee of the TUC. This body was clearly designed to put the anti-union case to MPs. It also publicized the effect of the recent legal decisions on the trade unions, and even published a book by W. J. Shaxby, *The case against picketing*, which emphasized how *Lyons* v. *Wilkins* had reinterpreted the law regarding picketing, and explained how picketing might now be challenged.

Something of a crisis had thus developed for the trade union movement at the end of the nineteenth century. The most urgent task appeared to be to strengthen their financial position, and in January 1899 a new organization, the General Federation of Trade Unions, was set up in order to amass a general strike fund. In fact, constituent unions of the TUC were not very willing to subscribe to this new fund: only 44 unions were willing to contribute, less than a quarter of the membership of the Congress. Plainly, they were reluctant to part with funds for what appeared to be a somewhat nebulous purpose. The other possibility to be explored was that of strengthening trade union influence in parliament. It has already been pointed out that the Lib-Labs had not achieved very much in the House of Commons since 1874. Their numbers were still limited, and not very likely to increase significantly. The Liberal Party had proved reluctant to adopt working-class candidates for election because they had no financial means of their own, and were unable to contribute to party funds. Although the unions supported the cause of salaries for MPs (for obvious reasons), salaries were not paid until 1911. The only alternative to persevering with the Lib-Lab arrangement seemed to be the creation of another separate Labour pressure group in the Commons, this time with direct trade union support. This was not a new idea; it had been proposed in the past, principally by Keir Hardie, but now the matter had become increasingly urgent.

Accordingly, at the 1899 TUC the proposal was made again for an investigation into the possibility of electing an increased number of labour MPs. The motion was put by James Holmes, on behalf of the Amalgamated Society of Railway Servants, a union that now had a strong ILP and socialist element. The somewhat wordy resolution ran as follows:

That this Congress . . . with a view to securing a better representation of the interests of labour in the House of Commons, hereby instructs the Parliamentary Committee to invite the co-operation of all the co-operative, socialistic, trade union and other working organisations to jointly co-operate on lines mutually agreed upon in convening a special congress . . . to devise ways and means for securing the return of an increased number of labour MPs to the next parliament.

This motion was debated for three hours. Although the TUC certainly wanted to make progress, not all thought that this was the way forward. Some members of the Parliamentary Committee were reluctant to add to the existing Lib-Lab arrangements. Others disliked the influence of the socialists, even though the resolution avoided any direct reference to the need for socialism. Some unions had their own special reasons for opposing, such as the miners, who had their own Lib-Lab MPs. The textile workers also had their own ways of influencing Lancashire MPs through a separate body, the United Factory Textile Workers Association. In any case, Lancashire textile workers included many Conservative voters who would not welcome the creation of a new political body. For all these reasons, the acceptance of the resolution was not a forgone conclusion. Finally it was passed with the solid support of the new unions by 546,000 votes to 434,000 – a comfortable but not overwhelming majority, with about a sixth abstaining.

Arrangements were then made for the special congress to be held in London at the Memorial Hall, Farrington Street, on 27 February 1900. Delegates included representatives from the trade unions, of course, but most of them were from the new unions; in all, they represented less than half the membership of the TUC. There were also delegates from the ILP, the SDF and the Fabian Society. The vital resolution was put by Keir Hardie. It advocated the setting up of a new parliamentary group:

> . . . a distinct Labour Group in Parliament, who shall have their whips, and agree upon their policy, which must embrace a readiness to co-operate with any party which for the time being may be engaged in promoting legislation in the direct interest of labour . . .

It will be noted that this wording avoids all reference to socialism, but concentrates on the "direct interest of labour". Further, it specifically refers to the need to co-operate with other parties, so that future co-operation with the Liberals and Lib-Labs was not excluded. Once this resolution was passed, a Labour Representation Committee (LRC) was formed, with seven members from the unions, two from the ILP, two from the SDF, and one from the Fabians (a disproportionate representation of the socialist bodies, of course). The election expenses of the LRC candidates were to be paid by the unions, unlike the expenses of the ILP. The secretary of the committee was to be a new and impressive leader in ILP circles, James Ramsay MacDonald, destined to be Labour's first prime minister. In 1906, the LRC was renamed, becoming the Labour Party.

In this somewhat unusual way, the Labour Party was born – certainly the greatest example of working-class self-help in the political field. Obviously enough, it was not the inevitable consequence of the growth of socialism, although socialist thinking played an important part. Rather it was a defensive action on the part of the union movement against the increasing hostility of some, but by no means all employers, and of the courts. To argue that with the extension of the franchise and the increase in class consciousness it was inevitable that the working classes should ultimately have their own party is to ignore the fact that the Liberal Party had been the party for working-class voters since the mid-nineteenth century. It might well have gone on representing both the middle-class and working-class electorate – Gladstone was held to be the "People's William" – but for its divisions at the end of the century over Ireland, the Boer War, and imperialism. It was out of office from 1895 to 1906, and when it finally embarked on a programme of social reform from 1906 onwards, the new Labour Party, though uncertain in its direction , was already well-established, as will be seen in the next chapter. These difficulties for the Liberal Party were reinforced by their failure, as mentioned earlier, to adopt working-men candidates, a lack of foresight which showed a serious misapprehension as to the future possibilities inherent in the working-class vote.

Inevitably the question arises, who deserves the most credit for the founding of the LRC, which afterwards became the Labour Party? It seems clear enough that it was Keir Hardie and his supporters who took the lead here. It is true that the TUC called the 1900 special conference, but as a body it was divided over the issue, and it was a new unionist and member of the ILP who moved the key resolution in 1899. The Fabians had never played an important part in trade union affairs, nor did they in 1900. As for the SDF, their programme was too extreme to gain much support, and a resolution put to the 1900 meeting for the creation of a distinct party, based on the recognition of the class war, and aimed at the socialization of the means of production, distribution and exchange, was heavily defeated. It can be said, therefore, that it was Keir Hardie's broadly socialist approach, non-doctrinaire and stressing the direct interest of Labour, which won the day. It was the trade union movement that provided the opportunity for the creation of the Labour Party, not in itself at the time regarded as being specially momentous, but it was Keir Hardie who was the real driving force. Beyond all others, he may be considered to be the founder of the Labour Party.

We turn finally to the general situation of the trade union movement at the end of the nineteenth century. Because new unionism represented a significant widening of the bounds of trade unionism in the 1880s, it is easy to see this development out of perspective. In reality, its strength was limited. Pelling has pointed out that in 1900 there was only one general or all-grade union (that of the gasworkers) among the ten largest unions, with only another two among the next ten largest. Only five new unions had more than 10,000 members each. So in numerical terms, the new unions were heavily outnumbered by the craft unions. One of the most important unions established at the end of the century was that of the South Wales Miners Federation founded in 1898, but it was led by liberals, not socialists, and was prepared to accept wage rates based on sliding scales, an increasingly out-of-date idea. In spite of the socialist belief in a more aggressive policy towards employers, and some increase in the number of strikes, more and more emphasis was being placed on the need for conciliation schemes. Thus, the Royal Commission on Labour recommended that a public department should have power to appoint arbitrators or conciliators on request, and suitable powers were given to the Board of Trade by the Conciliation Act, 1896 (it was not to prove particularly effective). The cotton strike in 1893 was ended with the drawing up of the famous Brooklands agreement on prices, while the 16-week strike by the National Miners Federation led to the establishment of a board of conciliation, and to similar boards in all mining districts by 1900, except in Scotland and Wales.

Yet if the national scene in 1900 shows a trade union movement increasingly accepted by the employers as an established part of the industrial scene – even the Final Report of the Royal Commission on Labour conceded that peaceful relations were on the whole the result of strong and firmly established trade unions (a kind of unavoidable necessity, one might say) – socialist thinking would not go away. Its greatest triumph was to prove to be not the creation of the Independent Labour Party, but the Labour Representation Committee. Socialism was in the air, reinforced by the social enquiries of the time, and by popular left-wing literature such as Robert Blatchford's *Merrie England* (1894), his weekly journal, the *Clarion*, and William Morris's Utopian fantasy *News from Nowhere* (1891). It was a very English kind of non-Marxist socialism, owing much more to the romantic and passionate anti-capitalism of Keir Hardie than to dialectical materialism. Nevertheless, it provided a driving force within the trade union movement that set it on the road to political reform and the more direct participation of the working classes in the affairs of the nation.

It may be true, as Professor F. M. L. Thompson has remarked, that new unionism was something of a flash in the pan, and he has suggested that its reputation in the annals of labour history has generally been inflated far beyond its real importance. This really is an interpretation similar to that found in the standard work on this period of trade union history by Clegg, Fox & Thompson. But however true this might be, the fact remains that the driving force behind many of the developments in new unionism came from socialist beliefs, and it was convictions of this kind that led to the famous conference in the Farringdon Hall and the setting up of the LRC. In this sense, new unionism was an expansion of the trade union movement into new directions, powered by socialist thinking, and no-one would argue that the entry of the movement more directly into the political field was of only minor importance. On the contrary, it was to have momentous consequences for working-class self-help, and for the history of the working classes in Britain in the twentieth century.

In concluding this chapter, a final general survey of the situation at the end of the century might be helpful. Self-help in the form of trade unionism was still a limited form of self-help for the working classes at this time. Total membership in 1901 was 2.025 million, distributed among some 1,322 unions. Of these unions, only 198 were affiliated to the TUC, leaving well over a thousand unions outside the TUC, with 625,000 members. Some of these unions were very small indeed. As for trade union densities, trade unionists were less than one in six of the occupied population in 1901, and were about one in four of adult male manual workers. The strength of the movement still lay in mining, metals, engineering, shipbuilding, cotton and railways. In mining in 1901, the trade union density was 56 per cent, although it was

157

much higher than this in some individual pits. In shipbuilding, it was 60 per cent. There had been some increase in white collar membership – for example, teachers numbered 44,000 in 1900, postal employees 36,000, shop assistants 19,000, and government employees 45,000 – but women's trade unionism beyond the cotton, linen and jute industries still hardly existed in any significant numbers at the turn of the century.

It is fair to say that trade unionism still influenced the working lives of only a minority of the working population in Britain at the end of the nineteenth century, and only a tiny proportion of working women. Nevertheless, it had become far more acceptable to employers by the end of the century than previously. As will be seen in the next chapter, the further development of collective bargaining and the growth of parliamentary representation were to bring a new element into labour relations – the direct intervention of the government into the settlement of national wage disputes. At the same time, the trade union movement was to expand greatly again just before the outbreak of war in 1914 with a further intake of semi-skilled and unskilled workers. The dawn of the twentieth century therefore saw the beginning of a new era in trade unionism.

Chapter Eight

The political and industrial scene 1900–1914

The beginning of the twentieth century saw the onset of a period of relatively peaceful industrial relations which lasted until 1907 or 1908, in spite of the employers' counter-attacks just before the turn of the century. This seems to have been due for the most part to the conciliation procedures set up in the cotton, mining, engineering and shipbuilding industries. However, this did not see the end of the unfavourable legal decisions described in the last chapter, and in 1901 there occurred the most serious of all as a result of a strike on the Taff Vale Railway in South Wales in 1900. This strike arose out of the alleged victimization of a signalman, and was quickly settled, but the railway company decided to sue the Society of Railway Servant,s which was responsible for the picketing during the strike. Finally in the House of Lords the case went against the Society, which afterwards had to pay £23,000 damages and its own costs, amounting in all to about £42,000. Hitherto it had been thought that as a trade union was an unincorporated body, it could not be sued for losses arising out of a strike. The Taff Vale case decided otherwise, and the trade union movement was faced by a sudden crisis. In effect, the right to strike had been directly challenged, for any strike henceforth might be followed by a similar action with serious consequences for the union concerned.

One view of the Taff Vale case is that it was simply the climax of the campaign waged by the employers against the unions since the mid-1890s, but it seems rather that the manager of the Taff Vale Railway was a very litigious person who had the support of the Employers Parliamentary Committee; he thought he had a good chance of success against the union, and was prepared to take a chance in court. It is often said, too, that the Taff Vale decision also had an immediate effect in causing unions to refrain from striking rather than risk their funds. In fact, it is difficult to be sure about this, because the period was one of peaceful industrial relations generally. One curious result of the ruling was that some unions were prepared to accept it as it stood, since they thought it could act as a useful restraint on younger, militant members in calling strikes. Most unions, however, could see the danger, and the Liberal opposition in the Commons were prepared to support legislation in the matter. Measures were proposed in 1904 and again in 1905, but were dropped after amendments at the committee stage. The Conservative government did appoint a Royal Commission on the matter, but without any trade union members, and the TUC boycotted it as a result.

Meanwhile, the Taff Vale decision had a remarkable effect on the fortunes of the Labour Representation Committee, set up in 1900. In the general election of that year, the LRC won two seats – those of Keir Hardie at Merthyr Tydfil, and of Richard Bell at Derby. However, the prospects for the new organization did not look too promising; affiliations from trade unions and trade councils were slow to come in: in the first year they represented only 253,000 members, and even after two years, this number had risen to only 455,450. The new threat posed to the legal position of the trade unions by the Taff Vale decision had a startling effect on affiliation numbers; by 1903 they had shot up to 847,315. Moreover, in 1903 the LRC decided on a compulsory levy to be paid by the unions for the support of LRC members of parliament. In the well-known words of the historian R. C. K. Ensor, a sudden wind filled the sails of the LRC and blew hard in its favour until the general election of 1906.

Another development helpful to the LRC was a secret electoral agreement drawn up in 1903 by Ramsay MacDonald, secretary of the new committee, and Herbert Gladstone, representing the Liberals. By this pact it was agreed that the Liberals would not oppose the LRC in the next election in about 30 selected constituencies while in return the LRC would support the next Liberal government. The agreement had advantages for both sides: it avoided splitting the anti-Conservative vote, saved Liberal election expenses, and gave the LRC a chance to improve their numbers in the House. Without the pact, there was every chance in a number of constituencies of both Liberal and LRC defeats if they opposed each other. It was thought better, however, not to make these arrangements public, since some rightwing Liberals might oppose any kind of bargain with the LRC, while some LRC supporters would be against any continuance of the old Lib-Lab alliance.

As it happened, these two developments – the effect of the Taff Vale decision, and the electoral pact with the Liberals – ensured not only the continued existence of the LRC, but also its success in the 1906 election, when it changed its name to the Labour Party. After the First World War the Labour Party was to go on to greater triumphs, becoming the official Opposition in the House, and supplanting the Liberal Party as one of the two major parties in Britain. This dramatic change in its fortunes could hardly have been predicted in 1903. Keir Hardie himself thought of it as merely another pressure group representing Labour in parliament, and even in 1905 remarked that he hoped that in time it might become an "influence second in importance only to that of the Irish National Party". Other socialists were similarly cautious about the future of the LRC. Robert Blatchford's socialist journal, the *Clarion*, made a comment that has become famous:

At last, there is a United Labour Party, or perhaps it would be safer to say, a little cloud, no bigger than a man's hand, which may grow into a United Labour Party.

So in this way, direct and independent representation of labour in parliament began, by a body pledged to advance the cause of Labour (but not of socialism), and in co-operation with any new Liberal government. From hindsight, it can be argued that the Liberals signed their own death warrant as a party in 1903. As one Liberal historian put it with feeling some years ago, commenting on the results of the general election in 1906, the Liberals should have strangled the infant Labour Party in the cradle. They failed to see future possibilities, and indeed can hardly be blamed for not anticipating the disastrous split in their own party during the First World War; but that is another story.

By the time of the general election in 1906, the number of LRC MPs had increased from two to four. Their election manifesto was very similar to that of the Liberals, emphasizing the need for free trade (the Conservatives were divided over the issue of tariff reform). In order to avoid any confusion, a trade union conference in the Caxton Hall, London in 1905 produced the "Caxton Hall Concordat", whereby it was agreed that all candidates in the next general election approved by either the LRC or the Parliamentary Committee (which still put up Lib-Lab candidates) should be supported by both bodies. In the election held in January 1906 a total of 29 LRC candidates were elected, one other MP joining their ranks shortly after. There were also an additional 24 Lib-Labs, making a Labour group of 54 MPs in all, according to Professor Pelling (Clegg, Fox & Thompson make the Lib-Lab total only 17, giving an overall total of 47). The LRC then acquired its new name of the Labour Party, and its 30 members became known as the Parliamentary Labour Party, with its own whips. Keir Hardie became chairman of this body, with MacDonald as secretary, and Arthur Henderson as chief whip.

Early in 1906 the Royal Commission on trade unions delivered its report, recommending the recognition of trade unions as legal entities, together with the protection of their benefit funds, and the confirming of the right to legal picketing. The new Liberal government thereupon introduced a bill to put these recommendations into effect. However, this bill ran into substantial opposition. The unions disliked the idea of legal incorporation, which would have allowed their own members to sue them. They simply wanted a return to the legal immunity as it appeared to exist before the Taff Vale judgement. Again, many Liberal MPs during the election campaign had promised support to the bill, which had already been before the House. The result was that the government withdrew its bill, replacing it by the earlier bill supported by the Parliamentary Committee of the TUC. This bill gave very substantial privileges to the unions: it provided that a trade union could not be sued "in respect of any tortious act alleged to have been committed by or on behalf of a trade union" – that is, it gave complete immunity from actions based on tort, an immunity not even limited to acts committed in a trades dispute. Further, picketing was redefined. It made it lawful for any number of pickets to attend:

> in contemplation or furtherance of a trades dispute . . . if they attend merely for the purpose of peacefully obtaining or communicating information, or peacefully persuading any person to work or abstain from working.

This was really a remarkable advance for the trade unions, and the eminent historian of trade unionism, Henry Phelps Brown, writing in the early 1980s, has examined the extent to which the settlement of

1906 seems to have been based on a backwards-looking, old-fashioned version of trade unions as peaceful bargaining bodies, on the whole respectful to employers. He suggests that in reality by 1906 their character had changed – they had become far less deferential and more critical in their attitude to social problems. Certainly at the time, the privileges given to the unions caused some alarm. Edward Carson, the famous Conservative lawyer and statesman, commented that immunity in tort would affirm that "the king can do no wrong; neither can a trade union". In addition, in the matter of picketing, Carson remarked (not without some justification, one might think), "I have always thought that the matter of peaceful picketing is a matter of absolute hypocrisy – peaceful persuasion is no use to a trade union". Later on, A. J. Balfour, leader of the Conservatives, spoke during the debate on the Coal Mines Bill in 1912 of the increased powers of the unions following the 1906 Act:

> The power they have got, if used to the utmost, is under our existing law, almost limitless, and there is no appearance that the leaders of the movement desire to temper the use of their legal powers with any consideration of policy or of mercy. Can anyone quote from history, in respect of any of the classes on whom are visited, and often justly visited, the indignation of the historical commentator, a parallel case? Has any feudal baron ever exercised his powers in the manner which the leaders of this great trade union are now using theirs?

Balfour was a great classical scholar, but of course this was to exaggerate somewhat wildly the extent and exercise of trade union power. Asquith, the Liberal prime minister, assured Balfour that the miners' claim was simply for a reasonable minimum wage for underground workers. Nevertheless, Balfour voiced the disquiet of many employers at the recent increase in power of the unions.

In retrospect, Phelps Brown concludes that the government did not have much choice in 1906. Their allies, the trade unions, would not accept compulsory arbitration and the outlawing of strikes (both of which were enforced in Australia and New Zealand before 1914), since this meant imposing authority from outside. Again, they rejected legal incorporation, and just wanted what they took to be their former legal immunity in tort. The simplest course of action was for the government to give them what they wanted; and this in fact was what the 1906 Act did. Even then, the courts were not done with the trade unions yet, as will be seen later in this chapter.

Once the new Labour Party had established itself in the House of Commons, it might be expected that they would begin to press powerfully for social legislation to benefit the working classes. One of its members, John Burns, had even become a member of the cabinet as President of the Board of Trade. In fact, he was to prove to be a somewhat ineffectual minister, very much under the thumb of his senior civil servants. The passing of the Trades Disputes Act had certainly been a considerable advance, and Clegg, Fox & Thompson say that the parliamentary labour representatives were conscious of much solid achievement up to 1910, at which date these authors end their authoritative survey of trade union history. Yet for the whole period 1906–14 the running was made by the Liberal government rather than by the Labour Party. In the earlier period up to 1909, it is true that a number of important social reforms were passed. They included the provision of school meals for children, medical inspection in schools, the codifying Children's Act, 1908, and above all, the Pensions Act, 1908. In and after 1908, a fresh wave of reforms began, such as the Town and Country Planning Act, the Labour Exchanges Act, the Trades Boards Act, and the People's Budget – all these in 1909. Then in 1911 there was passed the great National Insurance Act.

This is an impressive list, but in fact it cannot be said that they were passed as a result of pressure from the fledgling Labour Party. They owed much to the drive and initiative of Lloyd George, first at the Board of Trade and afterwards at the Exchequer, and to Winston Churchill, his successor at the Board of Trade. These two men were responsible for an astonishing amount of social reform that really owed very little to Labour MPs, who were relegated to a supporting role, or to suggesting amendments or criticisms of the legislation. For example, the Labour Exchanges Act was viewed with some suspicion by the trade unions who thought the exchanges might be used for the recruitment of blackleg labour. Then again, the Insurance Act, 1911, providing for national health insurance for all working men and women, and insurance against unemployment for 2.25 million workers, was disliked because of its compulsory deductions of contributions from wages. The support of the Labour Party for this measure was obtained only on the understanding that the government would introduce salaries for MPs, which promise was carried out in 1911. The Insurance Act, in particular, trespassed on trade union territory, with its limited scheme for unemployment insurance. As we saw in Chapter 3, the Act was made more acceptable to both the trade unions and the friendly societies by making them administrators of the schemes for insurance. Even then some Labour MPs criticized the health scheme for failing to get to the root of the matter, which was the poverty that caused the ill health.

All the same, the Liberal reforms constitute a mass of social legislation, much of it arguably providing the foundations on which the Welfare State was built by the Labour Party after the Second World War. It was not based on socialism, but was a product of the New Liberalism or Progressivism, designed in part to help the weakest who could not help themselves, and in part as supplying help through the insurance principle. Benefits were kept low in order to encourage savings. Yet at the same time there were elements of collectivism of the kind familiar to socialists in the Labour Party. The best example of this was old age pensions, which were non-contributory, and paid out of a national fund. Also, as we have seen, insurance against sickness and unemployment was compulsory for those covered by the Act. Miners' hours were fixed by the state, and machinery established for fixing their wages, together with wages in the sweated trades, under the Trades Boards Act. So, in spite of their disclaimers, the Liberal government introduced an increasing amount of state intervention into working-class lives, although not all of it was welcome at the time.

Of course, in assessing the contribution of the Labour Party to all this legislation, two obvious aspects of the political situation must be taken into account. The first is that the Labour MPs were not numerically strong enough to have much influence over Liberal legislative programmes, at least before 1911, and in any case they had undertaken to support the government under the terms of the Gladstone–MacDonald pact. There is the further point that they could hardly oppose in principle any of the social reforms, although they might quarrel with the details (in fact, they were consulted, and their co-operation sought in particular over the Labour Exchanges Act, the Trades Boards Act and the Insurance Act). The situation changed in 1910, when the two general elections of the year left the Liberals with only a tiny overall majority, so that the Labour Party and the Irish members held the balance. But even then, the Labour Party could not

afford to defeat the Liberals, for the consequence would have been
another general election, which the Labour Party could ill-afford, and
which might bring the Conservatives back into office – not at all a desirable outcome. So, as Professor Pelling put it rather elegantly some
years ago, circumstances made the Labour Party "the hand maiden of
Liberalism".

The second consideration is the nature of the Parliamentary Labour
Party itself in 1906. After an excellent start had been made with the
Trade Disputes Act, progress proved very disappointing. This was to
some extent the fault of Hardie himself, who was not a good chairman, although in 1906 the newly-created party could hardly avoid
honouring him in this way. He was too individualistic, too much given
to going his own way, and at times was inconsistent in policy. In addition, the party lacked a clear political programme, having only a general commitment to support the cause of labour. Then again, there
were divisions between the trade union members and the socialists,
and some mutual distrust. Party discipline was slack, and trade union
members were often absent from the House, being engaged elsewhere
on trade union duties. All in all, the record of the new party before
1914 was not impressive.

Signs of discontent with the party were seen as early as 1907, when
a leading member of the ILP, Victor Grayson, stood as an independent
Labour candidate in the Colne Valley by-election, and was elected
without Labour Party support. In the following year, Ben Tillett produced a pamphlet with the forthright title, *Is the Parliamentary
Labour Party a failure?* In this pamphlet Tillett declared that:

> The House of Commons and the country, which respected and
> feared the Labour Party, are now fast approaching a condition of
> contempt towards its parliamentary representatives. The lion has
> no teeth or claws, and is losing his growl, too . . .

Another pamphlet, issued by the ILP Council, the so-called Green
Manifesto (it was printed on green paper) was entitled *Let us reform
the Labour Party*. In 1911, some members of the ILP joined with the
SDF, which had withdrawn support from the LRC in 1901, to form a
new British Socialist Party (later to give rise to the creation of the
Communist Party of Great Britain in 1920). Shortly before this
breakaway, according to the ILP Annual Report of 1910, Keir Hardie

had declared, "At the present time, the Labour Party has almost ceased to count".

It would appear then, that the Labour Party did not make much of an impression in the House before 1914. In that year, Beatrice Webb recorded in her diary that the Labour members had lost confidence in both themselves and each other: ". . . there is little leadership, but a good deal of anti-leadership". Critics noted that Hardie spent much time in supporting the suffragette movement, and his close friendship with Sylvia Pankhurst was the subject of comment. Nevertheless, it is important to see the apparent lack of achievement by the Labour Party in perspective. On the whole, they retained a respectable degree of electoral support, their numbers increasing in 1908, when a group of miners transferred to them from the Lib-Labs, but declining again by two seats as a result of the two general elections in 1910 to a total of 42. Since there was a substantial loss of Liberal seats to the Conservatives in these elections, the loss of these Labour seats is not especially significant. Throughout the Liberal administrations, it should be noted again that the Labour Party leaders were frequently consulted on the drafting and organization of the various social reforms, and they made an important contribution in this respect. By 1914, the Parliamentary Labour Party was still there, their numbers standing at 37, while the Labour Party's numbers in the constituencies were growing. The chairman of the Parliamentary Party in 1914 was Ramsay MacDonald. Since taking office in 1911, he had proved a much more effective leader than Hardie, while Arthur Henderson (formerly of the Ironfounders Union) became secretary of the Labour Party itself. Both were very able men. For leaders such as these to be characterized by Ben Tillett in his 1908 pamphlet as "toadies", "sheer hypocrites", and "Press flunkeys to Asquith" was manifestly unfair. One can only comment that critics on both the left and the right are prone to use intemperate language, presumably to make their point. All in all, the Parliamentary Labour Party, in spite of its admitted deficiencies, did not do too badly in the difficult years before 1914.

Before turning to industrial relations, one last brush of the trade union movement with the law courts must be examined. This concerns the Osborne Judgement in 1909. The Walthamstow branch secretary of the Railway Servants Union (the same union that had figured in the Taff Vale case) brought an action against his own union for using part of his subscription for political purposes, that is, to support the Labour Party. This was a direct challenge to the principle of the compulsory political levy. The Webbs claimed that Osborne was "liberally financed from capitalist sources", but there seems no truth in this. He himself declared he was supported by individual workmen, and even by some trade unions. In fact, Osborne was a dedicated Liberal, who objected to the compulsory nature of the levy which was paid to a party that included socialists. The case went to the House of Lords, which ruled in Osborne's favour, finding that the compulsory levy was *ultra vires* the powers conferred by the legislation of the 1870s. As a result, the financial support that the TUC provided for MPs was cut off, and by February 1911, 22 unions had been restrained from making such payments. This was clearly a very serious matter for the trade union movement, and the TUC demanded legislation to reverse the judgement. (Osborne himself was expelled from his union, his eighteen years' contributions confiscated, and all benefits cancelled.) The situation was saved when salaries were paid for the first time to MPs in 1911 (£400 a year), and indeed, some unionists thought this was an appropriate solution to the problem. The TUC thought otherwise, and continued to demand legislative action.

Finally and after considerable delay, the Liberal government introduced the Trade Union Act, 1913. By this act, all unions who wished to support a political party had to ballot their members to ascertain whether they wanted to set up a political fund. If a majority was in favour, a political fund might be established quite separate from the general fund of the union. Any member not wishing to contribute to the political fund could say no, that is, "contract-out", and the whole of his subscription would then go into the general fund. The unions did not like the bill, and especially opposed the "contracting-out" provision (presumably Osborne would have approved of its voluntary nature). As it was, many trade union members who were not really supporters of the Labour Party must subsequently have paid the political levy because they couldn't be bothered to "contract-out". So the procedure was not without its advantages for the unions. There were still many trade unionists who were either liberals or conservatives, and this seems to be shown by the numbers voting against having a political fund when they were balloted on the issue. Thus the miners, who were predominantly Lib-Lab in outlook at this time, voted 261,643 for a political fund, and 194,800 against; the cotton weavers 98,158 for, and 75,893 against. In view of this, it can be argued that the original Osborne Judgement was as much in the interests of liberal and conservative trade unionists as it was the result of bias on the part of the law lords against the unions, although the latter was the view of the unions, of course.

The political activity of the infant Labour Party was obviously of interest to the trade union movement, but the great battles of the period immediately before the First World War were fought in the industrial field rather than in the political field. The years from 1907 to 1914 saw some of the most serious strikes in the history of the movement. The numbers of strikes, and of working days lost, are shown in Table 10.

Table 10 Strikes and working days lost, 1907–14.

Year	No. of strikes	Days lost
1907	585	2,150,000
1908	389	10,790,000
1909	422	2,690,000
1910	521	9,870,000
1911	872	10,160,000
1912	834	40,890,000
1913	1,459	9,800,000
1914	972	9,880,000

In 1907, there was a threatened national railway strike over a union demand for a wage increase for all grades of railway workers. The railway unions were still not recognized officially by the railway companies, with one exception, the North Eastern Railway Company. This in fact was the only company to accept the wage demand – all the others refused. The threat of a national strike on the railways – the first of its kind – led to government intervention, and Lloyd George, President of the Board of Trade, was able to persuade both sides to set up boards of conciliation for each grade of employment. In 1908, there was a serious strike by members of the Amalgamated Engineering Union in the northeast against wage cuts, but after being out for seven months they were forced into submission and to accept the cuts. In 1909, the principal cause of industrial unrest was probably the implementation of the Miners Eight Hour Day Act. Although beneficial in intention, this act had failed to define exactly what was meant by "eight hours"; in particular, how far it included "winding time". Fur-

169

thermore, hours and working practices varied considerably from coalfield to coalfield. For example, in the northeast pits, miners had their own custom of sharing shifts, while in the Midlands the shift had already been reduced to eight hours since the 1870s. For a variety of reasons then, the Act was unsatisfactory, and in 1910 the Durham and Northumberland miners went on strike against the new system, and were out for three months before they would accept it. In the same year, there was a serious and lengthy strike in South Wales, lasting ten months, by the miners employed by the Cambrian Combine. This strike was caused by the miners' refusing to accept new pay rates offered by a conciliation board. There was rioting and looting in Tonypandy, both London police and troops were drafted in, and one miner was shot dead.

The two worst years for industrial strife before the war were 1911 and 1912 (although 1913 and 1914 were not far behind). In 1911 there was again trouble in the docks. In Southampton there was a successful strike by seamen over pay. Further trouble erupted among transport workers, and there was a short general strike in the London docks, which was swiftly brought to an end by the government mediator, G. R. Askwith; the strikers obtained most of their demands. Another strike occurred in the Liverpool docks, where strike action was organized very efficiently by Tom Mann, although here a policeman and another two men were killed when troops were employed to stop a riot. In August 1911 the first national railway strike took place, the result of the lengthy deliberations of the new railway conciliation boards proving too slow for the unions. Once more government intervention took place. Lloyd George, now Chancellor of the Exchequer, negotiated with both sides, pointing out the dangers in the situation when war with Germany threatened over the Agadir crisis. Work was resumed after only five days. A Royal Commission was appointed; following its report, new conciliation boards were appointed, and the companies at last in effect gave official recognition to the unions. Although the strike was so short, troops were brought in (in London, they camped in the parks), and there was serious rioting in Llanelly where looting took place, two strikers were shot dead when trying to stop a train driven by blacklegs, and five men died as a result of an explosion among the freight. Hardie published a famous pamphlet on the subject entitled *Killing no murder: the government and the railway strike*.

Perhaps the worst year of all was 1912, certainly in terms of days lost at work – more than four times the number for 1911. In February the Miners Federation called a national strike for a minimum wage for miners – 5s a shift for men, and 2s for boys; there was also the vexed question of payment for work in the "abnormal places" (especially difficult seams). Once more there was government intervention, this time in the form of a committee of four ministers, led by the Prime Minister himself. A bill was soon introduced into the House for the setting up of local boards to fix district minimum wages, although not necessarily the rates demanded by the unions. After a ballot of their members, the miners went back to work in April. The Minimum Wages Act, 1912 was not altogether satisfactory, but its enactment showed the importance attached by the government to settling the dispute, and indeed the strike brought forth the attack on trade union power by Balfour quoted earlier in this chapter.

Another important strike in 1912 took place in the London docks where a dispute arose over the employers' right to employ non-unionist labour. Again a cabinet committee, this time of five ministers, was formed to deal with the strike, although an attempt by the National Transport Workers Federation to make it into a national strike collapsed by August. A far more intensive and long-lasting strike of transport workers broke out in Dublin, led by Jim Larkin, a well-known syndicalist of the time. After a long and bitter struggle, accompanied by much violence, the strike came to an end in January 1913. Further industrial strife occurred during the rest of that year, with a record pre-war number of strikes, and nearly ten million days lost, but without the involvement at length of any of the major industries. During 1914 there was some reduction in unrest, although the total of number of strikes and of working days lost remained quite high before war came on 4 August 1914.

Given the extraordinary number and severity of strikes from 1910 onwards, and bearing in mind the relative tranquillity of the preceding period, the question naturally arises, what were the causes? Historians have debated this at some length. One popular and very readable version of events, *The strange death of Liberal England*, by G. Dangerfield, published in 1938, advanced the idea that the industrial strife of the time must be seen in the context of escalating violence at home (the struggle over the Parliament Bill, with scenes of violence in the House, the suffragette movement, and the approach of civil war in

Ireland), and also of increased tension in European relationships. Only the outbreak of war, we are told, saved a mighty, revolutionary explosion at home. This is entertaining fantasy; there is really no evidence whatever to show that a revolutionary situation existed in Britain in the pre-war years. Instead, Philip Snowden, a Labour MP at the time, who was to become Chancellor of the Exchequer in both Labour governments between the wars, seems to have summed up a number of the causes fairly enough:

> In 1910 – a year of record trade – wages remained practically stationary. The cost of living increased, and the working people's desires rightly grew. But with stationary wages, the real condition of the workers is one of diminishing power to satisfy desires. This is one of the causes of unrest in the Labour world. With the spread of education, with the display of wealth and luxury by the rich, it is certain that the workers will not be content.

Undoubtedly a major factor in industrial unrest was that, whereas there had been a rise of well over 10 per cent in real wages between 1889 and 1900, from 1900 to 1910, there was a fall of nearly 10 per cent. Moreover, boom conditions after 1908 led to a high level of employment. Thus, conditions were ripe for continual protest by working people who found their wages were buying less and less. No wonder, as Snowden primly observed, they were not content.

A further important point, as Snowden indicated, is that the working classes were now better educated and could read about the ostentatious displays of wealth by the middle and upper classes in the new popular press. Undoubtedly the Edwardian period saw an increasing display of luxury and rich living by the better-off classes, following the example set by the new king. Rich dinner parties, elaborate and expensive dress and jewellery, glittering balls and other social occasions, the increasing use of motor cars – all this made a painful impression on the politically literate working man and woman, at a time when the extent of poverty in London, York and elsewhere was still in the public memory. Snowden did well to fasten on this aspect, although first and foremost must come the fall in real wages as a cause of unrest, for this hit all working men and women, whether trade unionist or not, where it hurt most – in the pocket, especially after a period of falling prices and rising real wages.

If declining pay levels are at the core of the discontent of the time, other causes must also be considered. One of these is the disappointment felt in left-wing political circles at the poor performance in the Commons of the Labour Party. This has already been discussed earlier in this chapter, and certainly helps to explain the increased militancy of some socialist trade unionists, who argued that the working-class cause would be furthered more by industrial action than by action in the House of Commons. Marxist ideas seemed to be gaining ground, and although not a major element in the situation, it is significant that in 1908 a dispute broke out at Ruskin College, Oxford (a college set up separately from the university in 1899 for trade unionists). The principal there wanted to introduce Marxism into the college teaching, and when permission was refused, removed to London and set up the Central Labour College. Associated with this was the establishment of another left-wing body, the Plebs League. Also in the early years of the century, an important advance in part-time working-class education on a higher educational level was made in 1903 with the founding of the Workers Educational Association, a left-wing but non-Marxist organization that received limited support from the TUC.

One distinct political cause of industrial discontent much discussed at the time was the spread of syndicalism. This movement derived its name from the French word for trade union, *syndic*, and had its origins in America, where the Marxist, Daniel De Leon, founded his Industrial Workers of the World Society in Chicago, and in France, where the movement was led by George Sorel. The basic idea of syndicalism was that a single big union should be created for each industry, which henceforth would be run for the benefit of the workers, not the employers. At an appropriate time, the workers in each industry would rise up and take political control of the state. Working-class rule would then be achieved not so much through parliament, but through industrial power, in particular through the use of the general strike. These ideas were set out in a statement in 1908, published in Edinburgh, and entitled, *The Socialist Labour Party: its aims and methods*. This party was strong on the Clyde, and supported the teachings of Daniel De Leon. After explaining that each industry should have its own industrial union, which would "palpitate with the daily and hourly pulsations of the class struggle as it manifests itself in the workshop", the manifesto continues:

When in the fullness of its strength, it is able through its political ambassadors to demand the surrender of the capitalist class, it will be in a position to enforce its demands by its organised might, and in place of the strikes of the former days, institute the General Lock-Out of the Capitalist class. Finally, having overthrown the class state, the united INDUSTRIAL UNIONS WILL FURNISH THE ADMINISTRATIVE MACHINERY FOR DIRECTING INDUSTRY IN THE SOCIALIST COMMONWEALTH.

Syndicalism received enthusiastic support from Tom Mann when he returned from Australia in 1910. He began to publish a monthly journal, the *Industrial Syndicalist*, founded the Industrial Syndicalist Education League, and also set up Amalgamation Committees in a number of industries. Also in 1910 he established the National Transport Workers Federation, including both dockers and seamen, but not railway workers. Syndicalist ideas understandably became attractive to socialist trade unionists, disappointed with the slow progress of the Parliamentary Labour Party. Syndicalism received substantial support in the South Wales coalfield, and in 1912 a body calling itself the Unofficial Reform Committee of the South Wales Mining Federation published in Tonypandy a pamphlet entitled *The miners' next step*. This set out, in very general terms, what had to be done as an "ultimate objective": this was "one organization to cover the whole of the Coal, Ore, Slate, Stone, Clay, Salt, mining or quarrying industry of Great Britain, with one Central Objective". According to Pelling, this pamphlet marks the high water of syndicalist influence in British trade unionism.

Thereafter the syndicalist tide ebbed. Mann's one real success in bringing about amalgamations of unions was the creation of the National Transport Workers Federation, but this was unsuccessful in bringing out transport workers in 1912 in a national strike. Attempts to bring about amalgamations of unions in the building trades led to a ballot in which less than a quarter of the membership voted, and the proposal was rejected. The one successful merger of unions that took place was the creation of the National Union of Railwaymen in 1913, when the Society of Railway Servants joined with the General Railway Workers Union, and one other smaller union of pointsmen and signalmen. However, this was by no means the creation of one union for the railway industry as a whole, for two important unions were still outside – the Associated Society of Locomotive Engineers and Firemen (ASLEF), and the Railway Clerks Association. It is clear that most unions still wished to retain their own separate existence and privileges.

One other move, if not to amalgamation, but to close co-operation, requires comment: this is the so-called Triple Alliance of 1914 between railwaymen, miners and the Transport Workers Federation. The idea was that the three partners to the Alliance should arrange that their contracts with employers should end at the same time, so that both the government and the employers would be faced with a national economic crisis if a dispute broke out in any one of the industries concerned. At first sight, admittedly, this looked like a proposal for joint action, possibly leading to a general strike. In fact, it seems that it was merely a practical proposal to ensure co-operation and avoid losses due to the unilateral action of any one of the unions concerned. During the miners' strike in 1912, for example, it cost the railwaymen's union £94,000 in compensation to their own members laid off during the strike. Of course, it was hoped that the alliance would influence both employers and government with the threat of a massive and widespread strike, but this is very different from the active plotting for a national strike. It proved difficult to work out the details of the alliance, and they were not finally completed till December 1915. When an effort was made to implement the Alliance in 1921, the railwaymen backed out, and the alliance collapsed in ruins. It seems, therefore, that the major idea behind the alliance in 1914 was not to prepare for a general strike, but to increase the bargaining-power of the three unions involved.

In summing up the influence of syndicalism before 1914, it is clear that it certainly added to the industrial unrest of the time, but it was never successful in gaining a secure foothold in the trade union movement. It was at its strongest in South Wales and among the leaders of the South Wales Miners Federation, where dissatisfaction continued with both the Eight Hour Day Act and the Minimum Wages Act – there was still argument over the interpretation of the latter act and over what payment was properly due for working the most difficult and inaccessible seams of coal. Feelings ran high in the coalfield, and it has already been noted that men were killed by the army during disturbances. Tom Mann himself was prosecuted for publishing the "Don't Shoot" appeal in the *Syndicalist* in January 1912. It took the form of an open letter to British soldiers:

Men! Comrades! Brothers!

You are in the Army.

So are we. You, in the army of Destruction. We, in the Industrial, or army of Construction.

We work at mill, mine, forge, factory or dock, etc., producing and transporting all the goods, clothing, stuffs, etc., which make it possible for people to live.

You are Workingmen's sons.

When we go on strike to better our lot, which is the lot also of Your Fathers, Mothers, Brothers and Sisters, you are called upon by your Officers TO MURDER US.

Don't do it . . .

Even today, the deaths at Tonypandy and Llanelly are not forgotten. The plain fact remains, however, that syndicalism made very little progress elsewhere, and if its success is to be judged by the extent to which its ideas were adopted by the trade union movement as a whole, then it had very little success indeed. Not a single industry went over to the notion of one industry, one union.

Yet it would be wrong to suppose that *all* the trouble at root was over the rise in prices and the failure of wages to keep pace. There was more to it than that. Although times were prosperous, many industrial employers were under the increasing pressure of foreign competition. The railway companies themselves had had their freight rates pegged by legislation in 1892. Coalmine owners had their own problems, with both the Eight Hour Day and Minimum Wages acts. More recently, the leading authority in trade union history, Professor H. A. Clegg, while accepting the importance of the fall in real wages, has argued that nearly all of the major strikes (14 in all between 1911 and 1914) can be largely accounted for by the boom in trade union organization (comparable with the 1871–3 and 1889–90 booms), and by the cost position of a few groups of companies, notably those of the coalowners and the railways. He points out that the earlier periods of booms and strikes did not follow a period of falling real wages.

As for the unions themselves, although conciliation procedures seemed to have worked well enough at the beginning of the century, conciliation boards found themselves caught more and more between employers who wanted to lower costs and unions who wanted to preserve the level of real wages. At grass roots, dissatisfaction was growing with the official procedures of the boards. They were often very slow, and the final award tended to be regarded merely as a comfortable agreement between employers and full-time trade union officials who had not themselves worked on the shop floor for many a year, and were out of touch with day-to-day realities. It is not surprising that in these circumstances the shop steward movement began to represent opinion on the shop floor, although it was to grow much stronger during the First World War, when trade union officials co-operated at the highest levels with members of the government.

Once all aspects of change are assessed, the eight years between 1906 and 1914 may then be seen as a really remarkable period in trade union history, both in the industrial field and in parliament itself. Yet one last development has still to be examined, and this is the growth of membership in the last few years, especially in and after 1911. According to Pelling (see Table 11), the figures show an astonishing growth. It can be seen that in 1913 there was an increase of 719,000 members – nearly three-quarters of a million extra members in one year alone. This remarkable increase owed a great deal to the coming into operation of the National Insurance Act, 1911 which required all working men and women to join a friendly society under the scheme for health insurance. Many therefore joined the trade union for their trade if it had a benefit fund, but this was not the only cause of the increase. Numbers of unskilled workers who were benefiting from the relatively full employment of the pre-war years came into the unions for the first time. The Workers Union, established in 1898, had a membership of 5,000 in 1910, and claimed an increase to 91,000 by December 1913. By 1914, the numbers of skilled and unskilled members were almost equal – a striking change from the 1890s when new unionists were outnumbered by skilled members by about ten to one.

Table 11 Numbers and membership of trade unions, 1911–14.

Year	No. of trade unions	No. of members	No. of TUs affiliated to TUC	No. of members affiliated to TUC
1911	1,290	3,139,000	201	2,001,633
1912	1,252	3,416,000	207	2,232,446
1913	1,269	4,135,000	–	–
1914	1,260	4,145,000	215	2,682,357

It is evident that the years of the Liberal administrations from 1906 to 1914 saw great changes in the growth and influence of the trade union movement. One of the most significant was the increasing intervention of the government into industrial disputes. The first instance of this was in 1893, when the prime minister, Gladstone, offered the services of Lord Rosebery as a mediator. *The Times* called this intervention "a doubtful step", but under the Liberal administrations such attempts at conciliation became a regular practice, as we have seen. Not only that, but the importance attached to solving industrial problems can be seen in the increase in the number of civil servants in the Labour Department of the Board of Trade, an increase from 105 in 1896 to 325 in 1913. At the same time, the Liberals supported the recruitment of trade unionists to government posts associated with industry. According to the historian, Halévy, by the end of 1912 nearly 400 posts had been created by the Liberals and staffed by trade unionists in the factory inspectorate, the Board of Trade, Home Office, National Insurance administration, and elsewhere in the Civil Service. The government also encouraged the payment of trade union rates by adopting a new Fair Wages resolution in 1909 for government contracts. In all these ways there was a direct recognition by the Liberal governments of the increased importance of the trade unions in the economic and social life of the country.

Indeed, when the nature of the Liberal social reforms such as the 1911 Act, old age pensions, school meals and medical inspection is taken into account, the question naturally arises of how far the need for working-class self-help had been diminished by these reforms. The answer to this must be, by not very much for as has been made clear, most of the acts were limited in their scope – old age pensions were kept deliberately small and subject to means-testing, health insurance did not extend to workers' families, unemployment insurance covered only a small minority of the working population, and so on. Again, it must be said that although collectivist in nature, the reforms were not socialist. According to Churchill:

> Socialism wants to pull down wealth, Liberalism seeks to raise up poverty . . . Socialism assails the maximum pre-eminence of the individual – Liberalism seeks to build up the minimum standard of the masses.

In actual fact, it was not always easy to distinguish between liberal progressivism and a mild, Fabian-like socialism. The middle-class conscience of the time was haunted by the revelations by Booth and Rowntree of the extent of poverty, by the scandal of the low medical quality of recruits in the Boer War, and by the further revelations of such works as Jack London's *People of the abyss* (1903), C. F. Masterman's *The condition of England* (1908), and not least, Leo Chiozza Money's *Riches and poverty* (1905). Then there were the contemporary anxieties about how the Empire could be maintained, about national efficiency and international competition, given the state of that section of the working classes below the poverty line. It was a time of intense political argument and controversy over the well-being of the nation and its future. For example, during the struggle with the House of Lords over the People's Budget, a famous attack was launched on the Lords themselves:

> The question will be asked, should 500 men, ordinary men, chosen accidentally from among the unemployed, over-ride the judgement – the deliberate judgement – of millions of people who are engaged in the industry which makes the wealth of the country? . . . Another question will be asked: who ordained that a few should have the land of Britain as a perquisite, who made 10,000 people owners of the soil, and the rest of us trespassers in the land of our birth?

The speaker was not a socialist, not a member of the ILP or the SDP, but the liberal Chancellor of the Exchequer, David Lloyd George (his Newcastle speech can be heard very effectively spoken by an actor on tape at the Lloyd George Museum, Llanystumdwy, near Criccieth, North Wales). So there was a good deal of concern and sympathy with the problems of the working classes, especially the poor inhabitants of the cities. This helps to put the Liberal reforms in context, but it must be repeated that, in themselves, these reforms in no way did away with the self-help activities provided by the trade unions.

Was trade unionism "transformed" between 1906 and 1914, as at least one historian has claimed? On the credit side of the account, there is undoubtedly the great increase in membership, partly the result of the 1911 Act, of course, but there was also an increase in unskilled membership. Then there was the trade union legislation, the acknowledged national repercussions of widespread strike action, government attempts at conciliation, and the new Labour Party in parliament. It was increasingly recognized that the trade unions had an important national role in both social and economic affairs in the regulation of industry. On the debit side was the slow recognition by the unions themselves of their increased national importance and responsibility. Their outlook was still highly traditional, concentrating narrowly on a fair day's pay for a fair day's work, although it was now clear that national strikes could have severe effects on the nation's economy. It was estimated that the miners' strike in 1912 reduced industrial earnings by 12 per cent, and made 60 per cent of iron and steel workers unemployed within three weeks. One historian has suggested that by 1900 trade unionism was probably among the most serious impediments to improved economic efficiency and a significant handicap in international competition, though admittedly the unions did curb wild-cat strikes and enforce collective bargaining. Then again their political future was uncertain in 1914, and so was the future of syndicalism, for the true import of the Triple Alliance had yet to become clear.

Administratively, too, the unions were very weak. The numbers of full-time officials per union varied considerably – Ben Tillett's union had 37 full-time officers for 15,000 members, while the gasworkers had only 15 officials for 32,000 members. The size of unions also varied greatly; some were very small. The figures given earlier in this chapter show that of the 1,260 unions in all in 1914, only 215 were affiliated to the TUC, representing only 2.7 million members out of the total membership of 4.1 million. Perhaps most serious of all, most unions were run on a shoestring. Officials were thought to have "cushy" jobs compared with their members in mine or workshop, and were paid only the pay of the average member. When it came to negotiations with employers, especially during strikes, trade union head offices were frequently at a disadvantage because the employers were so much better organized, and had better administrative resources. Suspicion among the rank and file of their own officials was common enough. In the ASE it reached absurd heights in 1912, when a delegate meeting elected a new Council but the old Council refused to resign, barricading themselves in the head office in Peckham Road, only to be thrown out when members of the new Council broke in from the house next door. Episodes like this were highly exceptional, of course, but they certainly did not improve the image of the movement.

Naturally, it is quite impossible to strike a simple balance between the two sides of the account. What is beyond any doubt is that the trade union movement had made enormous progress since the beginning of the nineteenth century. A firm legal position had been secured, and employers had finally come to accept their existence and indeed their value in establishing industrial discipline, although still given to criticizing their "tyranny" and "inflexibility" when disputes occurred. Moreover, their membership had expanded greatly, extending to include large numbers of unskilled workers by 1914. During the course of the preceding century, countless numbers of unionists must have been thankful for support from the union during wage negotiations, during strikes, and also in times of sickness and distress. But all this must not be taken too far. As late as the 1890s, unskilled workers formed only a limited proportion of the total membership. Among adult male manual workers in 1910, just over two out of three were still *not* unionized, and for women not in the unions, the figure was far higher. At the beginning of the twentieth century, women's trade unionism hardly existed outside cotton, linen and jute, although one encouraging sign was that in 1906 Mary MacArthur set up the National Federation of Women Workers, which had a membership of 6,000 after the Sweated Industries Act,1909 had come into operation, rising to 20,000 by 1914. By 1913, the total number of women who were members of trade unions was increasing rapidly, and by that year had amounted to about 433,000.

Finally then, to see trade unionism as an expression of self-help as the British people became an industrialized nation during the course of the nineteenth century is to acknowledge an important truth, but even in 1914 it was of no help to well over half of the working population outside the ranks of the unions. In particular, the 37.7 per cent of population in Booth's London, and the 30.7 per cent in Rowntree's York, who were below the poverty line (not to mention the submerged tenth in each city) had little or nothing to thank trade unionism for. It had not reached them, and this form of self-help was of no consequence to them. These lower ranks of society were the people of the abyss, so far sunk in wretchedness and degradation that steady employment and the chance of joining a union were beyond them. For these people, the Liberal social reforms, operating outside the scope

181

of a still largely unreformed Poor Law, offered at least a ray of hope.
Self-help in an industrial nation had its limitations, as it still has today.

Part Three

The co-operative movement

Chapter Nine

Before Rochdale

The idea of workers' co-operation was not new in the early nine-teenth century, nor that of community settlements. There are a number of earlier examples, ranging from the mid-seventeenth century Diggers to the Bishop of Durham's community store at Mongewell in Oxfordshire in 1794, although the latter was simply a philanthropic enterprise to help the poor. It was not until the period after the end of the Napoleonic Wars in 1815 that the idea of projects for both retailing and manufacturing goods by groups of workers began to take hold. This is not surprising, given the vast urban expansion of the time, the consequent boom in retailing, and the often shoddy nature of the goods on sale. More than that, in the post-French Revolutionary period there was much debate of a political nature on the expanding capitalist system, the value of labour, the nature of profit, social justice and related matters. This kind of discussion was greatly stimulated by the writings of Robert Owen, and in particular by his *Report to the County of Lanark of a plan for relieving public distress and removing discontent*, published in Glasgow in 1821. This famous work included a plan for the setting up of equitable labour exchanges, that is to say, places where goods could be exchanged (in Owen's words) "in the only equitable manner in which men can mutually dispose of their property, viz, its value in labour without the intervention of money". Since Owen was later to open two equitable labour exchanges in London, and one in Birmingham, the early history of the co-operative movement tends to be centred on Owen's ideas and activities. This can be somewhat misleading, and for more than one reason.

In the first place, Owen was by no means original in writing about the valuing of goods in terms of the amount of labour used in manufacturing them: the labour theory of value had been discussed in previous centuries by Thomas Hobbes, John Locke and Adam Smith. In Owen's own time, it had been explored by Thomas Spence, Thomas Hodgskin, and David Ricardo, the famous economist. What was new, it seems, was Owen's plan to price goods by labour notes instead of conventional currency. Secondly, Owen was not at first an advocate of "mere buying and selling" (as he put it), but was more interested in the setting up of communities on the land of both middle-class and working-class settlers. As pointed out in an earlier chapter, although often described as a socialist, and indeed sympathetic to the working classes, Owen is better described as a communitarian.

The 1820s were to see at least two Owenite enterprises that owed little or nothing directly to Owen himself. The first was the establishing of a small community of journeymen printers in Spa Fields, London in 1821 by George Mudie (it has been claimed that he was virtually the first Owenite). According to Mudie, this community lasted two years, and consisted of 21 families. Much more is known of a larger-scale undertaking at Orbiston, near Motherwell in Lanarkshire. Here the leading figures were A. J. Hamilton (son of General Hamilton), and Abram Combe, a well-off Edinburgh leather manufacturer. The settlement cost £19,995, and was housed in an impressively large building near the river Calder, which included a kitchen, bakehouse, library, drawing room, lecture room and dining rooms – the food was to be brought up from below "by means of a machine called an Elevator"; and shoes and clothes were all to be cleaned by machinery. The building was planned on a grand scale to accommodate 200 families, the first applicants being mostly weavers from Hamilton, but work was available for masons, sawyers, joiners, tailors, shoemakers, leather workers and agricultural workers. Later, printers and bookbinders were recruited, and an iron company and even an agricultural company were formed. The community opened in 1825, and by September 1826 it numbered nearly 300 settlers, divided into squads of 10–20 families each.

By mid-1827 the settlement seemed to be doing well. In July of that year, there were still 298 members, and a theatre was opened, with 300 seats. However, there was a shortage of ready money, and some problems with pilfering, and when Combe died in August 1827 it spelt the end of the enterprise. For a time it had seemed moderately successful, although the main building had to be finished off by the settlers themselves as the builders abandoned the site in April 1826. The whole project lacked clear direction, and Combe was inexperienced as an organizer; but the major problem was certainly lack of ready funds. Owen himself appears to have been unaware of the existence of Orbiston until some months after it had opened. He subsequently blamed its failure on the lack of principles he considered necessary in running a community, that is to say, principles laid down by himself.

Be this as it may, co-operative enterprises of a varied nature sprang up in the second half of the 1820s, from 1824 onwards when Owen was out of the country in America. In that year he left England to found a community named "New Harmony" in Indiana in the United States, and apart from a brief return in 1827, he was away from his native country till 1829. During this time, a number of trading societies were set up, some for simple retailing, others for handicraft manufacture, most of them aiming to use their profits ultimately for the purchase of land and the founding of communities. The first of these trading groups seem to have been the Union Exchange Society, 1827 run by a London umbrella maker, William King, in a room hired from the London Co-operative Society. In the same year, Dr William King of Brighton started a co-operative group, and wrote and published a monthly journal, *The Co-operator*, between 1828 and 1830. Unlike Owen at this stage, Dr King was a believer in trading, followed by manufacturing, when funds allowed it:

> What shall we do with our own surplus capital? The answer will be – employ one of your own members in manufacturing shoes, or clothes, etc., etc., for the rest; pay him the usual wages and give the profits to the common capital.

Thus, although at this time Owen's beliefs appear to have centred exclusively on communitarianism, many of his followers believed that the way to finance community building was through trading and the accumulation of capital to support it. Owen himself remained committed to the idea of community settlements, although his estimates of the cost of setting up a community were hardly encouraging – he quoted various figures, up to as much as £240,000.

In January 1828 the London Co-operative Society opened its own store in Red Lion Square, and further pioneering stores were established in Birmingham, Belper, Hastings, Oxford, and Poole between

1828 and 1829. According to Mrs Fletcher, there was "a dramatic countrywide interest" in co-operative manufacturing in 1829, and wholesale depots were planned in London, Liverpool and Manchester. By April 1830, if we are to believe *The Co-operator*, there were as many as 42 co-operative stores in London alone, all but three involved in trading, and mostly aiming to raise capital for communities. Of the ten societies in Manchester and Salford, two had also decided to share out their profits as dividends, although this idea was opposed by the Birmingham Society. Meanwhile, two equitable labour exchanges had been set up in the United States in 1827 and 1828, one in Cincinnati, and one in Philadelphia; a third was established in Paris in 1829.

When Owen returned from New Harmony, he was to find a very lively co-operative movement in being, mostly emphasizing trading activities, but with the long-term objective of setting up communities (naturally, this was assumed to be an expensive business, involving the purchase of land, given Owen's estimates). Various guesses have been made of the number of societies of all kinds in existence at this time – they are often said to number as many as 500, with a membership of at least 20,000 in all. Many of these societies were Owenite in conception, that is, they aimed to found communities along Owenite lines, but they were all going their own individual way, lacking the guiding hand of Owen himself. Already the Glasgow Co-operative Society, 1830–31, was claiming to use labour notes, while notes of this kind were certainly in use in the co-operative community at Ralahine in Ireland in 1831. So, whatever Robert Owen thought about "mere buying and selling", it seems that he was obliged to take action on his return to England in 1829 in order (as Mrs Fletcher puts it) to regain control of an idea that had got out of hand. The result was the setting up of the famous equitable labour exchanges in London and Birmingham in 1832 and 1833.

Yet even here, Owen was not personally a pioneer, breaking new ground; his exchanges were not the first of their kind to be established in London. They were preceded in 1832 by four separate Owenite exchanges: in Poland Street; in New Road, Marylebone (the Gothic Hall); in Red Lion Square and in Westminster Road. All these exchanges were open before Owen's National Equitable Labour Exchange began business in August 1832 in the Gray's Inn Road. A second exchange was opened by Owen in London in December 1832

– the First Metropolitan Branch at the Rotunda, Blackfriars. Owen was at first fortunate in that the spacious premises in the Gray's Inn Road were offered to him originally rent-free; but after a dispute with the landlord, he was forced to move the exchange temporarily to the Blackfriars branch, then later to rather smaller but adequate premises in Charlotte Street. Meanwhile, preparations went ahead for the opening of the Birmingham exchange, and in July, 1833 the First Provincial Branch opened its doors in Coach Yard, Bull Street, Birmingham. At this point, therefore, Owen had three equitable labour exchanges in which to demonstrate the viability of his schemes.

The basic principle on which all three exchanges worked (as did the other, independent exchanges) was clearly expressed by William King, the founder of the Independent Exchange Bazaar at the Gothic Hall, Marylebone:

> A person carries the produce of his industry and skill to the Bazaar, say that he is a shoemaker, we will suppose that he takes six pairs of shoes; parties who understand the value of the article inspect it, and the number of hours labour, which have been consumed in the making of these shoes is decided upon; he then receives a labour note for that number of hours . . . if he wants nothing which is in the Bazaar he puts the note in his pocket, if he does, he takes it, and receives the product of so many hours of another man.

This was the simple theory on which equitable exchange was based. Of course, the value of the raw materials had also to be taken into account, and at first this was expressed in cash terms, although later it was converted into a figure of labour time-value, based on sixpence as the worth of an hour's labour. Each exchange had an elaborate system of paperwork to assist in the valuation of incoming goods, to keep a check on the stock, and to issue the labour notes themselves, which were intended to be used over and over again. Each exchange also had an impressive array of administrative officers – a governor, directors, and a council of shareholders. Depositors at the National Exchange had to be of good character, and pay a shilling per quarter in advance.

How far then can Owen's exchanges really be considered examples of working-class self-help? In fact, their establishment was very much based on middle-class effort, and so was their day-to-day running.

Owen made no bones about his need for and use of middle-class assistance. In Birmingham, for example, he was anxious to gain the support of well-known local business men, and in his newspaper *The Crisis* referred to:

> the Attwoods, the Scholefields, the Muntzs, the Jones and many others, who have been long labouring in the public vineyard.

At least 12 of the 17 members of the Birmingham organizing committee were members of the Birmingham Political Union, which had been a major pressure group in securing the passing of the 1832 Reform Act. They included such leading figures as George Edmonds (solicitor), W. Hawkes Smith (manager of a foundry), G. F. Muntz (a very wealthy foundry owner) and William Pare (a tobacconist, later manufacturer, and strong supporter of co-operation).

As for the participation of working people in the running of the exchanges, it seems that in spite of Owen's desire to help the working classes, he never intended to use their talents in the administration of the exchanges. His approach was essentially paternalistic, and often autocratic. He really had no great faith in working-class ability to organize, in spite of his involvement in 1834 with the trade union movement. In October 1835 he wrote in his publication *The New Moral World*:

> The working classes never did direct any permanently successful operations . . . whenever working classes have attempted any complicated, important measure that required unity, patience, & perseverance to bring it to a successful issue, they have failed in every instance as soon as they have taken the direction of it.

Perhaps Owen was still smarting from the collapse of the GNCTU when he wrote this, but he certainly did not believe in active, working-class management of the exchanges. This is so much so that in July 1833 there was something like a revolt among the depositors and noteholders of the Charlotte Street Exchange who took over the running of the exchange for the remainder of its brief life. Most of the organizers in both the London and the Birmingham exchanges were comfortably-off manufacturers, retailers and gentlemen, together with a few master craftsmen (the noteholders who assumed control of the National Exchange in July 1833 called them "our more opulent friends").

What then of the users of the exchanges? They numbered about 800 in Charlotte Street, and about 746 in Birmingham. Very largely they consisted of journeymen and not of masters. In London, there were many specialist, expensive trades, and the goods brought in reflected this fact. In Birmingham, there was a preponderance of metal manufactures, and a good half of the depositors worked in these trades and supplied metal goods. In fact, Robert Owen had specified the kind of goods necessary to make the exchanges a success, and they included a very wide variety of products, including (most important) foodstuffs. Many goods of different types were essential if depositors were to be able to rely exclusively on the exchanges for their household needs. Obviously enough, workmen without manufacturing skills were not drawn to the exchanges, while ordinary labourers were largely excluded, in spite of the often-expressed, vague, general aim of helping the unemployed poor.

The story of the failure and collapse of Owen's equitable exchanges is well known. The whole system of labour notes was beset with difficulties from the beginning. At first it was proposed to pay staff in labour notes, but the very limited range of goods deposited made this impossible to implement, so that they were then paid at a flat rate of 25s a week. In fact, there was a continual shortage of cash, which had serious repercussions when it came to paying both wages and the rent. Then again, valuation of goods presented major problems: if goods were undervalued by comparison with market prices, they were in demand and soon exchanged. If they were overvalued, they simply remained on the shelves, which in time became full of unwanted goods. The method of valuation took no account of the state of the market, nor of the laws of supply and demand and their effect on price. Another major problem has already been touched on – the shortage of foodstuffs was acute in the exchanges, which were remote from agricultural areas. In any case, such foodstuffs as were deposited could very quickly deteriorate and become useless for exchange. Housewives therefore found shopping at the exchanges far too restrictive. Then there were workers who were put off by Owen's indifference to forms of government, whether democratic, monarchical or despotic, and by his known rejection of conventional religious belief. At the third Co-operative Congress, held in London in April 1832 a resolution was passed with the following significant wording:

> Whereas the co-operative world contains persons of every religious sect and of every political party, it is resolved that co-operators as such, jointly and severally, are not pledged to any political, religious, or irreligious tenets whatsoever; neither those of Mr Owen, nor of any other individual.

Owen's views certainly antagonized some potential supporters, but were not a major reason for the failure of the exchanges. The main causes of failure were rather the difficulties over valuation, and the limited range of goods on offer, especially the shortage of foodstuffs. Equitable exchange might have had a better chance of working had some sort of national network of exchanges come into being, as indeed Owen had hoped, with a much wider variety of goods on offer; but this never came about. Faced with the powerful competition of the retailers of London and Birmingham the exchanges had little chance of surviving. Significantly, only the small, closed agricultural community at Ralahine in Ireland was moderately successful, until it was brought to ruin by the gambling habits of its founder, John Vandeleur.

We return to the question of how far Owen's equitable labour exchanges can be viewed as examples of working-class self-help. The awkward fact is that although workers' co-operation is always thought to be an important aspect of working-class self-help, Owen's exchanges were not only a failure but were not set up or run by the working classes. They were certainly intended to help the working classes, but were essentially paternalistic in nature, conforming with Owen's beliefs in co-operation between the classes, with the middle class taking the lead. Indeed, it might even be argued that Owen did harm to the cause of co-operation by his insistence on his own idiosyncratic approach to the problem of labour valuation, and by the sheer impracticality of his schemes. This might seem a rather severe judgement, but it could be that the successful growth of retail co-operation that began in the 1840s might perhaps have begun sooner if the labour exchanges had not proved an abortive experiment and something of a false start. In fact, Robert Owen's heart was in his community settlements, rather than in co-operative trading or "mere buying and selling", and subsequently he was to start another community project at Queenswood in Hampshire in 1839.

This was based on a substantial estate of more than 700 acres, leased to the Owenites by a supporter, Isaac Lyon Goldsmid, who was an admirer of Owen's educational methods. It was the sole official community enterprise of the Owenites, and was subject to detailed rules, one of the most important being that the land was to be held as common property; the host of minor rules included the requirement that there should be uniformity of dress and furniture, "consistent with utility". The trustees took possession in October 1839 but it was not until August 1841 that the foundation stone of the main building, Harmony Hall, was laid. By 1842, £15,000 had been spent on it. The building was well-equipped, with piped water, kitchen, dining room, offices, library, lecture rooms, and individual bedrooms (there were refinements characteristic of the aristocratic households of the time, such as a miniature railway for conveying meals from the kitchen).

Financial support came from the main Owenite body, the Rational Society, and from an associated body, the Home Colonisation Society, set up in 1840. Numbers in the community varied from time to time; starting with 57 residents, they were down to only 12 adults and seven children in August 1840, but by May 1843 there were 45 adults and 25 children, 720 acres were under cultivation, and a number of handicrafts were being carried on. The school that had been started had 61 pupils, 35 of them fee paying, under a headmaster, Dr Oestreicher. Evening classes were held, including classes in drawing, music, geography, grammar and elocution, and dancing (dancing was a popular educational activity of the time; a female ex-employee of Robert Owen's at New Lanark claimed in 1833 that the dancing there was more exhausting than the actual work).

The existence of this community, sometimes called "socialist" and sometimes "communist", did not go unnoticed by opponents of Owenism. Virulent attacks were launched against it in the rightwing journals of the day. In 1840, the *Quarterly Review* claimed that:

> Every foul sink of doctrine which has been opened of late years in this country, all run together into this grand cloaca of Owenism. The present is a sewer drained off from the lucubrations of Benthamites.

One might think this was a bit hard on the Benthamites. This journal bitterly opposed what was termed Owen's atheism, and the spreading of his pernicious beliefs. One early victim of this hostility was William Pare, the Birmingham supporter of the equitable labour exchange in that town, who served for some years as governor at Queenswood, selling £500 worth of his railway shares to help finance the project before removing himself and family to Queenswood in 1844. Pare, perhaps the most active of the Birmingham reformers after Thomas Attwood, was forced by a campaign led by the Bishop of Exeter to resign from his post of Registrar of Births and Marriages in Birmingham on the general grounds that he was a socialist.

However, the community was not without its sympathizers, and gifts were sent to them from supporters all over the country. Furthermore, good relations seem to have been maintained with the local inhabitants including, surprisingly enough, some of the local clergy. The real problems of the settlement were to do with the lack of any forward planning of either agricultural or handicraft production, and above all, with the failure to provide any real financial budgeting. By far the largest source of income was the sale of agricultural produce. Against this had to be set such items of expenditure as rent, tithes, poor rate, window tax, insurance and, greatest of all, the purchase of food. Loans from the two Owenite parent bodies – the Rational Society and the Home Colonisation Society – were soon swallowed up. Financial difficulties were experienced from the very beginning. This was in spite of the fact that the members of the community, who in theory held all the property of the settlement in common, in practice were working for nothing except pocket money of a shilling a week. A further expense was the need to hire local agricultural labour, for this proved cheaper than using the labour of many of the community members who were artisans and unused to farm work.

The result of these financial problems was a declining standard of living for the community. Repeated economies were made in housekeeping expenditure. Skilled workmen found themselves living at or even below the standard of an agricultural labourer (it is remarkable that many of them stuck it out for so long – a tribute, perhaps, to their idealism). Meals became increasingly frugal in 1844, by which time vegetarianism had been adopted by some members. A visitor from another settlement, the Ham Common Concordium, noted that members were providing their own tea and coffee, the latter being known as "community mocha", made from wheat grain. The visitor remarked sympathetically that if the coffee "had not the exquisite fla-vour of the Arabian bean, yet I can assure my readers that to an indi-vidual devoted to the success of this place, a cup of Community Mocha is a pleasant beverage". A working-class writer commented in 1861 that the Queenswood settlement was "an attempt to convert skilled artisans, used to good wages, into agriculturists upon bad land; and to satisfy them with agricultural labourers' fare, and no money wages". This appears to be a fair if unsparing description of the real situation – something very different from the New Moral World en-visaged by Robert Owen.

By 1845 it was clear that a crisis point had been reached. It is not easy to discover precisely the extent of indebtedness reached by the community at this time, but there was certainly a heavy accumulation of debt – loans alone amounted to £24,496. The overall picture was that whereas the estimated value of the property was £25,676, liabili-ties were £39,915, the deficit thus being £14,239. It was decided to put Harmony Hall up for sale, but proceedings for its disposal proved lengthy and protracted. In June 1846 the premises were at last com-pletely evacuated and closed up. In March 1847 Harmony Hall was leased to a Quaker schoolmaster, and was renamed Queenswood Col-lege, later to become one of the most distinguished educational estab-lishments of the nineteenth century.

What can be said finally about the Queenswood venture? In the first place, it was bound to be an expensive undertaking, and it was there-fore vital that its development be planned carefully with due regard to the selection of settlers, and the marketing of products, agricultural or otherwise. All this was conspicuously absent, and the hard-earned savings of many working men, contributed to branches of the Rational Society, were all lost. This also applies to middle-class sup-porters who were also out of pocket. It was as if there was a naive, optimistic belief that somehow all would turn out for the best, given good will and the right community spirit. The harsh reality was otherwise.

Secondly, credit must be given to all those who took part in the experiment to put Owenite notions of community into practice. At a time when the new industrial society was still developing, it must have seemed not impossible to form a community based on mutual co-operation and respect in contrast to the relationships of the new industrial towns. Many of those who participated were certainly idealistic, and it must be remembered that the late 1830s and early 1840s were years of social ferment and of great reform movements – for example, Chartism, the Ten Hours Movement and the Anti-Corn Law League. Indeed, these may have drawn off some support that otherwise might have gone into the communitarian movement. However, the point is worth making that at the time, the founding of a settlement based on Owenite ideas did not seem as foolhardy and unrealistic as it might appear later in the century.

This brings us to a third point, the role of Robert Owen in the story of the Queenswood community. It is difficult to know how to sum this up. Owen was still a great hero, a leader to be followed by the working classes. In his history of co-operation, George Holyoake quotes one of the numerous acrostics based on Owen's name. It was written by one Mary Leman Grimstone:

O mnipotent benevolence, this is thy holy reign:
W oe, want, crime, vice and ignorance shall fall before thy fame;
E re long o'er all the gladd'nd earth shall thy full blaze be glowing,
N or leave a spot that shall not hear and bless the name of
OWEN!

Owen was undoubtedly much admired by working people, and had his supporters (as well as detractors) among the other classes. The prime minister, Lord Melbourne, even presented Owen to the newly-enthroned Queen Victoria (it seems that afterwards Melbourne thought this to have been a mistake). Yet Robert Owen contributed little to the running of Queenswood. In fact, as early as October 1839 he resigned as governor, complaining that the community was ill-conceived and premature. Subsequently he resumed office as nominal governor, only to resign again in July 1842. William Pare did more than Robert Owen in a practical sense as acting governor of the community between 1842 and 1844 (quite apart from lending £500, and bringing his family to live in Harmony Hall, as previously mentioned). All Owen's business acumen and powers of organization, so evident in New Lanark, seem to have deserted him. He really was of little practical use either in policy or in the detailed administration of Queenswood. In fact, in financial matters he was often wildly unrealistic, and when things went wrong he would claim that he was not responsible for the mistakes of others. Extraordinary as it might seem, according to a report in his own paper, *The New Moral World*, in 1840 in Nottingham, Owen denied that the Gray's Inn Labour Exchange was "of his contrivance", and when asked whether New Harmony was an attempt to carry out his principles, he answered, "My principles have never been carried out". To put it mildly, Owen was never an enthusiast for the Queenswood adventure, and it is little thanks to him that it survived as long as it did.

However, co-operation did not die out completely after the failure of the exchanges and of Queenswood. It is true that most of the other equitable labour exchanges (which Owen described as "evil" because they threatened to fragment the movement), faded out after a short while. For example, the Gothic Hall co-operative was wound up in July 1833 while the Ralahine settlement closed down in the following November. But not all disappeared immediately. Moreover, the independent exchanges appear to have been run by committees of ordinary working men, and were more democratic in nature, and rather more representative of working-class self-help than Owen's exchanges. Co-operative congresses also continued to be held – the first was in Manchester in 1831, the seventh meeting in Barnsley in 1834, and the eighth and last in Halifax in 1835. From time to time, short-lived co-operative enterprises were set up by workers thrown out of employment or on strike. Little trace remains of their organization or activities.

After the last of the early co-operative congresses had been held in 1835, Owen himself held annual conferences of his own followers from 1835 to 1846, and these led to the creation of the Owenite supporting bodies mentioned in connection with Queenswood. At the first of Owen's conferences, that of 1835, a new body was set up, The Association of All Classes of All Nations. In 1837 another organization was founded, The National Community Friendly Society. The country was divided into districts, each under a Social Missionary. In the following year, these two bodies merged into the Universal Community Society of Rational Religionists (from 1843 known simply as the Rational Society). In 1840, yet another society was established, the Home Colonisation Society, formed specifically to found community settlements. For a time, the term "rational religionists" was used of Owenites, although from 1841 onwards, they often took the name of "socialists", a word loaded at the time with derogatory implications.

These various bodies served as a means of organizing propaganda

197

for Owenite ideas. Branches of the Rational Society were set up. According to the Bishop of Exeter in 1840, there were 60 branches, operating in 14 districts, with missionaries lecturing in 350 towns, supported by the weekly *New Moral World* and the issue of half a million tracts a year. These large claims were more or less confirmed by the *New Moral World* in April 1842, which listed branches with so-called "halls of science" in numerous large towns, and "social institutions" in other towns, having accommodation in all for 21,000 people. Thirteen branches were registered as places of worship, nine ran day schools, and there were also twelve Sunday schools. Meetings were held frequently, both on Sundays and also monthly or quarterly, and festivals were also held.

All this looks impressive enough on paper, and it is true that the branches did provide valuable financial support for Queenswood. What is unclear is how far these branches, which were basically propaganda bodies, also carried on any form of co-operative trading. In Huddersfield, where there was a branch, there was also a large-scale grocery store, but this seems to have been exceptional. A contemporary, G. A. Fleming, writing in 1842, seemed to think that there were still a few co-operative societies in existence, but that except for the Huddersfield store, "their condition is anything but satisfactory". According to Holyoake, a few years previously in 1836, there were still six or seven co-operative societies in Carlisle, but Owen criticized them, remarking that although they were doing well, "as they think, making some profit from joint-stock retailing", this was *not* the social system of the *New Moral World*. Holyoake also comments that traces of co-operative societies become fewer and fewer in the pages of the *New Moral World* about this time. Dr King of Brighton, however, maintained some sort of exchange from 1835 to 1839, and in the latter year started the Independent Exchange Bazaar, followed by the London Bank of Industry in 1844, but these appear to be isolated examples. On the whole, it seems that co-operative trading was at a low ebb after the failures of the equitable labour exchanges and the Queenswood community.

It is interesting to consider just why Owenite ideas should have become so popular in the years following the end of the wars against France in 1815. It is necessary to recall that this was not only a time of great economic and social change, it was an age still experiencing the aftermath of French Revolutionary thought, which encouraged belief that all things could be made anew. It was not illogical to believe that fresh beginnings could be attempted in small communities based on more egalitarian principles, especially in the New World of the Americas. In the UK, Orbiston, Ralahine and Queenswood were not the only Utopian communities to come into existence. Other examples are the Manea Fen colony of about fifty settlers, set up in East Anglia in 1838, which lasted about a year. The Hanwell Commitorium, founded by Goodwyn Barmby near London, had a brief existence in 1843. The Leeds Redemption Society, established in 1846, had a full-blooded socialist programme and founded a settlement in South Wales in 1847 (there were also sister societies in Bury, Norwich and Stockport, and seven branches in all). The First Concordium community was founded on Ham Common near Richmond Park in 1841 – it was visited by Robert Owen in 1843 – while as many as five Chartist land communities were set up by Feargus O'Connor, the Chartist leader. Most of these communities were founded by men and women with strongly-held beliefs, often of an idealistic nature, and inclined to temperance and vegetarianism. George Holyoake, himself a life-long radical, wrote satirically of the First Concordium:

> The inmates were scrupulously clean, temperate, transcendental, offensive to anyone who ate meat, attached to Quakers, especially white ones, repudiated even salt and tea, as stimulants, and thought most of those guests who ate their cabbage uncooked. They preached abstinence from marriage, and most things else. Their cardinal principle was that happiness was wrong...

Evidently Holyoake could not take the Ham Common community very seriously, but its existence, and that of others, shows that community life had an appeal for those earnest seekers after a juster form of society, in which the labour of each man and woman received its proper reward.

Against this background, Owen's plans had their attraction, especially as they had middle-class support, and were based on class collaboration rather than class confrontation. As we have seen, funds were subscribed by both middle-class and working-class supporters. Moreover, Owen had a proven record as a benevolent employer, providing good working conditions and accommodation, and a school with progressive ideas. His community plans did not seem especially unrealistic or extreme, nor was his vision necessarily backwards-looking; he was not opposed to the use of machinery, although admittedly, funds were never available to permit it to replace the handicraft trades at Harmony Hall. It must also be said that he was a good, persuasive speaker, and personally kind and courteous to all who met him. Unfortunately, however convincing his ideas on paper, any settlement on the land inevitably cost a great deal of money, and this led to problems that were never solved. It was strange that in spite of his highly successful career as manager and joint proprietor at New Lanark, he seemed incapable of solving the practical difficulties that arose at Queenswood. It was as if once he had explained his theories to others, it was up to them to carry them out. If problems arose, that was their concern, and not his. As was remarked before, Owen was quite useless as a working administrator at Harmony Hall, and more of a hindrance than a help. It may be, of course, that by this time of his life he was growing old and impatient with the details.

To conclude, for any reader new to the subject of co-operation before the Rochdale pioneers, the story of the co-operative movement before 1844 may come as something of a surprise. It is not simply an account of efforts to promote retail trading of the kind that became famous after 1844. It was much more than this, as we have seen, and it emphasized strongly the importance of community, moreover of community life based on the common ownership of property. However, although this sounds socialistic in the modern sense, this could be misunderstood; Owen did not believe in the class struggle, indeed he believed in the necessity of class co-operation. Although he had sympathy for the plight of the working classes in an England being transformed by the Industrial Revolution, he certainly did not think the workers should rise up and take over the means of production, distribution and exchange. His lack of faith in the working classes being able to organize anything themselves was rooted in his strong belief that man was formed by his environment. Environment was all. Working people grew up having no experience of the direction of affairs, so how could they successfully take charge of any organization? That was the responsibility of the middle classes. Moreover, Owen was indifferent to forms of government, and at times even expressed hostility to democracy. So although a fresh start was necessary in society, it must take the form of communities based on co-operation between middle-class leaders and working-class men and women. He had no scruples, of course, about appealing for financial aid from middle-class supporters. This kind of co-operation was very different from the doctrines propounded by Marx and Engels in the *Communist Manifesto* in 1848, which envisaged a very different form of communism.

Robert Owen died in 1858, aged 87. His influence over the early years of the co-operative movement was immense, although it can be argued that it was not always a beneficial influence. It is true that he gave the working classes some hope for a better future, but it cannot be said that he was very active in encouraging self-help. Without faith in working-class initiative, his attitude towards the working classes was highly paternalistic, if not autocratic, the result presumably of his experiences at New Lanark. As we have seen, the equitable labour exchanges were almost forced on him by the success of the co-operative retailing establishments of the time, and even then, the organization of the exchanges was placed deliberately in middle-class hands. It may be that better examples of working-class self-help are provided by the work of such pioneers as Dr William King of Brighton and William King of London whose retailing establishments seem to have given greater scope for working-class participation. Their efforts were on a small scale, and the great days of co-operative trading were still in the future, but they provided precedents for later developments. In the second half of the 1840s, co-operative retail trading, based upon local self-help in Rochdale, really took off to grow into a great national enterprise. It has already been suggested that this might have happened earlier if Owen had remained in America, and had not returned to lead so obstinately in the wrong direction; but this admittedly is to pose unanswerable questions. The fact is that the modern history of the co-operative movement based directly on working-class self-help really begins in 1844. What happened before might perhaps be termed a kind of idealistic exploration of the possibilities of community life; what happened afterwards was a more successful and more realistic venture into retail trading and later into manufacturing.

Chapter Ten

Rochdale and after:
the Modern Movement

It often used to be said that the old style co-operation was virtually dead in the mid-1840s. George Holyoake's words are sometimes quoted in this connection to justify this view: "Thus it befell Co-operation, which after 30 years of valorous vicissitudes, died, or seemed to die, in 1844–5". Holyoake followed up this assertion in an extended and colourful passage in his *History of co-operation*, the second volume of which was published in 1879:

> The little armies on the once militant plain of social progress had been one after another defeated and disbanded. The standards, which had been carried defiantly over the agitated field with some daring and loud acclaim, had fallen one by one; and in many cases the standard bearers had fallen by their side. For a few years to come no movement is anywhere observable . . . The very air is cold and thick over the blank and desolate scene.

So it might have seemed to Holyoake, but although the failure of Queenswood was a blow to the co-operative movement, it had by no means entirely died out in the mid-1840s. The map showing the existence of co-operative societies, which G. D. H. Cole provided in his *A century of co-operation* (1945) to illustrate the position in England and Scotland before 1844, shows well over a hundred societies. Many of these had passed out of existence by 1844, of course, but a number still traded here and there, and the idea of co-operation still had a powerful influence, witness the founding of the Rochdale Pioneers Society itself in 1844, of the Leeds Redemption Society in 1846, and of the Christian Socialist Movement with their producers' co-operative societies beginning in 1848. More recent research suggests that the number of general retailing societies in the ten years before 1844 amounted to more than 120, with another 25 specialized stores supplying coal, bread, flour and manufactured goods. The Huddersfield Trading Society had nearly 500 members in 1840. These stores were located mainly in the West Riding, southeast Lancashire, and in Northumberland and Durham. What was noticeably missing before 1844 was anything like a national movement. This was to be the achievement of the Rochdale Pioneers, although it was hardly their avowed aim in 1844. In fact, although Holyoake went on to describe Rochdale as a "grim, despairing, sloppy hole of a town" (admitting in a footnote that it had improved since 1844), in reality it was normally a brisk, busy textile town, known for its political liveliness. Its branch of the Rational Society, No. 24, was established in 1837, and it had a programme of lectures, debates, and dancing. It sent financial support to the Queenswood settlement, one individual contribution amounting to £20, and another to £21. There had also been an earlier co-operative shop, which traded from 1833 to 1835. The setting-up of another co-operative enterprise was therefore not unexpected, although it is still not clear whether the failure of a local weavers' strike and the intention to start a producers' co-operative contributed to this. Certainly the aims of the new society were of the traditional kind. They included the setting up of a store, the provision of houses for members, the manufacture of articles by unemployed members, the purchase or renting of land, the establishment of a self-supporting home colony, and the setting-up of a temperance hotel. Here then was the possibility of a new Queenswood in the making – yet another society aiming at the creation of a co-operative community.

The rules of the society are of particular interest: they provided for a democratic form of organization, with a president, treasurer, secretary, three trustees and five directors, to be elected annually by the members (there were 34 subscribers originally, including four arbitrators, of whom 15 were Owenite socialists, and ten were weavers). Two rules are of especial significance. Rule 21 states:

> The officers of this society shall not in any case, nor on any pretence, purchase any articles except for ready money, neither shall they be allowed to sell any article or articles except for ready money. Any officer acting contrary to this law shall be fined in the

sum of ten shillings, and be disqualified from performing the duties of such office.

Rule 22 then deals with the distribution of profits:

> Interest at the rate of 3½ per cent per annum shall be paid upon all shares . . . the remaining profits shall be paid to each member in proportion to the amount of money expended at the store.

Curiously enough, the original rules contain no mention of principles afterwards considered fundamental to the Rochdale Society – the provision of pure food, true weight and political and religious neutrality. Starting capital amounted to £28, raised by weekly subscriptions, and the store began business (evenings only at first) on 21 December 1844 at its premises at 31, Toad Lane, Rochdale. Its opening stock consisted of 28 lb of butter, 56 lb of sugar, 6 cwt of flour, a sack of oatmeal, and some candles, worth £16 11s 11d in all.

There is no need to labour the significance of this beginning of the modern co-operative movement, although the view has been put forward recently that Rochdale was really part of the continuous history of an existing co-operative system, rather than a new beginning. This is one way of looking at it, of course. It is certainly true that the Rochdale Pioneers did not aim at the creation of a national retail organization. They did not reject the original Owenite notion of communitarianism – far from it. It was one of their basic objectives. Nor was there anything original in the paying of a dividend on purchases – we have seen that this was common enough before – or in the aim of keeping to cash transactions. What seems to account for the subsequent extraordinary success of the Rochdale Society is partly the business-like nature of their organization, and partly the up-turn in the economy in the second half of the 1840s and in the 1850s. No doubt the dividend on purchases and the banning of credit played a part, as did the provision of pure food and true weight – features of Rochdale practices all praised afterwards by historians of the movement. At a time when foodstuffs were frequently adulterated and false weight was common, the Rochdale shop and its imitators provided a valuable service, while the dividend was a useful form of working-class savings, made more secure by the insistence on cash transactions. Nevertheless, it was the growing prosperity of the skilled working classes at the mid-century that allowed the increased trading of the retail movement, and the nationwide success that followed. In theory, this should have led to the creation of numerous self-supporting communities. In practice, it was otherwise. This did not go unremarked at the time, but it was left to others, especially the Christian Socialists, to try yet again to set up producer co-operatives.

As for the Rochdale Society, progress was slow at first. At the end of the first year's trading, there were still only 74 members, sales amounted to £710, and profits to £22. It could be that the failure of the Rochdale Savings Bank in 1849 encouraged working-class savers to put their savings into the co-op. At all events, there was substantial growth in the years 1848–50. Membership rose from 140 to 600, trade from £2,276 to £13,180, and profits to £991. A butchery department was begun in 1846, drapery in 1847, and tailoring in 1849. Meanwhile, a newsroom was opened in 1848, and an old corn mill acquired in 1850. The 1850s saw further progress. It is said that by 1851 there were at least 130 societies in existence similar in nature to the Rochdale Society, which opened its first branch in 1856, and another in 1859. Boots and shoes were sold from 1852 onwards, and in 1853 the subscription to the newsroom and library was abolished, their financing in future being provided by a 2.5 per cent grant out of profits (afterwards known as the educational grant). In 1854, the Rochdale Co-operative Manufacturing Society was established – at last a venture into co-operative production. Rented premises were acquired, and 96 power looms were installed. The society's own mill was erected later. Workers were to be given a bounty or share of profits, based on their earnings, but the idea was unpopular with shareholders, who eventually succeeded in abolishing it in 1862. From then on the company became a simple joint-stock company, so that this really ended the Rochdale experiment in producers' co-operation.

Meanwhile, as indicated earlier, further efforts were made to set up producers' co-operative societies by the Christian Socialists. The leaders of this group were of the middle class, and eminent in other spheres: J. M. Ludlow, who became Registrar of Friendly Societies in 1872; Thomas Hughes, author of *Tom Brown's schooldays*; Charles Kingsley, author of *Hereward the Wake*, *Westward Ho!*, and *The water babies*; and Frederick Maurice, Professor of Theology at King's College London, later dismissed for his heterodox views. These men believed in co-operation as a practical example of Christian brother-hood. In their own words:

> that the remedy for the evils of competition lies in the brotherly and Christian principle of co-operation – that is, of joint work with shared or common profits; and that this principle might be widely and readily applied in the formation of Tailors' Working Associations.

The reference to the tailoring trade was due to the fact that tailoring in London was a notoriously sweated trade. In 1850, therefore, the Christian Socialists set up the Working Tailors' Association, which opened a co-operative workshop in Oxford Street. After a successful start, a further organization was established, The Society for Promoting Working Men's Associations. In all, 12 of these associations were set up. Meanwhile, the Leeds Redemption Society was forming similar associations, and Ludlow was impressed by what he saw on a tour of Lancashire and Yorkshire. In 1851 the newly-formed Amalgamated Society of Engineers seemed likely to support the movement for producers' co-operatives – both Allen and Newton were enthusiasts for it – but this support faded away after the depletion of the funds of the ASE in the lock-out of 1852.

For a short time in the early 1850s it seemed that co-operative production had a promising future, based on the increasing prosperity of the time. In fact, all the Christian Socialist ventures had collapsed by 1854, due mostly (according to the Christian Socialists themselves) to a failure to select carefully enough the workers in their associations. Certainly there was disagreement over the distribution of bonuses and profits, but there was more to it than this; criticisms were also made of the rigid middle-class control and financing. As for the provincial societies, they too petered out in the course of time, being faced with much more difficult marketing problems than simple retailing, based for the most part on the supply of foodstuffs. Nevertheless, all was not entirely lost in the cause of producers' co-operatives, as will be seen later, not only in the growth of manufacturing enterprises by the Co-operative Wholesale Society, but also in the co-partnerships and profit-sharing ventures later in the century. However, the fact remains that although for a while it appeared that the Rochdale mode of retailing would be matched by a new burst of producers' co-operatives, the Rochdale type of consumers' co-operatives was soon left in charge of the field.

One last contribution by the Christian Socialists to the cause of co-operation must be noted – their contribution to the law relating to the co-operative movement. Before 1846 there was no separate body of co-operative law, and the Friendly Societies Acts of 1829 and 1834 gave societies little protection. Although they could register under these acts, they could not legally buy land, or trade with non-members, or invest other than in government stock. The 1846 Act did give limited recognition to co-operative societies as well as to friendly societies that had been formed, in the words of the act,

> for the frugal investment of the savings of their members, for better enabling them to purchase food, firing, clothes or other necessities, or the tools or other implements of their trade or calling, or to provide for the education of their children and kindred.

This gave basic trading rights to co-operative enterprises, but they could still not hold personal property except through trustees, and real property had to be conveyed absolutely to such trustees. Furthermore, societies could still trade only with their own members. However, the Christian Socialist leaders were able to have a House of Commons Committee appointed to consider the legal position of co-operative societies, and the favourable report of this committee resulted in the Industrial and Provident Societies Act of 1852. This act greatly improved the legal standing of the societies, but still failed to give them limited liability. This was granted by the Industrial and Provident Societies Act; 1862, which also allowed a society to hold shares in other societies. The way was therefore cleared for a further advance, this time in the direction of co-operative wholesaling.

This was by no means new in itself in the 1860s. A number of attempts had already been made at wholesale organizations in the 1850s, and the Rochdale Society itself had set up a wholesale department in 1851, selling to other co-operative societies, but it had lost money and closed down in 1858. Those who could still see the need for a wholesale society, based on a federation of societies, persisted in putting the case for it, and their arguments were give publicity in the pages of the new monthly periodical, the *Co-operator*. Following conferences in Rochdale and Manchester in 1860, a bill was drafted, and this in due course became the Act of 1862. Another Manchester conference in 1863 led to a society being set up and registered under the name of The North of England Co-operative Wholesale Industrial Provident Society Ltd (the title was understandably shortened later to the Co-operative Wholesale Society, CWS). The initiative for its creation came from a group of societies in southeast Lancashire, especially from Rochdale, Oldham, Manchester and the surrounding towns. This new body started in a relatively small way. In October 1864 its total membership was only 18,000, and its capital only £2,455. Ten years later, membership stood at nearly 200,000, capital was £61,000 plus £193,000 in loans and deposits, and turnover was nearly £2 million. The need for a national system of wholesale purchasing had been amply demonstrated, individual societies becoming members and obtaining dividends on their wholesale purchases just as individual members gained dividends on their own retail purchases. Four years later in 1867, the Co-operative Insurance Company was set up, originally to meet the need to insure the increasing amount of property owned by the movement. In 1868, the Scottish Co-operative Wholesale Society (SCWS) was established, since it was considered that the English CWS in Manchester was at too great a distance to serve the Scottish societies.

It soon became evident that further steps were necessary to construct some form of national organization. As early as July 1865 William Pare, the veteran Birmingham supporter of co-operation, wrote to the *Co-operator*, advocating the setting up of a national organization of societies and the holding of annual congresses. In 1869 a congress attended by 57 societies and nine trade unions, including the ASE, appointed a committee to arrange a congress for the following year. In that year, a separate Lancs and Yorks congress agreed to merge with the main congress, which met in Manchester. At that congress, a Central Board was elected, divided into a London Board and a Provincial Board. Two further annual congresses followed, in 1871 and 1872, and then at the Newcastle conference in 1873, a further reorganization took place.

This took the form of replacing the Provincial Board by five sections representing the Scottish, northern, northwestern and Midland areas, the fifth section being the Southern area, replacing the London Board. These five boards together constituted the Central Board. A committee was also elected, consisting of two representatives from each sectional board (the northwestern had three), which was to meet quarterly. The committee was named the United Board. The new organization became known simply as the Co-operative Union, with offices rented in Corporation Street, Manchester. Meanwhile, the movement had acquired a new mouthpiece, *The Co-operative News*, which began publication in 1871. In 1875, Samuel Bamford became editor, a position he retained until his death in 1898. One historian of the co-operative movement has termed these events "the End of the Beginning", arguing that "powerful idealism ... created the national organizations. This was formed of the currents of Owenism, Christian Socialism, and the practical Co-operation of more ordinary folk ... ". He goes on to argue that many of those who created the national movement were the old idealists, such as William Pare, and that many saw the need to go beyond the narrow confines of self-supporting communities. This may be so, and certainly the whole idea of both the wholesale societies and of the national framework answered the practical needs of the day. Nevertheless, there were still some who must have regretted the abandoning of the concept of self-sufficient communities. William Pare himself was still talking of self-supporting co-operative villages at the 1869 congress, and even spoke of labour notes. As late as 1870 he commented that "if the old co-operators erred in sentiment, certainly the present ones err in the direction of materialism". Self-help had proved highly successful, achieving large-scale organization on a national basis, but older critics no doubt joined Pare in lamenting the loss of idealism.

The 1860s and 1870s were years of continued expansion for retail co-operation, and G. D. H. Cole provides a useful survey of the main areas of growth and activity. In Scotland, new societies were founded in both the Edinburgh and Glasgow areas, and also in Aberdeen, although progress was interrupted by the failure of the Glasgow Society in 1864, which had overreached its resources. Nevertheless, plans went ahead for the creation of the Scottish Co-operative Society in 1868, by which time the movement had begun to recover in Glasgow. In England, Lancashire and the West Riding remained the major areas of growth, but substantial development also took place in the northeast, where the iron and steel industry and shipbuilding were booming. Between 1859 and 1875, 39 societies were founded in Durham, 31 in Northumberland, and 8 in Cleveland, all still in existence in 1912. In the eight East Midland counties, 86 societies came into being in the years 1844–75. The West Midlands, however, were much less active in the 1860s, with only a few scattered societies in Warwickshire, Staffordshire and Worcestershire. Birmingham, once a great centre of Owenite activity, had become a "co-operative desert", and London was not much better. Separate efforts were made in the capital to get wholesaling off the ground – the Metropolitan and Home Counties Purchasing Association lasted in a small way until 1869, while the Central Co-operative Agency, designed to market goods of the kind manufactured by societies, was taken over by the CWS in 1874. Some signs of growth were to be seen in the founding of the Stratford (East London) Society in 1860, and of the Royal Arsenal Co-operative Society in Woolwich in 1868, destined to become one of the very largest of the societies.

Elsewhere, growth was patchy. Around London, except to the east, there was little development, although there was an active group in Berkshire and Oxfordshire. There was a good sprinkling of societies in Essex and Suffolk, but only one society in Norfolk, at Norwich, dating from 1875. In Kent, growth was moderate, while in the West Country, the movement was comparatively strong in Somerset, Wiltshire and Gloucester, but weak in Devon. Wales had been late in coming into the movement, and still had to show much advance. It is said that the mining villages in South Wales were too much dominated by truck, and later on by grocers who were prepared to give credit. Summing up, it seems that as might be expected, retail co-operation progressed most rapidly in Lancashire and the West Riding, and then in other expanding industrial areas such as Glasgow and the northeast, while slower progress was made elsewhere, as in London, the southern agricultural counties, and Wales.

Cole also draws attention to the revival of producers' co-operation in the prosperous decades after 1850 – there were 163 co-operatives of this kind registered under the Industrial and Provident Societies Acts, 1862–1880, and many more registered as joint-stock companies. Of these enterprises, the so-called "Working Class Ltds" deserve a mention. Mostly centred on Oldham, they paid high dividends during the boom of the early 1870s, but were not really co-operatives at all. Another group of ventures consisted of companies with workers as partners, sharing in the profits. There were several companies of this kind in the mining industry. For example, in 1872 co-operative mining enterprises started up in Newcastle, Leeds, Ecceshall and Darwin. A Manchester scheme supported by a number of consumer societies ended in 1882. Other schemes collapsed before this – the Newcastle project, which was designed to become nationwide, ended in 1877, and the Derbyshire and Notts Co-operative Mining Company ran out of capital in 1878. Perhaps the most ambitious scheme of all was in engineering, not in coal mining like so many others. This was the Ouseburn Engineering Works on Tyneside, purchased by local co-op societies in 1871, making marine engines and boilers. At one time the works employed 800, and an industrial bank was started. When the boom of the early 1870s ended, the firm ran into trouble. Faulty management and inadequate financing led to the liquidation of both the company and the bank in 1875. The works were taken over by the CWS, the Halifax Society, and five other co-operative societies, but were finally closed in 1881.

Rather more successful (but not invariably so) were the manufacturing activities undertaken by the CWS, and later by the SCWS. Following the creation of a banking department of the CWS in 1872, the CWS opened its first factory for the manufacture of biscuits in Crumpsall, with another factory for making boots and shoes in Leicester in the same year. In fact, progress in manufacturing by the CWS proved very uneven, and there were a substantial number of failures at first; for example, the CWS lost £8,000 in the Ouseburn affair. However, manufacture of its own brands ensured the production of unadulterated foodstuffs, and of well-made goods, which were an essential part of the service provided for co-op members. Both the CWS and the SCWS therefore persevered with the production of their own brands. The SCWS also had its misadventures, losing £10,427 in the ill-fated Scottish Co-operative Ironworks, but began to make progress with the manufacture of shirts in 1881. Similarly, the CWS extended its manufacturing activities in the 1880s, and especially at the turn of the century. A variety of foodstuffs and goods were provided, including footwear, clothing, bedding and furniture, hardware, brushes, paint, soap and tobacco. The value of CWS productions rose from £133,106 in 1881 to £9,051,646 in 1914, when a workforce of 20,000 was engaged in production. Some of this activity was greeted with hostility by rival shopkeepers, and also by soap manufacturers such as Lever Bros. It must also be remembered that individual societies also manufactured their own lines, and in total their production figures actually exceeded those of the CWS, rising from £4,293,000 in 1900 to

£15,705,000 in 1914.

On the whole, the Great Depression did not affect to any marked degree the progress of the co-operative movement. It is true that unemployment increased at the time, but it affected the unskilled rather than the skilled workmen who constituted the vast majority of co-operative members. Then again, as pointed out in previous chapters, the Great Depression was accompanied by a fall in prices, especially of foodstuffs, and by a significant increase in real wages, so that again the co-operative movement would have benefited as a result of the increase in purchasing power. Giving evidence before a Select Committee on Co-operative Societies, 1878–79, George Holyoake spoke of the advantages enjoyed by the retail societies over their competitors.

> Our ambition is that Co-operation shall signify genuineness in food and honest workmanship in articles of use. We take no fees; we give no commission, we accept no credit; and we permit no debt among our members . . . Then we care for our members; we set apart a portion of the profits for their instruction, because you cannot make co-operators out of the ignorant.

However, as already noted, by the 1890s, opposition was mounting from other retailers. One witness before the Royal Commission on Labour, 1892–94, alleged that co-ops frequently broke their rule of not giving credit, and members under the Rochdale system paid higher prices than in other shops, and sometimes got back only a small proportion of the extra price charged. It was further suggested that private traders would welcome the abolition of the dividend on purchases, and for it to be replaced simply by selling goods at cost plus the cost of distribution – a somewhat odd proposal.

After recording these criticisms, the Final Report of the Royal Commission on Labour provides a good deal of interesting general information about the co-operative movement. For example, the report describes in detail the Rochdale Society. It notes that in 1891, it had 11,647 members, funds of £370,792, sales of £296,025, and made a profit of £36,823. The report goes on:

> Of the net profits, 2½ per cent is appropriated to educational purposes. By this means, the society has instituted a large central

newsroom, and provided 18 branches with libraries, containing an aggregate number of 67,318 volumes, and has organised science, art, and technology classes, which have been attended during the current session by 345 students, paying £121 in fees.

Another town selected for comment was Oldham, and the report remarks that nowhere has the movement made greater progress than in this town in which there were five principal societies. Each member must belong to a different household, so that the membership included fully 50 per cent of Oldham households. The aggregate sales of the town's societies over the previous 20 years amounted to £11,735,589. The number of cottages built through loans (presumably to members) was 1,026. The average annual purchases per member of the Industrial Society (one of the two largest societies) amounted to £30.

The report gives a good number of facts and figures regarding both retailing and the CWS. We are told that in 1887 there were 919 co-op retail distribution centres, with 5,010 shops, selling a range of goods, including beer, wines and spirits (this is interesting, given the fact that the movement was opposed to the sale of alcohol). Information regarding the CWS contains a reference to the society's fleet of six steamers, built at a cost of £84,500, with a gross tonnage of 3,898 tons (in fact, they were all quite small, and were sold off by 1914). Reference is also made to the CWS depots in Ireland, Denmark, Germany and New York. (Later on, depots were also set up in France, Canada, Sweden, Spain and Australia, and tea estates were acquired in Ceylon in 1913). The report then supplied a useful reminder that in addition to the manufacturing outlets of the Co-operative Union, there were at the time 88 independent productive societies in England, with a membership of 8,081, making profits of £25,214 (evidently they were quite small enterprises). These sometimes shared both profits and management, sometimes not. In addition, there were 47 co-partnership productive societies, where the workers had a share in, but did not monopolize, either profits or management. Their membership numbered 11,000, their aggregate annual sales were £666,000, their profits were £37,000, and they employed 3,653. There was a third class of society where the workers shared in the profits, but not the management. This was the case with nearly all the Scottish societies in this class (it should be mentioned that unlike the

CWS, the SCWS paid bonuses to its employees on their wages at the same rate as its dividends on purchases).

Cole provides further details that may help to put this information into perspective. He points out that there were still some advocates of producers' co-operatives within the Co-operative Union. The Co-operative Productive Union was established in 1882 to encourage such co-operatives, together with a Productive Committee and a Labour Association. This last body stressed the need for the co-operative movement and for employers generally to give their workers a share of the profits and of the control of industry. Cole also says that the number of profit-sharing schemes rose after 1894, peaking at 126 in 1903 (a separate report to the Board of Trade by a Mr D. F. Schloss, which is included in the Royal Commission's Final Report, lists and names 114 such societies).

Cole was a guild socialist, with a special interest in worker control in industry, and this perhaps explains his obvious interest in productive co-operatives and profit-sharing. He does emphasize that most of the productive co-operatives at the end of the century were on a small scale, many of them being in the East Midlands boot and shoe industry. Thus, in 1897 there were 20 firms of this kind making footwear, with a turnover of £166,000. There were also others in the clothing trades and in printing, usually employing skilled labour, but using low-cost capital equipment. They sold mostly to consumer societies. By way of comparison, in 1900 the CWS produced goods in its own factories of more than £2,600,000 in value, and the SCWS goods valued at £1,146,000. Again, according to Cole, co-partnership schemes also grew up about this time – there were 79 profit-sharing firms started between 1881 and 1890, a further 77 in the period 1891–1900, and 80 in the years 1900–1910. However, the total number of employees in all such schemes was less than a quarter of a million, so that by the end of the century it is clear that profit sharing in production was only a relatively insignificant survivor of earlier co-operative ideals.

Three last aspects of co-operative development in the second half of the nineteenth century require examination. The first is the role of women in the movement. In fact, although the housewife was the person who did the family shopping at the co-operative store, membership of the society was usually in the name of her husband, not herself. He alone had a legal right to the dividend. However, with changes in public opinion in the later nineteenth century, the issue of women's rights became more and more a matter for debate. In 1883, Mrs Alice Acland, who had been put in charge of a "Women's Corner" in the *Co-operative News*, successfully proposed at the annual Congress that the Women's League for the Spread of Co-operation be set up. It was to start with a membership of fifty, and a subscription of 6d a year. Its aims were carefully worded so as not to upset male co-operators:

> . . . to spread a knowledge of the advantages of Co-operation; to stimulate among those who know its advantages a greater interest in the principles of Co-operation; to keep alive in ourselves, our neighbours, and especially the rising generation, a more earnest appreciation of the value of Co-operation to ourselves, to our children, and to the nation; and to improve the conditions of women all over the country.

The wording was soothing enough, indeed positively emollient, although perhaps there was a sting in the tail. In spite of its apparently innocent nature, the guild was not popular. Men suspected the thin edge of the wedge, and the danger – as they saw it – of petticoat rule. But slowly it made progress, at first under the leadership of Mrs Acland, then under Mrs Mary Laurenson (of the Royal Arsenal Society), and then, above all, under Margaret Llewelyn Davies, who became Secretary in 1889 (according to Cole, "by far the greatest woman who has been actively identified with the British Co-operative Movement"). Membership grew from 500 in 1886 to 5,000, in 100 branches, by 1892. The new organization, known generally as the Women's Guild, did much to train women in administration, and to encourage educational work in the branches. Missioners and lecturers were sent out to spread the message from 1894 onwards. Women's membership of educational committees increased from 42 in 1886 to 73 in 1891. By this latter date, about 100,000 women were among the million shareholders in the retail societies.

However, some of the ideas of the guild leaders were bound to excite opposition, in particular their belief in the need to bring co-operation within the reach of the poor, rather than confine it to the better-paid working classes. To this end, they advocated stores that would have loan departments and club rooms or settlements, proposals that to many opponents smacked of charitable works and soup kitchens. It was not easy to find any society willing to experiment on these lines, but finally in 1902 the Sunderland Society opened a "People's Store" in Coronation Street, which had a grocery, a butcher's shop and a flour store. It also had a soup kitchen, an assembly hall, and a settlement staffed by two social workers. There was a full programme of activities, classes were held, and a library installed. It was very successful, actually making a profit in the first year, and declaring a dividend of 2s in the pound.

Unfortunately things then went wrong. The social workers quarrelled with the society directors, and thereupon resigned. The directors recommended that the settlement be closed down, and the store became an ordinary branch store. It was the end of what had been a very promising experiment. The fact is that it was all too adventurous for the more conservative male members, and no further attempts were made to establish similar establishments before the First World War. The Women's Guild turned its attention to other issues such as women's suffrage, the campaign for a minimum wage, and for shorter shop hours, including shorter hours in co-op stores. In the course of time, some worthwhile results were achieved within the movement. More women were to be found in senior posts. In 1904, a woman, Miss Spooner, was in the chair of the United Board of the Co-operative Union. Women also occupied two places on the Union's Education Committee, 11 places on the Association of Education Committees, 30 places on management committees, and 283 places on the Education Committees of 108 societies.

It will have been noted that women's services were thought particularly appropriate and valuable in the field of co-operative education, although education was regarded by many rank-and-file members as of only minor importance among co-operative activities. In theory, 2.5 per cent of profits were supposed to be devoted to education in every branch. In practice, what happened varied from society to society. Rochdale provided a good example of educational practice, as we have seen, but in other branches the 2.5 per cent provision was quietly ignored. In the 1880s renewed efforts were made to encourage educational activities. In 1882 a class studying co-operative principles was begun in London, and a scheme for instruction in the basic principles was drawn up by Alice Acland. In 1883 a new central education committee was appointed, and area committees were also set up. The aims of co-operative education were stated to be:

> primarily the formation of co-operative character and opinion, and secondarily, though not necessarily of less import, the training of men and women to take part in industrial and social reforms and municipal life generally.

Courses in bookkeeping and related subjects were made available to employees, and correspondence courses were started in 1890. In 1900, 1,154 students undertook courses, and 582 sat examinations in Co-operation, Industrial History, Citizenship and Bookkeeping. Junior classes for children began in 1898–9, and 942 children sat the junior examination in 1900.

By the beginning of the twentieth century, the co-operative movement was clearly making renewed efforts to improve its educational work, but there were those who thought that what was being done was too narrowly vocational, and that something involving deeper and more extended study was required. To meet this need, the Workers Educational Association (WEA) was founded in 1903, based on the ideas of Albert Mansbridge, a clerk employed by the CWS. It had strong support from the movement, and at the end of the first year, eleven co-operative societies had affiliated to it, and there were 135 members. The first local branch was in Reading, and in 1905 another branch was formed in Rochdale, where the first university tutorial class began in 1908 under the guidance of R. H. Tawney; the two-year course, on which 43 students were enrolled, was in economic history. WEA courses were run in conjunction with local universities. Meanwhile, more vocational courses were organized by the Union, and funds devoted to this purpose rose from £64,147 in 1900 to £113,226 in 1914. The number of students also increased from 3,216 to 20,094 between these years. In 1913, the first co-operative summer school was held, and a proposal was adopted in 1914 for the establishment of a co-operative college; but the coming of war in August of that year prevented any further action. Efforts were not lacking to spread the ideas of co-operation before 1914, but there was still the problem that many branch members of the movement had little interest in co-operative activities beyond the range and price of goods on sale, and their dividend on purchases.

Lastly, a word or so on political issues: throughout its history, the modern movement asserted its neutrality in political matters, although the Rochdale Pioneers were themselves strongly influenced by Owenism, and certainly the general tone adopted by co-op leaders in the middle decades of the century was Liberal rather than Conservative. This was so much so that in 1869 the Rochdale Society split, and a Rochdale Conservative Co-operative Society was formed. Again, friendly links were maintained with the trade unions, especially the ASE. Nevertheless, when the first Lib-Labs were elected in 1874, the co-operative movement did not follow the unions' example and seek parliamentary representation; and when a resolution in favour of representation was discussed and passed at Congress in 1897, the societies afterwards showed little interest. When they were circularized and asked for their opinions, only 160 societies out of 1,659 replied, and of those which replied, only 60 were in favour. Efforts were made in 1905 to secure joint action by the movement and the new LRC, but they were opposed, and a second canvassing of opinion resulted in only 141 replies, 129 being opposed to parliamentary representation. Finally, at the 1914 Congress a motion was carried for political neutrality in party politics. Therefore, in spite of the apparent trend towards some form of co-operation, if not actual union, between the Central Union and the labour organizations, nothing was achieved before 1914.

By 1914 it is quite evident that the modern movement had made vast strides since its beginnings in 1844. There is no lack of figures to show this. On the retail side, trade increased from £15,411,185 in 1881 to £87,964,229. Dividends were often high, and about the turn of the century sometimes reached 5s in the pound. The size of individual societies also increased. In 1880, only three had more than 10,000 members. In 1900, the three largest had over 25,000 members, and by 1914, the top three had over 40,000 each. In 1914, there were 1,385 societies with an average size of 2,083, and a total membership of 3,054,000. Meanwhile, the central organization had been refined, with new sections being added – the western section in 1878, the southwestern in 1895, and the Irish section in 1889–95. There were more district associations, and more central committees. The Co-operative Union was registered under the Industrial and Provident Societies Act, 1869 as a federation of co-operative societies. A new headquarters was acquired – Holyoake House – in Manchester, where the CWS took over large warehouses in Balloon Street. In many ways, all this progress looked like unqualified success, and indeed it is not unreasonable to view it in simple terms – first the creation of a national retailing network, then the establishing of the CWS and the SCWS, then finally the manufacture of own brands, both by the CWS and by the retail organizations. What could be more straightforward?

Nevertheless, it must be admitted that this is not what the founding fathers of the movement had looked for. Robert Owen certainly had a vision beyond mere shopkeeping, and so did the original Rochdale Pioneers. Their major aim had been to escape from the marketplace, not to compete in it. They wanted to break away altogether from the capitalist system, and not merely provide an alternative system of retailing. This is why William Pare made his remark in 1870, which has already been quoted, that if the older co-operators erred in sentiment, the present ones erred in the direction of materialism. It also explains why throughout the history of the Co-operative Union there is intertwined the story of successive attempts to set up various forms of co-operative production and co-partnership, whereby the workers exercised some ownership and control over the product. None of these efforts ever gained anything like the success of retail co-operation, selling products drawn from a variety of sources, both commercially manufactured and also made in their own factories. Few if any of the producers' co-operative factories under the control of the retail societies had any form of profit-sharing, certainly not the Rochdale Pioneers Manufacturing Society, or the factories of the CWS (only the Scottish CWS retained a form of "labour bounty" in their manufactories). There were even some problems among co-operative employees regarding labour conditions and wage levels. In 1891 the Amalgamated Union of Co-operative Employees (AUCE) was set up, and in 1907 Congress adopted minimum wage scales. When some societies failed to adopt them, the AUCE set up a strike fund. Some officials then left the AUCE, and established the Co-operative Secretaries Association in 1908, and the Managers Association in 1912. Subsequently the TUC called union members of AUCE to join the industrial unions, whereupon the AUCE left the TUC. Again, all this is somewhat different from the kind of fraternal relationships originally looked for.

On the other hand, it might well be objected that the achieving of economic and social change is based on the art of the possible, no less than the practice of politics. Plainly, Owenite ideas of communitarianism had been put to the test again and again in the first half of the nineteenth century, both in this country and in North America, but they had failed. It may be remarked in passing that ideas of community life, untarnished by the sordid materialism of everyday life, have an enduring appeal even today, especially if based on religious or ethical conviction; but in the circumstances of the developing industrial capitalism of the nineteenth century, they simply didn't work. A peaceful replacement of the existing economic and social system by self-supporting communities was never the remotest possibility. Consequently, it can be argued that in the second half of the nineteenth century, co-operators went for the next best thing – pure foodstuffs, true weight, goods of assured quality at a fair price, and the incentive to save through the dividend. These were the essential achievements of the co-operative movement in the nineteenth century, and as such they received the support of the Webbs, who backed consumer co-operation, and were opposed to producer co-operation, which they thought was based on profit-making, and "not a step forward in the moralisation of trade".

How far was the co-operative movement after 1844 based on working-class self-help? The original group of Rochdale Pioneers was certainly composed of working men, including as many as 20 weavers, although this number rapidly fell to ten. The number of Owenite socialists among them shows clearly that they were men of superior intellect who thought for themselves, and men of this quality led the movement in the early days. But as pointed out before, the movement catered very largely for the more skilled and better-paid workman, not for the *lumpenproletariat*; and this helps to explain the failure of the Sunderland Coronation Street experiment before the First World War. In this respect, the co-operative movement resembled the friendly societies in serving the needs of the better-off among the working classes, and not the working classes as a whole. There was a further resemblance, too, in that many of the national leaders of the co-operative movement in the second half of the century were middle-class in origin, and in time a class of branch managers emerged who inevitably adopted a more middle-class lifestyle. However working-class in origin, therefore, by the end of the century the co-operative movement owed a good deal to middle-class leadership, although at grass roots level in the branches it was still largely respectable working-class in nature. In this respect, the co-operative movement remained overwhelmingly a working-class organization at the beginning of the twentieth century.

Conclusions

Throughout the ages, and certainly in nineteenth century England, working-class self-help has taken a variety of forms beyond the three major aspects examined and discussed in this book. In particular, there has always been much communal self-help among working-class men and women, especially between members of the same family, in times of sickness or adversity. It is wrong, therefore, to think of self-help in Victorian England purely in terms of middle-class striving for success, a kind of early Thatcherism based on self-centred advancement. The sense in which the term "working-class self-help" has been used in this book is to indicate the major ways in which the working classes helped themselves collectively to improve conditions of employment, to afford protection against ill health and the threat of a pauper's grave, and to co-operate in the production of foodstuffs, goods and services. As pointed out in the Introduction, its essence was co-operation, rather than individual striving after achievement. However, this did not exclude individual endeavours to add to family earnings. Not all working people worked exclusively for others, for in addition to their full-time employment, many had spare-time jobs, taking in washing, selling firewood, and so on, of the kind recently described as penny capitalism. It has even been claimed that in 1900 penny capitalism was the chief support of up to 10 per cent of all working-class families, and the partial support of at least 40 per cent. So although in this book the emphasis has been placed on three outstanding forms of working-class self-help, individual efforts to increase income are by no means to be excluded from any broad definition of self-help. They do, however, take one in the direction of Smilesian doctrines of self-help, which was not the purpose of this book, and no effort has been made in these pages to examine either part-time or full-time entrepreneurship by working people.

To turn to those three major forms of working-class self-help, and to comment finally on them: the trade union movement has been given the lengthiest treatment, for reasons touched on in the Introduction. There is the further reason, of course, that trade unionism was to have repercussions on not only working-class lives but on the lives of the nation as a whole. It started out at the beginning of the nineteenth century as a means of safeguarding the livelihoods of the skilled working classes. As such, it was undeniably exclusive, although in the 1830s, in some quarters, it briefly entertained ambitions of extending to include all kinds of working men and women. Only towards the end of the nineteenth century did it begin to include the unskilled, or that half of the working population – the female half – which still played little part in the movement. Yet already with the extension of the franchise, the movement was heading in a new direction, into politics and the creation of a new, working-class political party. Thus, trade unionists, whose former outlook had been limited to the concept of a fair day's work for a fair day's pay, found themselves actively participating in national politics, and ultimately in national government. This did not happen overnight, of course, but by the 1880s the possibilities had begun to appear. It became apparent that trade unionism had more to offer than merely a fair deal in the workplace – indeed, it was argued that in order to achieve this, it was necessary to enter into national politics. The point remains that self-help aimed at obtaining a fair wage and good working conditions ended up with far greater dimensions.

Something of the same kind might be said of the co-operative movement, although here the change was in a different direction. Whereas the trade union movement still appeared content with only limited perspectives in the mid-nineteenth century, co-operation began with far loftier ideals earlier in the century. Society was to be transformed, and a new ideal world created on the basis of communitarianism – a form of socialism based not on class struggle and the triumph of the working classes, but on class co-operation in productive communities. It didn't happen, although attempts at co-operative production and at profit-sharing went on throughout the century. The concentration on retail co-operation that evolved was certainly deprecated by some of the founding fathers of the movement, who still hankered after productive communities; but others would argue that

224

it was a realistic adjustment to a changing economy. Certainly when the CWS went in for production, it was not to create new communities, but simply to provide goods for the assured markets in the retail co-operatives; and its employees took no share of the profits, at least not in England.

So it can be argued that the co-operative movement changed its objectives very markedly after 1850, concentrating realistically on very practical and attainable targets. It is true that at the end of the century, the development of new educational ambitions seem to indicate a change in outlook, but it cannot be said that the change went very deep. The fact is that the average co-op member was not very interested, being more concerned with the size of the dividend and the price, quality and range of goods on offer than anything else. The failure of the People's Store in Sunderland at the beginning of the twentieth century is significant. Although thinking and better-informed co-operators were becoming more and more concerned at the state of the lower echelons of the working classes, the average rank-and-file member was suspicious of social experiments of the kind attempted in Coronation Street, Sunderland. The nineteenth-century co-operative movement must certainly be credited with many worthy achievements, but the fact is that it remained relevant to only the better-off sections of the working classes.

This brings us conveniently to the third movement which has been investigated – the friendly societies. Here again is a movement springing from the better-paid sectors of the working classes, and doing an excellent job in safeguarding them against sickness and disability, and at the same time involving very large numbers of the working population – far more than were members of trade unions. There can be no doubt about the value of the services provided by the friendly societies (including the building societies, tontines, savings clubs, and the rest) during the nineteenth century. The lack of any social services, other than that of the detested Poor Law authorities, ensured that the friendly societies would have a ready clientele. But again it must be stressed that that clientele was limited in size for the simple reason that the lower ranks of the working classes could not afford membership. The Submerged Tenth, which William Booth, the founder of the Salvation Army, wrote about in his *In darkest England and the way out* (1890), had no money to spare for friendly societies. His namesake, but no relation, Charles Booth, described this lowest class (Class

225

A in his classification of working people) in his *Life and labour of the people of London* (17 volumes, 1889–1903) as follows:

> Their life is the life of savages, with vicissitudes of extreme hardship and occasional excess. Their food is of the coarsest description, and their only luxury is drink ... They render no useful service, they create no wealth; more often they destroy it. They degrade whatever they touch, and as individuals are perhaps incapable of improvement.

These are harsh words. It is true that they applied to only 0.9 per cent of Londoners, but the class above (Class B) constituted 7.5 per cent, and the classes above that, Classes C and D, were 22.3 per cent. In all, while Classes A and B were in abject poverty, all four classes (30.7 per cent) were regarded by Booth as being below the poverty line. They were very unlikely candidates for friendly society membership. At most, they might afford the odd copper or two a week for a burial club.

How far was working-class self-help limited by the existence of these socially degraded strata of the working classes, the *residuum*, those lower orders who caused so much anxiety among the middle classes of tender conscience towards the end of the century? The answer must be that self-help of the conventional kind was of little relevance to them. They simply lived from hand to mouth, and from day to day. It could be that as much as anything, the coming of compulsory education in 1880 impressed their existence on the middle classes. Here were the children from the slums, the offspring of the people of the abyss, ill-nourished, ill-clad, often stunted in growth, the children of the truly poor. The result of their coming into the state educational net was to be free school meals for the needy, and medical inspections in schools. Moreover, there were repeated demands for old age pensions to keep the aged poor out of the workhouse. The story of how old age pensions were finally provided by the state was traced in Chapter 3. Although in one sense their provision was a relief to the friendly societies because it lessened the financial strain on their funds, the coming of state aid was ominous for them. The instituting of national health insurance in 1911 was even more so, not merely because of the preferential treatment given by Lloyd George to the commercial insurance companies, but because it showed clearly that the state was at last prepared to offer support for the working classes as a whole when suffering from ill health. A start was also made in the same year on relieving unemployment, although the scheme was on a small scale.

It may therefore be seen that although working-class self-help in the three major forms surveyed in this book achieved great things by 1914, it had proved inadequate as a means of succour for the working classes as a whole. Put simply, the very poorest did not have the resources to help themselves, and it was for them that Churchill and Lloyd George spread the net over the abyss. For them, state aid had become inevitable. Of course, this was more than a philanthropic gesture by the government, and it has already been pointed out that fears about the physique of the nation, about its economic future in increasingly competitive international markets, and about the maintenance and well-being of the British Empire, all contributed to this fear of national decline. As Sidney Webb put it, and Asquith agreed with him:

> What is the use of talking about Empire if here, at its very centre, there is always to be found a mass of people, stunted in education, a prey of intemperance, huddled and congested beyond the possibility of realising in any true sense either social or domestic life?

No doubt political expediency was another factor, and helps to explain the coming of the pre-war Liberal reforms; but for whatever reason, working-class self-help had been weighed in the balance and found wanting. Government aid had become unavoidable, because neither the problems of ill-heath and old age, nor the problem of unemployment, could be left to the friendly societies and the trade unions.

In one sense then, the Liberal reforms closed an epoch in the history of working-class self-help. Its heyday undoubtedly had been during the nineteenth century, and its development is a testimony to the resilience and hardy spirit of the working classes in this country. They were the first people in the world to experience the traumas of industrialization and urbanization, and in the Introduction the point was made that the history of development in all three areas – friendly societies, trade unions, and co-operation – may be seen as the response of working people to their changed environment. It is hoped that enough has been said to explain how the pace and nature of that response was conditioned by change in the economy as a whole. It must be reiterated that the improvement of real wages in the second half of the century is a valuable key to understanding the progress made, although it is not the only factor, since the revival of socialist thinking, of a kind very different from Owenism, also helps to explain the new direction taken by the trade union movement.

In the final analysis, it would be satisfying to be able to say which aspect of self-help was really of the greatest value to the working classes in the nineteenth century. It is certainly tempting to have a last fling in this direction: but on reflection it seems wiser to resist the temptation. The disparate nature of the three forms of self-help makes it difficult to draw firm conclusions. Perhaps it could be said that the friendly societies provided valuable services to working people from the very beginning of the century, and especially from the 1830s onwards. In terms of numbers involved, they would certainly have a claim to have been of the most use, whatever their dwindling influence between the wars and subsequently.

On the other hand, the trade unions often had a hard time of it in standing up to employers for fair treatment, and in maintaining solidarity when on strike, often enduring great personal privation and even near-starvation when standing out. It could thus be argued that it was the trade unionists who had the roughest time of it, for they frequently had to face the hostility not only of the employers but also of the middle classes generally, and of the government itself. Furthermore, even if trade union membership is often contrasted unfavourably with friendly society membership in the nineteenth century, it must be remembered that trade unionism began to play a part in national affairs from 1874 onwards, and especially with the formation of the LRC and of the Labour Party. Thus, it was the trade unions who took the cause of the working classes into parliament itself, and created a national party to represent them. How is this to be weighed against the numerical superiority of friendly society membership?

Lastly, the co-operative movement tried valiantly, but failed to change materially the development of industrial capitalism in the early nineteenth century. For this the founding fathers, Robert Owen and the two Kings of London and Brighton, William Pare and George Holyoake, and many others, all deserve credit, though their attempts at community building were of no avail. The best that can be said of their achievements, perhaps, is that they tried to make co-operative communities a success, but were defeated by the practical difficulties involved. Nevertheless, their ideals remained to inspire leaders later in the century, when retail co-operation had such success, providing literally millions of satisfied members with goods of assured quality, and a useful dividend. Again, how should these very solid services be evaluated in comparison with those supplied by the trade unions and the friendly societies?

Lastly, it is fitting to pay tribute to the many men and women who devoted their lives to helping their fellow workers in all three areas of self-help. It is true that in the second half of the nineteenth century a middle-class element began to appear here and there in both the friendly societies and the co-operative movements, but this seems to be less so in the trade unions. Even then, both the friendly societies and the co-operative societies had a solid working-class membership, and this was very much the case with the trade unions. Especially in the middle years of the nineteenth century, working-class men spent long hours after work on union business – indeed, many gave their lives to it. They were honourable men, dedicated to the cause of their unions, but drawing very few material gains from holding office, although gaining much from a sense of comradeship and the respect of their fellow men. These humble branch officers were the true pioneers of the union movement, and their patient work made possible both model unionism and new unionism. Their names are not often recalled today, but they laid the foundations of modern trade unionism. The social historian is accustomed to making his generalizations and to drawing cautious conclusions, carefully balancing one argument against another, always on the look-out for some new interpretation. Yet in labour history there are at base only the activities, the opinions and the thoughts of the many thousands of ordinary men and women who collectively made self-help possible. It is right that we should pause from time to time, stand back, remember these humble and unknown heroes, and salute them.

Select bibliography

It should be stressed that this is not a complete list of all authorities consulted during the course of writing this book. It is a select bibliography intended to guide the reader in search of further information to some of the basic sources for the text. The place of publication is London unless otherwise stated.

Official publications

Select Committee on Artisans and Machinery, 1824, Reports.
Select Committee on Laws respecting Friendly Societies, 1825, Reports.
Select Committee on the Combination Laws, 1825, Reports.
Select Committee on Manufacturers' Employment, 1830, Report.
Select Committee on Combinations of Workmen, 1838, Reports.
Royal Commission on Trade Unions, 1867, Reports.
Royal Commission on Friendly and Benefit Building Societies, 1870, Reports.
Royal Commission on Labour, 1891–94, Reports.

The economic and social background

Ashworth, W., *An economic history of England, 1870–1939*, 1960.
Bédarida, F., *A social history of England, 1851–197*, 1979.
Best, G., *Mid-Victorian Britain 1851–75*, revised edn, 1973.
Crafts, N. F. R., *British economic growth during the industrial revolution*. Oxford, 1985.
Crouzet, F. *The Victorian economy*. 1982.
Floud, R. & D. N. McCloskey (eds), *Economic history of Britain since 1700*, 2nd edn, 1994.
Harris, J., *Private lives, public spirit*. 1993.

231

Harrison, J. F. C., *The early Victorians 1832–51*, 1971.
Harrison, J. F. C., *Late Victorian Britain, 1875–1901*, 1990.
Hopkins, E., *A social history of the English working classes 1815–1945*, 1979.
Mathias, P., *The first industrial nation*, 2nd edn, 1983.
Royle, E., *Modern Britain: a social history 1750–1985*, 1987.
Thompson, F. M. L., *The rise of respectable society: a social history of Victorian Britain 1830–1900*, 1988.

Part One: The friendly societies

Bruce, M., *The coming of the British Welfare State*, 4th edn, 1968.
Crossick, G., The Labour aristocracy and its values: a study of mid-Victorian Kentish London. *Victorian Studies*, **XIX** (3), 1976.
Crossick, G., *An artisan élite in Victorian Society: Kentish Town, 1840–1880*, 1978.
Friendly Societies: seven pamphlets 1798–1839. New York: Arnos Press, 1972.
Fraser, D., *The evolution of the British Welfare State*, 2nd edn, 1984.
Gilbert, B., *The evolution of National Insurance in Great Britain*, 1986.
Gosden, P. H. J. H., *The Friendly Societies in England 1815–1875*. Manchester, 1961.
Gosden P. H. J. H. *Self help*, 1973.
Hay, G. R., *The origins of the Liberal welfare reforms 1906–1914*, 1975.
Hennock, E. P., *British social reform and German precedents: the case of social insurance 1880–1914*. Oxford, 1987.
Hopkins, E., *Birmingham: the first manufacturing town in the world 1760–1840*, 1989.
Hutton, W., *History of Birmingham*, 1781.
Scott, W., *Essay on public charities*. Stourbridge: Unitarian Church, 1810.
Thane, P., *Foundations of the Welfare State*, 1982.

Part Two: Trade unions

Aspinall, A., *The early English trade unions*, 1949.
Biagini, E. F. & A. Reid (eds), *Currents of radicalism: popular racialism, organised labour and party politics in Britain 1850–1914*, 1991.
Brown, H. P., *The origins of trade union power*. Oxford, 1983.
Brown, K. D., *The English Labour movement 1700–1951*, 1982.
Brown, K. D. (ed.), *The first Labour Party 1906–1914*. Beckenham, 1985.
Burgess, K., *The challenge of labour: shaping British society 1850–1930*, 1980.
Clegg, H. A., A. Fox & A. F. Thompson, *A history of British trade unions since 1889*, vol. I, 1889–1910. Oxford, 1964.

Clegg, H. A., *A history of British trade unions since 1889*, vol. II, 1911–1933. Oxford, 1985.

Cole, G. D. H. & A. N. Filson, *British working class movements: select documents*, 1951.

Dinwiddy, J. R., *Chartism*, 1987.

Dobson, C. R., *Masters and journeymen: a prehistory of industrial relations 1717–1800*, 1980.

Epstein, J. & D. Thompson (eds), *The Chartist experience*, 1982.

Fox, A. *History and heritage: the social origins of the British industrial relations system*, 1985.

Fraser, W. H. Trade Unionism. In *Popular movements c. 1830–1850*, J. T. Ward (ed.), 1970.

Fraser, W. H. ,*Trade unions and society: the struggle for acceptance 1850–1880*, 1974,

Hobsbawm, E. J., *Labouring men*, 1964.

Hunt, E. H., *British labour history 1815–1914*, 1981.

Jones, G. S., *Language of class: studies in English working class history 1832–1982*. Cambridge, 1983.

Kirby R. G. & A. E. Musson, *The voice of the people: John Doherty 1798–1854*. Manchester, 1975.

Laybourne, K., *A history of British trade unionism 1770–1990*, 1992.

Laybourne, K., *The rising sun of socialism*, 1991.

Leeson, R. A., Business as usual – craft union development 1834–51. *Bulletin of the Society for the Study of Labour History* 49, 1984.

Lovell, J., *British trade unions, 1875–1933*, 1977.

Mather, F. C., *Chartism*, 1975.

McLean, I., *Keir Hardie*, 1975.

Morgan, K. O., *Keir Hardie*, 1975.

Musson, A. E., *British trade unions, 1800–1875*, 1972.

Oliver, W. H., The Consolidated Trades' Union of 1834. *Economic History Review*, 2nd series, XVII, 1964–5.

Orth, J. V. The legal status of English Trade Unions, 1799–1871. In *Law making and law-makers in British history*, A. Harding (ed.). Royal Historical Society, 1980.

Orth, J. V., *Combination and conspiracy: a legal history of trade unionism, 1721–1906*. Oxford, 1991.

Pelling, H., *A short history of the Labour Party*, 9th edn. New York, 1987.

Pelling, H., *A history of British trade unionism*. 4th edn, 1987.

Pimlott, B. & C. Cook (eds), *Trade unions in British politics*, 1982.

Prothero, I. J., *Artisans and politics in early nineteenth century London: John Gast and his times*. Folkestone., 1979.

Reid, F., *Keir Hardie*, 1978.

Roberts, E., *Women's work 1840–1940*, 1988.

Rule, J., *The labouring classes in early industrial England 1750–1850*, 1986.

Rule, J. (ed.), *British trade unionism 1750–1850: the formative years*, 1988.
Rule, J., Labour in a changing economy 1700–1850. In *New Directions in Economic & Social History*, vol. II, A. Digby, C. Feinstein & D. Jenkins, 1992.
Thompson, D., *The Chartists*, 1994.
Thompson, E. P., *The making of the English working class*, 1963.
Ward, J. T. & W. H. Fraser (eds), *Workers and employers: documents on trade union and industrial relations in Britain since the eighteenth century*, 1980.
Webb, S. & B., *The history of trade unionism*, 1920.

Part Three: The co-operative movement

Armytage, W. H. G., *Heavens below: Utopian experiments in England 1560–1960*, 1961.
Beales, H. L., *The early English socialists*, 1933.
Beer, M., *A history of British socialism*, 1921.
Bonner, A., *British co-operation*. Manchester, 1961.
Fletcher, L. J. *Robert Owen's Equitable Labour Exchanges*. BPhil. thesis, Open University, 1984.
Garnett, R. G., *Co-operation and the Owenite socialist communities in Britain, 1825–45*. Manchester, 1972.
Garnett, R. G., *William Pare, cooperator and social reformer*. Co-operative College Papers, **16**, 1973.
Gosden, P. H. J. H., *Self-help*, 1973.
Hall, F., & W. P. Watkins, *Cooperation, a survey of the history, principles and organisation of the cooperative movement in Great Britain and Ireland*, 1934.
Hampton, E. W., *Early co-operation in Birmingham and district*. Birmingham, 1928.
Holyoake, G. J., *The history of co-operation in England* (2 vols), 1875.
Pollard, S., Nineteenth century co-operation: from community building to shop-keeping. In *Essays in labour history*, A. Briggs & J. Saville (eds), 1967.
Purvis, M., Co-operative retailing in England 1835–50: developments before Rochdale. *Northern History* **XXII**, 1986.
Webb, S. & B. Webb, *The consumers' co-operative movement*, 1921.

Index

affiliated 12, 25, 27, 28–35, 47, 55
ages of members 18
attitude to national insurance 66, 67, 68
benefits 9, 12, 19, 28–9, 30, 34, 69
female societies 11, 46, 60, 69
fines 18–19
Foresters, Ancient Order of 17, 28, 30, 31, 31–2, 32, 48, 61
funds 19–20
influence of 62–3
Manchester Unity of Oddfellows 17, 28, 30, 31, 32, 33–4, 47–8, 48, 55, 61, 69
membership numbers 9, 10, 13, 24, 31, 32, 33–4, 51–2, 60, 69
middle-class attitude to 13, 14
officials 17–18, 30
origins 9
Rechabites 28, 33, 55
sick relief 3, 20, 34
social activities 3, 29, 35, 70
subscriptions 18
tramping benefits 28–9
tables 31, 34, 56
Fyson, Robert 107

Garnett, Thomas 138
"gas and water" socialism 142
Gascogne, Col. 80
Gast, John 90, 91
General Federation of Trade Unions 153
general practioners 67, 68
General Railway Workers Union 174
general strike 175
General Strike, 1842 112–13
George, Dorothy 80, 81, 86
German insurance schemes 65
Germany 54, 63
Gilbert, Prof. Bentley 60, 66, 69
Gladstone, Herbert 160
Gladstone, W. E. 49, 132, 141, 148, 155, 178
Glasgow 36, 49, 84, 85, 86, 89, 90, 97, 101, 109, 112, 116, 125, 145, 185, 210, 211
Glasgow Co-operative Society 188
Gloucester 76, 211
Goldsmid, Isaac Lyon 193
Gosden, Prof. 9, 38, 42, 60
Gospel Oak 84
Gothic Hall 188, 189, 197

government intervention into industrial disputes 158, 171, 178
Graham, Cunningham, M. P. 143
Grand General Union of Cotton Spinners 97–8
Grand National Consolidated Trades Union 101, 102, 105, 106, 107, 108, 115, 118, 140, 190
Grand Union of England 98
Gray's Inn Road Exchange 188, 197
Grayson, Mr 88
Grayson, Victor 166
Great Depression 53, 56, 125, 135, 136, 137, 138, 139, 140, 213
Great Exhibition 116
Great Victorian Room 27
Great Western Railway 44
GWR Sickness Benefit Fund Society 44, 125
Guile, Daniel 125

Halévy, Elie 178
Halifax 151, 197
Halifax Building Society 56
Halifax Society 212
Hallam, Sam 129
Halls of Science 198
Ham Common Concordium 194, 199
Hamilton, A. J. 186
Hammond, J. L. & Barbara 78, 81
Hampshire County Society 15
Hanwell Comitorium 199
Hardie, Keir 67, 144, 147, 148–9, 150, 153, 154, 155, 156, 157, 160, 161, 162, 166, 167, 170
Harle, W. J. 38
Harmony Hall 193, 195, 200
Harnott, Richard 130
Harrison, Frederic 127, 130, 131, 132
Hastings 187
hatters 86, 102
Hawkes Smith W. 190
health insurance 54, 65, 66–7
Hearts of Oak Insurance Company 43–4, 57
Henderson, Arthur 162, 167
Higham, Mr 39, 41
History of co-operation 203
Hobbes, Thomas 186
Hobsbawm, Eric 74
Hodgins, Jonathon 99
Hodgskin, Thomas 186

Liberal Party 67, 150, 153, 154, 155, 160, 161, 167
Liberator Society 56
Lib–Labs 138, 143, 148, 150, 153, 154, 162, 167, 168, 219
Life and labour of the people of London 141, 226
Lincolnshire 10
Lindley, James 129
Link, The 143
liquid rent 35
Liverpool 33, 34, 36, 38, 41, 75, 80, 83, 84, 86, 88, 93, 105, 126, 170, 188
Liverpool carpenters 85
Liverpool, Lord 92
Liverpool–Manchester Railway 116
Liverpool Protective Benefit Society 36, 37
Liverpool Shipwrights Society 85, 86
Liverpool Victoria Legal Society 59
Llanelly 170, 176
Lloyd George, David 63, 64, 65, 66, 67, 68, 69, 164, 169, 170, 179, 226, 227
Lloyd George Museum 179
Locke, John 186
Locomotive Steam Engineers and Firemen Society 44
London 38, 40, 42, 74, 84, 86, 90, 98, 100, 102, 105, 106, 107, 113, 116, 120, 121, 126, 132, 133, 142, 143, 145, 170, 171, 181, 185, 188, 190, 191, 192, 211
London Bank of Industry 198
London Co-operative Society 187
London County Council 149
London Docks Strike 144
London Dorchester Committee 105
London Gas Workers Union 134, 143, 145
London, Jack 179
London Society of Taylors 19
London Temperance Land and Building Society 39
London Trades Council 123, 125, 126, 127, 132
Loveless, James and George 104
Loyal Order of Ancient Shepherds, Ashton Unity 32
Ludlow, J. M. 206, 207
Lyons v. Wilkins 151

MacArthur, Mary 181

MacDonald, Alexander 123–4, 133, 138
MacDonald, James Ramsay 155, 160, 162, 167
Manchester 23, 30, 39, 41, 81, 90, 96, 98, 100, 102, 105, 109, 113, 114, 132, 135, 188, 197, 208, 209, 210, 212, 219
Manchester Caledonian Society 48
Manchester cotton workers 96
Manchester Guardian 99–100
Manchester Trades Council 132
Manea Fen Colony 199
Mann, Tom 140, 141, 142, 143, 144, 145, 170, 174, 175
Mansbridge, Albert 218
Mansion House Committee 144
March of unemployed in London 143
Marx, Eleanor 143, 144
Marx, Karl 91, 140, 143, 173
Masterman, C. F. 179
Match Girls Strike 143
Mather, Prof. Fred 112
Maudsley, Henry 83, 84
Maurice, Frederick 206
Mayhew, Henry 121
McCall, Samuel 82–3
McCulloch, J. R. 82
Mearns, Arthur 141
medical inspection in schools 65, 226
Melbourne, Lord 196
Memorial Hall, Farrington Street 154
Merrie England 157
Merseyside 145
Merthyr Tydfil 150, 160
Metropolitan and Home Counties Purchasing Association 211
Metropolitan Police 116
Middlesex 42
Midlands Iron & Steel Wages Board 125, 136, 137
Miners 76, 84, 102, 126, 131, 135, 157–8, 167, 168, 169–70, 171, 175, 180
Miners Association of Great Britain and Ireland 115
Miners' next step, The 174
miners' yearly bond 115
Money, Leo Chiozza 179
Mongewell 185
Moore, Peter 82
Morgan, William 16

Parry, Mr 88
paternalism 50, 116
Peel, Sir Robert 82, 89
Pelling, Henry 152, 162, 166, 174, 177
penny banks 49
penny capitalism 223
pensions
  old age 54, 61, 62, 63, 64, 65, 226
  widows and orphans 68
Pentrich Uprising 82
People's Budget, 1909 179
People of the abyss 179
Perkin, Prof. Harold 117
Peterloo 82
Petty sessions 77, 80
Phelps Brown, Henry 162–3
Philadelphia 188
Philanthropic Hercules 98
Philanthropic Society 98
piecework 130, 131, 138
Pioneer, The 103, 105
pit clubs 44, 59
Pitt, William 15, 75, 79
Place, Francis 74, 82, 83, 87, 90, 91
Plebs League 173
Plug Plot 101, 112, 113
Poole 187
Poor Law relief 2, 3, 4, 9, 14, 51, 54, 62, 63, 145
population 1, 10, 14, 27, 30
Portsea Island Society 56
Post Office Savings Bank 50, 57
Potter, George 121
potteries, the 30, 108
Potters Union 108–9
poverty line 145, 181, 226
Pratt, John Tidd 17, 41, 46, 47, 48, 49
Preston 22, 27, 108
Price, Dr Richard 16
Price, S. J. 22
producer co-operation 206, 207, 211–12, 214, 215, 221
Progressive Party 149
provident societies 21
Prudential Insurance Company 57, 66
public houses 12, 13, 74
pure food 205, 221

Quarter Sessions 77, 80, 91
Quarterly Review 193
Queenswood 193–5, 196, 197, 198, 199, 200, 203, 204

Queenswood College 195

Railway Clerks Association 175
railway friendly societies 44–5, 59
railwaymen 175
Ralahine 188, 192, 197, 199
Rational Society 193, 194, 195, 198, 204
"rattening" 128
Rawlinson's Report 13, 13–14
Red Lion Square 187
Reform Act, 1832 27, 102, 107, 117, 133
Reform League 126
Registrar of Friendly Societies 17, 128, 131, 133
Renshaw, Robert 129
Report to the County of Lanark 185
residuum, the 54, 64, 70, 226
Revolutionary and Napoleonic Wars 2, 4, 14, 15, 185
Ricardo, David 186
Riches and poverty 179
Roberts, W. P. 115
Rochdale 30, 99, 102, 201, 204, 205, 208, 209, 218
Rochdale Conservative Co-operative Society 219
Rochdale Co-operative Manufacturing Society 206
Rochdale Pioneers 203, 204–6, 208, 213, 217, 219, 220, 221
Rolfe, Baron 128
Ropemakers of London 108
Rosebery, Lord 64, 148, 178
Rowntree, B. S. 179
Royal Arsenal Co-operative Society 211, 216
Royal Commissions
  Aged Poor, 1895 61, 62
  Agricultural Depression, 1879 139
  Depression of Trade and Industry, 1886 139
  Friendly Societies, 1870 4, 24, 28, 31, 36, 37, 38, 41, 42, 45, 46, 51
  Labour Laws, 1874 133
  On Labour, 1892 53, 54, 56, 59, 144, 156, 213, 215
  Railways, 1911 170
  Trade Disputes and Trade Combinations, 1903 160, 162
  Trade Unions, 1867 124, 127, 138

INDEX

Taff Vale Railway Case 159–60, 161
tailors 86, 102, 105, 107, 131
Tarleton, General 80
Tawney, Prof. R. H. 218
Taylor, Mr 83, 84
Taylor, Richard 84
Teeside 124
Temperton v. Russell 151
Ten Hour Movement 106, 196
Thames 9
Thompson, E. P. 80, 117
Thompson, Prof. F. M. L. 51, 60, 157
Thorne, Will 143
Tillett, Ben 142, 143–4, 166, 167
Times, The 104, 178
Tolpuddle Martyrs 103, 104, 108
Tontines 45, 59
Tonypandy 170, 174, 175
town life 1, 54, 226
Town Porters Friendly Society 17, 19
trade councils 125, 142, 147
trade fluctuations 2, 172
trade, home and abroad 2
trade unions
  administration 74, 180
  benefits for members 3, 75
  case for and against 144–5
  closed unionism 136
  committee organisation 74
  effect on economy 180
  hostility towards 4, 76–8, 115–16
  membership numbers 115, 121, 146,
    157, 177, 179, 181
  model unionism 119–21, 137, 229
  new unionism 134, 136, 137, 139–40,
    143, 144, 145–7, 156, 157, 229
  origins and nature 73–4
  picketing 131, 133, 151, 159, 162
  subscriptions 74
  Trade Union Congress 108, 132, 134,
    147–8, 150, 153, 154, 155, 157, 160,
    168, 173, 180
  violence during strikes 85, 86, 97, 127,
    129, 137, 170, 171, 175
  white collar unions 158
  women's unions 135, 158, 181, 224
Trafalgar Square riot 143
tramping 74
Triple Alliance 175, 180
Trollope's, builders 126–7
Trollope v. London Trades Federation
  151

true weight 205, 221
trustee savings banks 48–50
Tunbridge Wells Equitable Building
  Society 59
Tyne keelmen and sailors 81, 90

unemployment 53, 135–6, 143, 164,
  165, 227
Union Exchange Society 187
Union of Working Men's Clubs and
  Institutes 46–7
*Union Pilot and Co-operative Intelli-
  gencer* 100
United Factory Textile Workers Associa-
  tion 154
United Insurance Company 58
United Philanthropists of London 18, 19
United Trades and Co-operative Journal
  98
Universal Community Society of Rational
  Religionists 197
University Tutorial Classes 218
Unofficial Reform Committee 174

Vandeleur, John 192
vegetarianism 194, 199
Victoria, Queen 196
vitriol throwing 86, 88, 110, 132
Voice of the people 99
voting at the TUC 147–8

wages, real 5, 27, 30, 38, 50, 53, 135,
  176, 228
Wales 51, 133, 135, 170, 172, 174, 199,
  211
Walker, Samuel 84
Wallis, Graham 141
Warehousemen and Clerks Friendly
  Society 48
Warwickshire 10, 211
Wastnidge, George 129
watch clubs 12, 21, 24
Waterloo 81
Wear, R. 9
weavers 90, 221
Webbs, Sidney and Beatrice 67, 73, 78,
  80, 81, 87, 92, 106, 107, 111, 112,
  113, 115, 119, 120, 125, 133, 135,
  137, 139, 141, 142, 145, 167, 168,
  221, 227
"welters" 111
Welfare State 165

245

INDEX